I Wish I Were a Wolf

The New Voice in Chinese Women's Literature

Compiled and Translated by
Diana B. Kingsbury

New World Press   Beijing, China

First Edition 1994
Second Printing 1996

ISBN 7-80005-124-2
I Wish I Were a Wolf: The New Voice in Chinese
Women's Literature / compiled and translated
by Diana B. Kingsbury.

Published by
New World Press
24 Baiwanzhuang Road, Beijing 100037, China

Distributed by
China International Book Trading Corporation
35 Chegongzhuang Xilu, Beijing 100044, China
P.O. Box 399, Beijing, China

Printed in the People's Republic of China

To my mother, who teaches spirit and courage,
and to my Chinese sisters

Contents

Preface

One winter day in 1990 I read an article in the *China Daily* about a young woman writer who'd recently published her first collection of short stories. The article described how she'd worked her way from doing sales in a department store to writing for a major Beijing newspaper. There was a picture with her four-year-old son in her arms. What captured my attention was the paragraph about the title story in her book *Rejecting Fate*, the story of an unmarried woman who has an abortion. That such a *risque* topic, even in today's relatively open atmosphere, had made it to print and found its way into the English-language newspaper surprised me. I clipped out the article and put it in my drawer.

Her story made me wonder: What else are Chinese women writing about, aspects of life only they could know about as women in this rapidly changing society? In my search for women's works in English, I was disappointed to find the collections were merely re-prints of stories from the early eighties (more recent editions have since come out). None, moreover, focused on women writing about women, of women talking about what it is to be a woman in China today. I pulled the article from my drawer and proposed such a collection to my director at New World Press, Ms. Chen Xiuzheng. She gave me her full support.

Thus began the two-year project of collecting, translating and editing that has come to realization with this book. My guidelines were simple but difficult fulfill. I wanted women's writing: 1) about women, taking a woman as the central character, describing life from a woman's point of view; 2) written within the last five years about life today; 3) of previously untranslated work; and 4) of reasonably good quality. I looked especially for material that broke the mold, that walked outside convention and told me something about Chinese women I wasn't expecting to hear. Hoping to create a collection of diverse literary works, I read short stories,

1

poems, magazine articles, plays and interviews. The seven pieces in this volume — three short stories, one experiential account, one novella, one four-act play and an interview-based article — represent the women's writing which both fit my guidelines and told me something new.

Every compiler comes to the task with a bias; I understood through my work I was searching for an image that may be based more on hope than reality, an image of a self-actualized Chinese woman free of old ideas, living life as she wants. The pieces I chose present characters that challenge the stereotypes. They buck the system and struggle to break the chains of tradition and social expectation binding them in an everyday way. They struggle against forces — in themselves, in their families and in their communities — that resist change. They are women who, as Li Xiaojiang argues in the *Introduction*, make claims to personal rights from the strength of their awakened sense of Self as women.

Do such women exist in China today? They do, but as a drop in the sea. According to the 1989 census, women of the urban intellectual class make up less than two percent of the total women's population. Less than two percent are, as the characters presented in this collection, professionals with university educations — teachers, editors and doctors. Less than two percent are women with growing economic independence and access to ideas from the outside world. Their sisters in the countryside, on the other hand, the illiterate or semiliterate women who till the soil and for the most part live bound within the patriarchal clan, comprise about eighty percent of the total. For them, problems of personal development, self expression and lifestyle choice are an unimagined luxury. (In some of the poorer areas, a woman may be up against female infanticide, limited access to basic education and sale into forced marriages or prostitution rings — extreme cases, but realities nonetheless.) Though many women writers have delved into the peasant experience, their most insightful material generally centers on what they know best — the life of the urban and educated two percent.

The image of the challenging, self-realizing Chinese woman must be viewed in its proportion and as an expression of the class from which it grew. It should not be dis-

2

counted for its paucity of membership but understood as a beginning — the shining, newly sharpened tip of a cumbersome, out-dated spear. Women on the cutting edge are bound in spirit and substance to their under-valued, over-burdened sisters everywhere. The shining tip of Chinese women who are crying out for change, poking, first tentatively, then boldly piercing the wall of old ideas and habit, carry with them a tremendous load. They make the critical mistake, however, of perceiving themselves not as one unified spear, but as a thousand tiny arrows. Like the characters in these stories, Chinese women stand alone. Though there is an occasional reach out for help, ultimately each must find her own answer and draw strength from within. They have no community support; they do not collect and empower themselves with other women; they struggle with the wall in isolation. Unassailable, concrete change will come only with connection, collection and organization.

Life moves in circles. Several months of research passed, the article forgotten in my drawer, when an editor at Chinese Literature Press brought in a friend he thought I should meet. I liked her from the start — her inquisitive eyes and candid smile. Before leaving, she gave me a signed copy of her short story collection. It took a few minutes to sink in — that compact woman in sandals and shorts was the inspiration for my book project. I ran down the hall and caught her by the stairs. Two years later, she's still an inspiration and one of my closest connections. She calls our meeting the work of "Fate." Perhaps it was.

Diana B. Kingsbury
November 1992

Acknowledgments

Every book is the child of many parents. I would like to thank first of all Ms. Chen Xiuzheng of New World Press for her encouragement and direction when the idea was conceived. Without her, it wouldn't have been possible. My thanks also to the countless friends who offered leads and provided books and magazines in Chinese. Special mention goes to Mr. Peng Xingguo of Chinese Literature Press for his ready supply of short stories, Ms. Min Dongchao of Tianjin Normal University for her enthusiasm and help uncovering new material, and Ms. Li Xiaojiang of Zhengzhou University for her theoretical insights.

Though most of the translation work is my own, special thanks go to those who prepared drafts for select manuscripts. Michael S. Weiss laid the base for Li Xiaojiang's *Introduction* and Lisa Spollen for *I Wish I Were a Wolf*. Chinese Literature Press kindly allowed a re-write of Ms. Guan Yuehua's translation of *Friend on a Rainy Day*.

Having made China my home for the last four years, friends constitute my immediate family circle. I am indebted to everyone, in China and the States, who supported and encouraged me through this project. My thanks especially to Darou Niang, Mary Wiseman, Julie Crawford, Suk-hi Cho, and Ms. Han Chunxu. A final thanks to my colleagues at New World Press, who provided invaluable behind-the-scenes support at every stage of production.

Introduction

Li Xiaojiang

An introduction to a book of literature by contemporary Chinese women writers requires first an explanation of the road women in China have taken toward liberation. This road is the shared background to their creative voice.

Real change for women began not with the May Fourth Movement of 1919[1] but with the establishment of the People's Republic of China in 1949. Socialism marked a new age; the lives of both women and men underwent enormous change, breaking for the first time with Chinese tradition.[2] For women, change was manifested in the legal right of "sexual equality," in the ideology of "men and women are the same" and in a new era of social practice where "women hold up half the sky."[3] Women entered the workplace and, through participation in society, began to acquire some political power.

Contemporary Chinese women's literature sprang from the soil of these new conditions. Unlike women's literature of the May Fourth Movement, it has developed in an atmosphere of sexual equality, raising as never before the banner of "women."

"Women," as an issue, has posed a challenge — a challenge to the rights, already won, that are threatening to revert to traditional ways; a challenge to the thousands of years of that tradition; and a challenge to the new tradition of "sexual sameness" which has predominated social relationships in China for the last forty years. Making "women" an issue and confronting these challenges has opened a new page in the Chinese women's liberation movement — the awakening of group consciousness.[4]

It took Chinese women nearly a century, from the first

5

steps of social and ideological change in the late nineteenth century, to come to this awakening. The period between the end of the Cultural Revolution[5] in 1976 and the onset of urban reform[6] in the eighties marked the end of this road and the beginning of a new awareness of ourselves as women. Our women writers have taken part, with their lives and their pens, living and recording this process in its becoming.

Looking back over the last fifteen years of works by Chinese women authors, we can discern two main periods: The first, from the late seventies to the mid-eighties, dealt primarily with the awakening of a women's consciousness. Zhang Jie's "Love Must Not Be Forgotten" (1979) sparked a literary genre which portrayed the unique experience of women (as compared to men) in the previous thirty years, particularly during the Cultural Revolution decade. Describing the inner journey of women's unavoidable awakening, the most prominent pieces of that time lit the fire to raising group consciousness.

The second period coincided with the urban reforms of 1986. New images of awakened women with a sense of Self began to appear. Confident of women's social status, literature of this period raised a series of claims to "women's rights," claims that cut deeper to the root of the women's problem than the usual discussion of rights in society.

Two collections of literature by contemporary Chinese women writers are scheduled to come out in English this year. Professor Zhu Hong of the Chinese Academy of Social Sciences has compiled a book of short stories from the early eighties. Her selections, drawn from the first period outlined above, highlight the process of women's awakening. The pieces in *I Wish I Were a Wolf: The New Voice in Chinese Women's Literature*, on the other hand, were written in the latter half of the eighties. They're about awakened women making claims to their rights as women.

China's legal system guarantees sexual equality. What other rights could these writers be talking about? In contrast to the feminist movement in the West, little is said about rights in society; in contrast to previous demands made by Chinese women (up through the modern period), the question of "sexual equality" is deliberately avoided. Women already awakened, they find expression to critique their present state: The rights they lay claim to are exactly those which their sisters of the older generation discarded on the path to that awakening.

What claims are made in this collection?

A Woman's Right to Love and Be Loved

The notion of love as a woman's "religion" has been covered from every angle, exhausted beyond possibility. To love a man — not any man, but her husband alone — this was the religion of every Chinese woman in years past. Han Chunxu's "Rejecting Fate" tackles the topic with a different twist. On the surface, it's the story of an "outside lover," a young woman who gets pregnant out of wedlock. Facing the unborn life inside her that she's forced to give up, she comes to analyze the meaning of her own. A woman, and yet she says: "How I wish I could be a real woman, as lovely as a poem, a woman who understands love, who knows how to love, who loves with warmth, with passion, with delight; to be a *lover*, a *wife*, a *mother*. And to experience all the sensibilities of a woman for myself."

In prose as beautiful as the emotions conveyed, Han's protagonist defies tradition — both familial norms and moral values. Having bent to external pressure, her ultimate victory lies in her true and whole-hearted love. She claims the right to say: "What is it we shouldn't forget about the love, so Chinese, that Zhang Jie writes of in 'Love Must Not Be Forgotten'? A love like that, so shrunken, so pitiful, so hideous...."

Liu Xihong's "You Can't Make Me Change" and Wang Anyi's "Brothers" tackle the issue from a different angle. They explore admiration and affection between women, and doing so, challenge conventional love. The writers offer no moral judgment. Their characters act; they record. The stories do, however, appeal for a revaluation of what is considered reasonable behavior. Further, they render aesthetic actions which would undeniably incite criticism in both the old and new societies. Who can resist this aesthetic? We can only admit their right to love as they will.

7

A Woman's Right to Sexual Expression

Unlike love, sexual expression is a new topic for Chinese women writers. In that sex fit into the scheme of marriage, Confucian ethics dictated for women a passive role. Yet the repugnance Chinese women have felt all along for the sexual act and insistence on linking sex to love does not necessarily result from Confucian training. These ideas are more probably related to self-hatred stemming from unwilling resignation as an instrument of "sexual service" for their husbands' pleasure.

Reform in the eighties did not prompt landmark discussions about "sex." Nor has there been the "sexual liberation" that took Western countries by storm in the sixties. Ideas about love and sex among the new generation of women, however, have changed dramatically. By the late eighties, sex had become a regular topic in the work of women writers. Speaking through their female protagonists, they either bind sex to love or treat it on its own, allowing interpretation to swing from "sexual repression" of real life to "sexual liberation" of fantasy.

Xiang Ya's on-the-spot reporting in "Women Speak" takes the air out of free interpretation by using real stories to chronicle real change: the onset of a sexual revolution, a revolution that has come full cycle for some women. Her article did not incite a whirlwind when it appeared in 1988 because, for most intellectual and career women, a base of social equality and group consciousness had already been laid. Shatter the traditional view of sex, and claims to the right of sexual expression follow.

One voice in particular in this stream of changing ideas clamors for attention. Asserting that sex should be freed from the confines of marriage, an interviewee in "Women Speak" asks: "Your world is so big, how can you fit a man in?" A woman with little faith in men, she says: "Sex and love are two different things. If you can't find a man worth loving, are you going to give up the chance to enjoy sex?" Right or wrong, this voice circulates today among educated women. Claiming the right to sexual expression, while part of a woman's personal liberation, remains thus, on some level, a dilemma for women already "liberated."

8

A Woman's Right to Choose Her Own Lifestyle

In the old society, women endured the same pattern of life for thousands of years. Marriage, the only respectable route allowed, defined two primary occupations: wife and mother. Women were thrust into society and granted new rights in 1949, but traditional roles in the family held fast; they merely became "working" wives and mothers. Tradition, the invisible lasso, continued to bind, pulling women down the same old road, a road marked with the sign: "You have no choice."[7]

Awakened women boldly claim the right to control their own destinies. The narrator in "You Can't Make Me Change" demonstrates her independence by pursuing her own career and freely socializing with friends of both sex. The young woman in "Rejecting Fate" likewise determines to call her own shots. She will have love regardless of marriage. "The present is all I need," she says. "That is enough."

Though such claims are gaining acceptance today, ten years ago even, they would have been decried as heresy by men and women alike. Take, for example, another interviewee in "Women Speak" who has her own ideas about the way she wants to live:

"...I do want a child. I don't think it's anybody else's business but my own who the father is. I went at lunchtime to have a talk about this with the Party Secretary.

" 'I plan to have a child,' I announced to him. He looked happy to hear the news. 'Well then,' he smiled, 'when are you getting married?'

"I'd been thinking over the problem for some time; when he said that, I broke out angrily: 'What makes you think I should get married to have a child?!' Food from his chopsticks splattered all over his lap.... He stared at me for the longest time, then asked, 'Why are you bringing this up? Is it morally right?'

"I got even more excited: 'Why bring it up? Because it's my right! I'm a woman, and it's in my na-

9

ture to have children. Restricting my right as a woman to give birth is inhumane! Nature has given me not only the ability to procreate but also the inclination to do so. Giving birth is my right!' ''

A Woman's Right to Self-development

Self-development and "women's liberation" are two different but related pursuits. The goals of "women's liberation" are group-oriented; the struggle is directed against opposing forces inherent in a male-dominated society where women have always been the "second sex." A woman's claim to the right of self-development, on the other hand, is one outcome of this movement toward liberation. It's the cry raised by women who are saddled with the dual responsibilities of career and family.

Ma Zhongxing's "I Wish I Were a Wolf" portrays the typical married working woman's life in urban China. Shen Rong first tackled the subject in 1980 in "At Middle Age," depicting the despair and powerlessness of a woman doctor caught between the demands of career and family. "I Wish I Were a Wolf," written in 1988, takes a different bent. The protagonist describes herself as a "sheep" herded by her mother-in-law, sacrificed to husband and sons. "I am oppressed, suffocated, ground down, stupid and lowly." Like her illiterate, jobless mother-in-law, she is "...strangled. (Their) lives have flowed from different streams into the same current of household slavery." But there's a difference: As a college instructor, she must get up to lecture in front of class. "Failing would not only mean my career; it would affect me spiritually."

Ma's protagonist, when caught between the demands of career and family, thinks: "I've wondered a thousand times whether I could've endured the loneliness of staying single. Every time I start to sink under the tremendous weight of life, I berate myself: Why couldn't I have had enough sense and determination as a young woman to choose that path?" In the end, she comes to the conclusion: "If I could live my life over again, I'd be a wolf and not a sheep."

To be a "wolf" represents the resistance a woman

10

must put up to protect her chances for self-development. What happened when Xia Zhixian, a central character in the play by Bai Fengxi, "Friend on a Rainy Day," played the wolf? She is quoted on the title page as saying: "A woman is not the moon. She can shine by her own light." The price she paid for illumination, however, was divorce from the man she loved. A woman of crowning achievements, she says: "Don't you think it's hard on a woman who wants to develop her professional skills but in doing so has to give up the pleasure of a family? Is that supposed to prove she's strong? Of course not!" She tells her daughter who's bent on taking the same path: "I don't want to see you make the same mistakes I have."

From the differing negations of Self expressed in "I Wish I Were a Wolf" and "Friend on a Rainy Day," we can see that for modern-day women, the claim to self-development is multi-directional. It's the claim to overall growth toward a more well-rounded life.

In fact, though most of the stories in this collection express claims to specific rights, all reflect a desire for well-rounded development. The "wholistic consciousness" written into the female protagonists lies at the heart of the women's movement in China today.

In our quest for "wholism," however, we inevitably run into a wall of opposition. What makes up that wall? To whom do we submit our claims? The wall is not built from law or society, the family, or even men. The wall is simply the tradition from which we ourselves have grown.

In the overhaul of the old social system, antiquated ideas like "a woman's place is in the home" were repudiated and new concepts of "sexual equality" absorbed. Women hold up not only "half the sky" by working and participating equally in society, but with their responsibilities at home, are required, in fact, to shoulder the *whole sky*. Tradition, nonetheless, envelops and binds our "new society" like a giant net. Traditional values flow through our veins; we carry them inside us and pass them along. How can we escape when we ourselves are the tradition?

It's not surprising, therefore, that while the works in

11

this collection rebel against tradition, they do not champion women's rights *per se*. They attack the stock of old ideas, beliefs and behaviors we and our communities are made of — the tradition which hinders our development. Tie Ning's "Octday" is a case in point. Divorced at thirty-four, "...every time (Zhu Xiaofen) thought about her age and her divorce, she felt so happy she wanted to jump rope...." From the eye of tradition, divorce is a tragedy; everyone is sympathetic. Tie Ning turns on her wit in free-flowing language to enumerate good intentions gone awry. Untangled, as it were, from the web of marriage, Zhu Xiaofen falls into a web of divorce. Who is she up against? Those who good-heartedly contribute to her post-marriage discontent are none other than colleagues, boss and close friends. The narrator in "I Wish I Were a Wolf" has a similar experience. Who forces her to become a "wolf" but those most intimate — husband, sons and mother-in-law.

Two claims, for Chinese women today, stand out above the rest: the right to love, drenched as it is in tradition, and the right to equality in the work-place. The latter, a forty-year-old legacy of socialism, has placed women in the social arena and ensured economic self-sufficiency, thus laying the base for all other demands.

In the stories presented here, when danger of losing other rights looms, the protagonist invariably looks to work for compensation. She'd give up everything, even love and family, rather than lose the base to her "rights in society." Whereas her sisters of yesterday would have sought refuge in the family, today's woman reaches outside of herself to work, to what she has in society. Grasping this point is critical to understanding the thought, emotion and spirit behind the works in this collection. *It is the key to understanding contemporary Chinese women.*

Finally, how do men fit into these works by women authors? None of the stories follow the traditional romantic narrative. Women take the leading roles, men play second fiddle. In Wang Anyi's "Brothers," the three women, contrary to custom, label their men "family." Love, nonetheless, appears to exist. No matter how great their disappointment in men, they do not reject them completely. It is through loving men they create a vision of what it means to be women.

On this point, "Brothers" is a highly symbolic work. The thoughts and emotions, interrelations and unfolding destinies described in the story represent those of contemporary career women. The so-called "brothers" are three women. Implied is that women today are equal to, if not better than, men in school and at work. The characters "overstep" their bounds, not only in the classroom and society, but also at home. "Lao Da" disregards her husband and takes over the house with her friend. "Lao Er" decides irrespective of her husband whether or not to have a child. "Lao San," on the other hand, betrays her "brothers" to leave with her husband. She goes not because she has no choice, but because she chooses her husband's love over a job in the city. Like her "brothers," she takes responsibility for her own fate.

The "brothers" constantly point out what is lacking in men, but in the end, despite the strength of their fraternal union, they still choose them. Though men take no principal part, the male role is obvious: In school, the three women "compete" with the men students; they call themselves "brothers," their husbands are "family." The minute a man shows up, however, they are forced apart and back to their original state — that of women. They ask themselves: "What is a man anyway?" and answer: "He is the natural complement and companion to a woman."

All the works in this collection express women's willingness to compromise and cooperate in their love relationships with men. This is an accurate reflection of the attitude prevalent among Chinese women today. Rather than reproach ourselves for being too traditional, we should respect this grip on the past — it in itself is a form of resistance. We live in an era of change — modern culture is replacing tradition; material culture is subverting human links of empathy and love; the woman's movement is upending conventional relationships between women and men, calling for independence at the cost of personal happiness.

In this world of changing values, the hold contemporary Chinese women maintain on their right to love in a "traditional" fashion requires courage and vision. Humanity, after all, is comprised of both women and men. If men cannot be liberated, can there be a women's liberation or human liberation? Without women's tolerance and love, is the liberation of men possible?

Notes

1. The May Fourth Movement is named after the student demonstration on May 4, 1919 that protested the bartering away of Chinese territory at the Paris Peace Conference. This urban-based movement, lasting through the early 1920s, marked the turning of young, disillusioned intellectuals—mostly sons and daughters of the old gentry and new commercial classes—toward radical political activism. Critique of the Confucian family system and women's position in traditional society was an integral part of their search for alternative values and ideals to rejuvenate a degenerating China. May Fourth writers attacked the "iron net," the "flesh-devouring" monster of the old extended family system; they sought a family image based on gender equality, mutual love and free choice. But though family reform and women's rights issues developed into an important component of the current intellectual and political dialogue (centered in the cities), it took a comprehensive overhaul of the social system (as what happened in 1949) to effect real change.

2. The 1950 Marriage Law laid the grounds for women's break out of the traditional family order. It abolished arranged marriages, outlawed paying any price in money or goods for a wife, outlawed polygamy, concubines and child marriage, prohibited interference in the remarriage of widows and guaranteed the right of divorce to women as well as men. Furthermore, land reform in the countryside gave women legal rights to property ownership. On paper, these measures redistributed property and power in the family and granted women equal rights with men. Practically speaking though, change came slowly and through much struggle.

3. Mao Zedong's declaration that women must work side-by-side with men in all manner of productive activity—based on the Communist Party's stated belief that paid employment outside the home was the key to liberating women and building a gender-equal society.

4. For urban women who grew up in the "new society," in post-revolution "women are the same as men" years, the realities of personal experience (e.g. marriage, where one is knit into a web of relationships reinforced by traditional expectations; and work, where increasingly men are favored over women in a new age of economic competition) revealed the falsehood of that claim. Women studies theorists in China

14

call this revelation of gender identity, where "women are not the same as men," and the new-found appreciation of themselves as women, the awakening of group consciousness.

5. The Great Proletarian Cultural Revolution (1966-1976) was a mass movement of unprecedented vigor and duration led by Mao Zedong against the Communist Party machine. Feeling that the Party was losing its revolutionary zeal and capitalism loomed on the horizon, Mao encouraged class struggle to combat the rise of a new bourgeoisie. The first three years, from May 1966 to April 1969, were the most chaotic; students had responded enthusiastically to Mao's call to form Red Guard organizations to seek out and destroy the "ghosts and monsters" in China and "criticize the small handful of people in authority taking the capitalist road." They held mass rallies, traveled for free around the country, had license to attack their teachers, raid homes of suspected bourgeoisie and beat their victims. External calm was restored by 1969 through intervention of the army; the Red Guards were shipped off to rural and border areas to be re-educated by the peasants and steeled through manual labor. The suspicious death of Mao's designated successor, Lin Biao, in 1971 was a great shock to the young idealists exiled to the countryside. The next six years before Mao's death in 1976 saw a partial return to normality. The few city youth who could manage it filtered back home; schools re-opened; people began to rebuild their lives. The Gang of Four, the group responsible for the extremist policies during that period, headed by Mao's wife, was arrested several days after Mao's death, marking the unofficial end of the Cultural Revolution.

6. Economic reforms were launched in 1979 in the countryside with a series of new central government provisions. The most significant of these was the contracting of land to the peasant household, effectively terminating the system of collective agriculture. In the early 1980s, reforms followed in the cities, as expressed in the slogan "Opening to the outside world and invigorating the domestic economy." Special economic zones were created and special conditions laid for foreign investors to this end. Most state-owned factories and enterprises are now required to make a profit—to do this, they must compete with the booming number of small private businesses. Reform of the political structure—characterized by tight vertical bureaucracy, central planning and decision-making concentrated at the top—came next. 1986 saw the experimental beginning of administrative reform, a move designed to untangle overlapping interests and personnel in the government and Party. In 1987 broad principles of political reform were adopted. The most important of these were: separation of Party and state, release of decision-making power to lower levels and restructuring of organizations. "Opened" to the outside world, China has let in more than foreign capital and management skills. Increasing contact with peoples from abroad and access to foreign books and mass media have fostered new ideals of Western liberalism and individual rights.

15

7. The title of a highly-acclaimed short story by woman writer, Liu Suola, published in 1985, about the social and systematic constraints on lifestyle choices of university students.

I Wish I Were a Wolf

Ma Zhongxing

I

Lugging two large sacks of books, one slung over a shoulder, the other heavy on my arm, I trudged into the elevator at 14 Xuanxi Street. Little Zhang, the young elevator operator, stared at me enviously.

Earlier in the day, leaving the school library, this same armload of books had attracted one look after the next.

"Well, Teacher Ding, taking the whole library home with you, eh?" teased my colleague, her eyes sparkling with mischief.

Next came the department head: "Preparing for class? That's quite a stack of reference books you've got there." Eyes of suspicion.

I didn't care what they thought. Like a lost planet adrift in the universe, I'd once again found my orbit. I'd returned to the work world.

Little Zhang likes to have a quick chat with me when we're alone in the elevator. "You're amazing, teaching at a university and all," she sighed.

"Amazing? I've wasted over twenty years of my life. I don't know what I'm doing now," I protested, depressed at the thought. I didn't have my whole life ahead of me like some lucky young women.

"But you're still better off than we are. At least you got a decent education. We didn't learn a thing during the Cultural Revolution."[1]

Her words shocked me. What an enormous vacuum that time was!

17

I unlocked the door to apartment 1204. We have two rooms: Old Liu [2] and I occupy the twelve-square-meter room, and our two sons and Popo, my mother-in-law, share the larger fifteen meters.[3] There's not much space, but having moved often over the past twenty years, accumulating few personal possessions along the way, we don't feel cramped here. Three small beds and a home-made couch and coffee table set fill the larger room. A bed, a square table from the fifties — both dining room table and desk — and several stools take up the smaller. Our tiny entry is crowded with coats hung on pegs and a bench. The one source of charm is our narrow balcony. It offers an unobstructed, twelfth-story view of the city, where in the evenings we can look out on millions of twinkling lights and feel the warm glow from the homes below.

I deposited my books on the table but couldn't sit down. Before all else I had to pay my respects to Popo. The ceremony is quite simple: I poke my head in her room and say, "Ma, I'm home."

An unwritten law decrees that everybody in the house must shout four times a day to the old woman — when we get up in the morning, go out for the day, come home in the evening and go to bed at night. Four times a day. A simple "Ma!" or "Grandma!" is enough.

None of The Four Daily Shouts can be omitted. Over time they've become rote, formulaic, lacking any inspiration whatsoever and sometimes outright absurd. For example, first thing every morning, I go out to empty the chamber pot, but if I meet Popo in the hallway, I have to beat a quick retreat to my room, put down the pot, and then stick out my head to greet her. That business finished, I can get back to the pot.

Popo's adult sons and grandsons feel foolish with the ritual and have rebelled. Their wives have followed suit, leaving me to uphold the law. No doubt that's why Popo favors me. She often brags: "That Maomei has the sweetest tongue!" What's really at stake is that, since her rule is largely ignored by the others, my adherence to that single syllable ''Ma'' paints me an old-fashioned woman, modest and respectful to my elders.

Many a time she's told me her experience as a young daughter-in-law. Every evening she had to wash her popo's feet in a basin of hot water. She couldn't retire until she'd seen her popo to bed, but sometimes the old lady fell asleep after dinner without her foot-wash. She'd wait outside the room, baby in arms, until, unable to stand it any longer, she'd give the baby's bottom a good pinch. Wakened by the wailing, the old woman would sleepily grumble, "What are you doing standing there with the baby crying like that? Go to bed."

It's an enlightened Popo who's confided in me, "Life was too hard for young women back then. We had to get rid of those old customs. But," she's insisted, "if there's one thing I require, it's that you all pay your respects to me four times a day, every day."

"Ma!" I called. Popo, perched on the sofa looking at a photo album with her reading glasses, quickly raised her head. Her enormous eyes, clouded with age but as cunning as ever, peered up at me over the black rims. "Ah! Maomei! You're home."

Her tone was normal.

Next came my anticipated reward.

"There's a bowl of sugared tomatoes on the table for you."

If I hadn't stopped to greet her, the scenario would have taken another course. Should I later ask a simple question, she'd snap back, "Don't know!" without looking up. She'd spend the rest of the day sighing unhappily, a pained expression distorting her face. She's nearly eighty. At this point, it's not worth upsetting her.

I sat down at the table for my tomatoes, and loathe to waste a minute, began to flip through the stack of books before me.

Life is said to be like a circle: The closer you get to the end, the closer you approach the beginning. Over twenty years ago, when I was young and strong, I'd been asked to teach at a university. It hadn't seemed so crucial to me at the time. But then I'd been sifted out, and years of humiliation had left me sluggish, muscles slack, heart bruised.[4] I was back at the beginning, back in front of the classroom door. None of my youthful arrogance remained. All I had left was timidity and the anguish of wasted years.

I'd been assigned to lecture on the Analysis of Dramatic Works.

An old classmate had given me a tip about the first class. If I could make a big hit in the first session, one student would tell ten, ten would tell a hundred, and soon the whole school would be talking. The students' faith in me would spur on my self-confidence, and the classroom would become a garden for my ideas to blossom into words elegant and profound.... That's what she said anyway.

Everyone had been sure to tell me about my predecessor, the teacher whose course failed so dismally that only eight or nine of a hundred made it to the end. I'd gone to other institutes to listen in on their "analysis" classes and found smatterings of students, hiding magazines in notebooks, writing letters camouflaged as class notes, reading hefty novels buried in their laps ... and the teachers, huffing and puffing behind the podium, pumping up the classroom with hot air.

They'd also told me about the professor whose "analysis" class had won acclaim in both academia and the art world. She wasn't teaching the course at the time, but I'd listened to her lectures on tape. Thoroughly familiar with the theater, she gave detailed analysis and quoted with ease from innumerable sources. Her lectures were lucid, substantive and exciting. With over ten years of experience, her lecturing skills, as everyone had said, were superb.

How depressing to listen to those tapes. I'd worked in the theater, factories, and on farms for over twenty years. I'd never be able to speak like that.

But I had to do it. I had to make it come off. How else could I hold up my head? How else could I face my students and colleagues? Failing would not only mean my career; it would affect me spiritually. I needed to regain my honor and dignity that had been trampled in the dirt of those rough, bitter years. I needed to hold on to my self-respect. Without that, I was nothing.

From my seat at the old square table, I took my first step up that long, arduous slope. Theories, some antiquated, some simplistic, and arguments, fresh, abstruse, incisive, leapt from the pages, filling me with a new sense of purpose. I had stepped into the intriguing world of academics.

"Maomei! What's for dinner tonight?" Popo's bellow nearly blasted me out of my chair. Her reading glasses lowered, she shuffled over to my desk with a cheery grin.

I glanced at my watch. Only four o'clock. "Mama," I implored, "Let me read for another half hour and then I'll make dinner, okay?"

She fiddled with my books and sighed sympathetically, "So many books you have to read! You must have been very wicked in your past life to deserve such punishment." Before I had time to respond, she was on to a new thought:

"But it's just wonderful what you can do. You'll be teaching at a university and making over a hundred *yuan* a month."

Amazing. Wonderful. Two people called me that in one day.

After a long pause, Popo muttered, "Not like me. I've always lived off other people."

She often says that. It has several different meanings, depending on her mood. There are the times she's itching to give us a piece of her mind and knows we're ignoring her, or the times she's lost in a daze, reflecting on the past, or the times she's feeling lonely and has nothing to do.

I've tried to console her, recounting again and again all she's been through for her husband and six children. I've clasped her gnarled, callous hands in mine and sung songs of praise for wives and mothers. I've reminded her that her husband relied upon the honorable practice of medicine to make a living. I've told her she's had nothing to do with exploitation.

But I've never been able to convince her.

She stubbornly believes that reliance on her husband and sons for "room and board," having never had a job of

21

her own, means she's gotten by on the exploitation of others. Her other favorite saying is: "A man is your god." If one of the sons or grandsons ever noticed she was busy and offered to go pick up some soy sauce or peel the vegetables, she'd always chase him away, "No, no! Get out of here! Men have important things to do. You have to make money and support the family. I don't want you wasting your time in the kitchen."

I make money to support the family and still waste my time in the kitchen.

I remember how once, many years ago, Popo needed water for something. The basin was empty, and though it should have been my job to fill it up, my three-year-old son Linlin wouldn't budge from my lap. I turned to my husband and said, "Mama needs water. Will you go get a bucket for her?"

Popo flared with irritation (my words must have sounded like a veritable assault upon the laws of nature) and reprimanded me in a low, stern voice, "I do not like to hear you ordering him around."

Popo may be uneducated, but she's steeped in traditional Chinese etiquette. A natural sense of superiority props up the men in her family, convincing them they are entitled to a lifetime of obedient service from the weaker sex.

But her sadness also runs deep. She sat down on the bed beside me and began reciting the same story I've heard countless times before. "I was only sixteen when I married the old man. He was way over thirty. Every day I'd lean up against the window to watch the girls in their white blouses and black skirts go to school. Boys and girls in class together. What fun! I thought. I told the old man I wanted to go too, but he just threw that old Confucian saying back at me: 'A woman's virtue is her ignorance.'"

Popo chattered on. Immersed in one of my Greek tragedies, I let out an occasional "Hmph" to satisfy her.

She's used to that kind of treatment. No one in the family, not even the children, pays attention to her chatter. She didn't get angry, but took my silence as an opportunity

22

to have her say:

"After Liberation,[5] classes were organized in the neighborhood for us illiterates. One day I went home and said to the old man, 'A woman's virtue is her ignorance, huh? Well, I've had enough of virtue. I've signed up for a literacy class, and every night after I've made dinner, bathed the kids and turned down the beds, I'm going to go learn to read and write.'

"I got perfect scores on all my tests. Only once, on a dictation quiz, I couldn't remember the character for 'situation.' Try as I might, I just couldn't picture it. I got all the others but not that one. It broke my heart to get a ninety-nine. I was class supervisor. How could I take charge with a pitiful ninety-nine?"

Popo rebelled against the "virtuous woman" tradition and joined neighborhood-organized projects to help other women fight for their emancipation. Her neighbor, Mama Wang, had been sold as a little girl to work as a servant. She'd been raped by her master and had spent her entire life under his roof as a concubine and slave. Popo said to her: "Every day they beat you and scream at you. We can all see your face black with bruises. You have wings to flap and a voice to cry out, but you still can't fly away. I want to break open your cage and set you free." Mama Wang cried. "Don't cry," Popo said, brushing away her own tears. "Your tears make me cry all the harder." She arranged part-time work for Mama Wang at the neighborhood kindergarten and, to give her more time, took on some of her household chores. "I built bridges for those in need," she's told me.

A newly liberated woman has endless potential. Popo had been kindergarten supervisor, head of the neighborhood dental clinic, elected representative of this, model worker of that. She'd even spoken once before several hundred people at a meeting for military families. Those were her golden years.

They lasted until 1957 when her third son (my husband) was labeled a Rightist.[6] She went back home, back into the kitchen. Those thrilling days, like a flash of lightening, had illuminated her life for an instant, then passed

23

away forever. Her passion to eradicate old customs and ideas cooled down and eventually died.

It was almost five o'clock and time to buy groceries. Time to put away my books and papers so we could use the table for dinner. Would I ever be freed from the anchor of three meals a day? Would I ever have a desk of my own to spread out on without having to flip through everything to find my place when I sat down again?

Popo helped me tidy up. Suddenly, out of nowhere, she came up with the thought: "The Women's Federation doesn't hold classes anymore, but if it did, I'd still go. If you don't have smarts in this world, everyone looks down on you. And that's a fact."

Eighty years of age and so many regrets. I saw myself in Popo. The reflection made my blood run cold.

II

In terms of time management and strategic planning, grocery shopping is no less complicated than preparing for war. First to the outdoor market, where I stuffed my backpack with vegetables. Then to the grocery store: one line for lean meat, another for fish, and finally a short wait in the cooking oil section for eggs. My hands were full beyond use, but there was still soy sauce and cooking wine on the list. By the time I'd stuffed these bottles, so intertwined with my existence, into my shopping bag, I'd metamorphosed into a small, bulging pushcart. Straining under my load, I trudged deliberately home.

It's then, all I wish is for my husband or son to come out and give me a hand. The wish waits inside me, waits, and is still waiting.

That time in the elevator, Little Zhang's stare was one of pity. "Just you wait, girl," I thought, "Your day will come."

I was met at the front door by the pounding beat of disco music. A woman's voice crooned, "You don't know ... You alone are in my heart; You alone I can't forget...."

24

Yimin, my older son, was lounging on the sofa, a portable cassette player in one hand, a cup of tea in the other. Scraggly hair hung over his head, small atop his long body. One skinny leg crossed over the other bounced to the beat. Popo hovered beside him with spiced melon seeds and crispy sugar-nuts. Whenever Yimin comes home, treats from Popo's private cabinet appear. Beaming with pleasure, she excitedly circled round him like the earth around the sun.

In 1957, when Old Liu ran into political problems and was sentenced to penal labor in the countryside, I was carted off to a farming village and Yimin sent to the old family home to be raised by Popo. He's still her favorite.

Though the apartment resounded with the strains of disco, I had to march to the beat of my own drum. Spurred on by the call to attack, I charged into the kitchen. Wash the rice, chop the meat, scale and gut the fish, wash and chop the vegetables, peel the scallions, wash the ginger.... Whenever Yimin comes home, I have to put out seven or eight dishes. Popo knows he doesn't have much clout, so she uses her own to make sure he's well fed. "Us old folks need meat to fill up," she likes to tell us. "I go hungry every time I come here." (Popo can move as she likes from one son's house to the next.) "Go buy me some meat," she'll order, pulling out twenty *yuan* from her bag. Popo has many sons and thus many sources of income; she's the "moneybags" of the family.

The music changed to a Brahms serenade, soft and distant. I could see Old Liu, just home, through the open door. Barely seated, he pulled the newspaper off the table and began to read. My younger son Linlin, also just back, sat flipping through the magazines his father had brought home with him.

Men engage their energy in higher affairs of the world. Mealtimes, they enjoy tasting and commenting upon every dish, but other than that, they never dirty their hands with household matters. They have no idea what it took to find fresh fish and reasonably priced vegetables in the market. They don't know the time I spent in line to buy grain or the calculation required to pack it home. They certainly don't know my anxiety over my lecture as I stand there,

25

peeling vegetables and chopping meat. They call themselves "hard worker" and "good student" and praise me, the one who makes possible their hard work and good study, a "good housekeeper." As if I were born a second-class citizen ... their bondservant. And if I don't like my place, they think there's something wrong with me.

I've wondered a thousand times whether I could have endured the loneliness of staying single. Every time I start to sink under the tremendous weight of life, I berate myself: Why couldn't I have had enough sense and determination as a young woman to choose that path? It didn't even occur to me. It's natural to want love. But it's also natural to seek professional success. I never realized how, for a woman, the two are incompatible.

I watched through the open door as Popo ceremoniously drew a key from her pocket, unlocked her cabinet and excitedly pulled out the dish of crispy sugar-nuts she'd made the day before. Preparations for the day-long endeavor had begun by dragging a stool into the kitchen. She mixed shelled peanuts with sugar (that she'd sent me out specially to buy) and boiled them in water for ten minutes. When they were drained, she heated a wok and fried the peanuts in salt for an hour until they burst open. Cooled at last, she locked them up in her cabinet for their debut.

From my spot in the kitchen, I could imagine Popo, cheeks slightly flushed, proudly bearing the dish of nuts to the table to offer son and grandsons. "How do you like these peanuts?"

Her men, caught in a heated philosophical argument, grabbed a couple handfuls and popped them in their mouths, unaware of either Popo or the nuts. Only after she repeated her question did they respond, "Huh?... Oh, yeah... Good."

Popo was satisfied. Her hard work had earned her the greatest of all rewards.

I felt her loneliness. It's that reflection that horrifies me more than anything.

I remember one visit to the old family home not long after Old Liu and I were married. Popo had been running

26

around all day to feed her brood of sons and grandsons. After dinner they pushed in their chairs and moved upstairs to continue their debate on the history of world literature. I remember hearing a soft sigh from the stairs. It was Popo, finished with the dishes, pulling herself up along the banister and groaning with the strain. Rushing over to help her, I lashed out at everyone in the room, "Who are all of you to talk about Shakespeare and Tolstoy?! Look how tired your mother is. Who even thinks of lifting a hand to help her?"

The brothers sat dumbfounded.

Popo tore her arm away and glared at me. "I am happy to serve them!" she declared. "I don't want them to help me. My sons will not set foot in the kitchen! They will attend to important matters!" She then plunked down in a chair, reached for a fan and, seething with anger, began to fan herself furiously.

All eyes turned on me. I guess I should have kept my mouth shut.

Then there was the time, ten years ago, when Popo had gone to visit us in the countryside and, seeing how hard our life was, decided to stay and help out. One evening after dinner when she'd gone to wash the dishes, I turned to Old Liu and said, "All Mama does every day is cook. In the evening, she just sits around waiting for us to come home. She must be so lonely. We should try to spend more time with her."

When she came back in from doing the dishes, my husband suddenly said, "Why don't I tell you all a story!"

Why on earth would he want to tell a story? But on second thought, I realized he was right. What could we possibly talk about with his mother?

The prospect of a story excited everyone. Linlin, a first-grader at the time, threw down his homework and leapt into his father's lap. Popo's face broke into a happy grin. I reached for some old clothes and mended while he spoke. At the close of his second tale, my husband stopped abruptly and returned to his reading. I got Linlin back to his homework and sat down to prepare my English lesson for the next day. Quietly registering the situation, Popo crept back to her little bedroom. I could hear her fiddling with the stations on her transistor radio until she found a theater program. "I'm so lonely!" came a woman's voice over the radio.

"You're lonely? I'm lonely, too." Popo murmured.

The emptiness and misery in her voice chilled me.

When I whispered this to my husband, he replied without looking up from his book, "Well, what do you want me to do? She's a casualty of her time. I can't sit around trying to make her feel better."

History the sculptor. Whistling over oceans and seas, it had blustered its way into my destitute little house. Popo's sorrow, caught and rolled in the tempest, unfurled into nothingness.

Born into a capitalist family that believed in "ladies first," I'd little imagined the misery that women are subject to in this world.

I graduated from college in the fifties facing a wide, easy road. When we began to talk about marriage, I told Old Liu, "I can't cook, and I can't sew." He waved away my concern, "I'm looking for a wife, not a maid." As if I'd expressed some obsolete notion or told an old, worn-out joke.

We ate at the school cafeteria or in restaurants. All our clothes—even the handkerchiefs—we sent out to be washed. Then came the day we went through every pocket and found only two *mao*.[7]

Old Liu sat down in the rattan chair, threw his bare feet on the desk and began to read.

"What are we going to do?" I asked, plopping down on the bed.

"Why don't you write a story about our predicament today," he suggested.

So that's what I did.

I can't remember how we solved our food crisis, but one thing stands out in my mind: It was one of the few times my husband praised my writing. For that, I'll always treasure our day of hunger.

The mighty march of history takes an occasional detour to play a little mischief. Old Liu was labeled a Rightist, and like autumn leaves, we drifted from Beijing to a provincial city, and from there to a steel town, an ashen-skyed, foul-watered, smoke-belching workers' compound built during the days of the Japanese occupation.[8]

We lived in a leaky, tumble-down shack. In the night, an armed division of rats would crawl from their barracks to chew at the books we'd stuffed under beds, in corners and closets and atop cabinets. Their "crunch crunch" gnawed at us till, in our frustration, we'd rap angrily on the bed. A moment of silence, then slowly, a tentative "crunch," two, and finally the melee would crescendo to its former intensity. Pulling on the lamp, we'd find a rug had appeared out of nowhere, a rug of cock-roaches that, equally startled, would scurry from the light back to their dark corners.

The workers in the compound had fixed up their own shacks. They'd laid bricks in the dirt floor, patched the walls and built new roofs. They'd cut out a plot of land to plant vegetables and dug a cellar for storage. They knew how to make their own pots, pails, kettles, ladles and oil lamps.

My family had been pulled out of the modern world and dropped into a medieval peasant village, a New Stone Age. It's ludicrous for city folks to step back into the Stone Age. Our urban survival skills were useless, incompetence in their way of life a given. The workers used to gaze curiously at us, pitying the two pale, paralyzed intellectuals and their fragile three-year-old boy.

My husband, ordered around all day like a slave, had an especially hard time. I didn't have the heart to press him with housework at home. I took it all on myself, grappling with our Stone Age life every day after work.

Lenin wrote in *A Great Beginning*, "Women are slaves to the home because the triviality of housework oppresses them, suffocates them, makes them stupid and lowly. It strangles them with cooking and child-care: non-productive, trivial, exhausting, stupefying, grinding work saps them of their spirit and energy...."

I am oppressed, suffocated, ground down, stupid and lowly. I am, like Popo, strangled. Our lives have flowed from two streams into the same current of household slavery.

I'd returned to the work world as an old, gray-haired woman. How I longed to throw off the shackles of housework, to break free from my role of household slave! How I wished for my husband and boys to know my labor. How I wished they'd step into the kitchen to help me chop a few scallions or peel the garlic. Just to stand there and say a polite word or two would be enough. But the wisdom of great scholars, the delicacy of renowned composers with all their dreams and aspirations, had snuffed out my spatula-wielding, negligible existence.

I threw open the kitchen door and hollered into the noisy, brightly lit room, "Dinner's ready!"

My voice thundered like the roar of a lion. Aware that something was amiss, they leapt to their feet, and with cries of "Okay!", "Right away!", "Coming!" they rushed about wiping down the table and carrying out the food.

Each in turn glanced over to gauge my mood, but without a look in their direction, I stormed out to the bathroom to wash my hands and face.

Seating myself at the table, I picked up my chopsticks but couldn't swallow a bite. I took a few deep breaths. I slowed the pounding in my chest. I forced myself to calm down.

The men were still at it, comparing the ontology of limited existence with the egoism inherent in Descarte's methodology. Popo and I, the two idiots, were incapable of contributing a word of our own. A chill took me. In my mind's eye, I could see countless other women throughout history—ignorant, benighted, slow-witted—I could see myself in their faces. All I knew how to talk about was "firewood, rice, oil and salt."[9]

Yimin glanced over in quiet moment and whispered to Linlin, "Such good music, and Ma doesn't even notice." I realized then the tape-recorder had been moved up on the windowsill next to the table. It was a tape of Liszt waltzes. I hadn't noticed.

"Trivial, exhausting" housework insulates me, cuts me off from music, art and thought. Takes away my peace of mind. Robs me of my time and self-worth, my wisdom and my tolerance. I was sinking.

Could I really stand up to speak behind the university lectern?

III

I stood in the kitchen.

Greasy dishes covered the counter; pots and pans littered the floor and stove top. I had to get moving.

Mechanically, I pulled out the washtub, poured the hot water, added cold ... in with the dishwashing liquid, but, too late, I realized I'd grabbed the vinegar. I emptied the tub, poured the hot water, added cold and reached for the liquid. Slosh, scrub ... I soaped up each plate and bowl and spoon and splash, whish ... rinsed them under the faucet.

Zhu Ziqing [10] once said: "Wash your hands; the days slip down the sink. Eat your meal; they slip down your bowl. Do nothing; they slip away before your glazed eyes." My days were slipping, and though I reached out to draw them back, they were stealing through my fingers and sliding away.

Smash! A ceramic spoon shattered on the floor.

I stooped to pick up the splinters and toss them in the garbage.

My days were slipping away while I picked up broken pieces.

Years and decades had slipped away.

My time was withering away.

My class preparation was withering away.

My life was withering away.

I was no longer a young woman. I was a wrinkled old lady.

How many days did I have left? In the little time I did have left, how could I escape this punishment?

There was no hope. I'd been sentenced for life to dull, trivial, stupefying housework!

I brushed off one hand, then the next.... Brushed away the bloody stink of fish and meat. Brushed away the laundry

31

stains. Brushed away the weariness of pushing needles and pulling thread.

Brushed away the stupidity binding my life.

Give me back the freedom of my youth!

How did I ever get to this?

I pulled myself together, straightened my shoulders and walked into their room of music and laughter.

They were all there. I strode over to the sofa and planted myself before my husband to make my announcement, "I have three options: get a maid; jump out the window; or leave." Resentment clung to my throat, twisting my words strangely.

Their laughter switched off. The tape-recorder's bouncy tune blared alone through the empty space.

Popo's hard, biting eyes widened with surprise.

Old Liu peered up from his book.

Yimin cracked into a grin, as if I'd just told a good joke.

Linlin, sensing an oncoming storm, sat nervously still.

I'd destroyed their peace, invited chaos into their pleasant, quiet evening.

I waited.

Old Liu attempted a little humor to soften me up. "Don't scare me like that," he said laughing, "or I'll be the one out the door."

Popo got up and moved over to the doorway of the balcony to look out over the lights below. I couldn't tell if she needed the fresh air or was considering inviting me to jump.

A stalemate ensued.

Old Liu adopted a bargaining tone, "Maomei, sacrifice for me for just two more years...."

I already knew the rest: " ... I've just started a new job. I need time to get settled in."

Two years!

Could I sacrifice two more years?

Could I bungle my way through classes for two years? Were my students to laugh at me up on the lectern for two years? Was I to be humiliated at the university for two years?

After two years of disgrace, would I be able to redeem myself and start over again? More likely I'd be ousted from my position and reassigned a new job. That would shatter me.

Some say there are two value systems at play in the development of intellectuals — spiritual and physical. The spiritual emphasizes dignity and freedom. The physical places existence and career first. All I once had in the physical world, all desire for material gain, had long been stripped away. I only had a little "personal dignity and spiritual freedom" left, battered, but still my most basic need. I could throw away my life in an instant but never give up my dignity.

Leaving no room for discussion, I turned to Old Liu and said, "Please consider my three options."

I knew he was thinking about the money. Calmly, he offered his response, "That's fine. Write a story to earn some money for this household and you can have a maid."

My temper flared.

"I will not write a story! I will use my time as I want. If I want to work, I'll work. If I want to relax, I'll relax. But no matter what, I want a maid!"

No response.

Popo, meanwhile, had pooled her energy. Twisting her head around to look at me, she let out a long, laborious sigh, "Modern women are all so busy ee-MAN-cipating themselves." She drew out the word, as if suppressing extreme dissatisfaction under its weight.

"Our whole lives," she said, "we must serve parents-in-law, husbands, sons, older brothers-in-law, younger brothers-in-law.... It's our duty to feed and clothe the family, to lower our heads obediently and do what's expected of us as women. Emancipated women in our new society won't be slapped around or yelled at, but we still have to serve the people. We all have to do our share to serve the people...."[11]

That was Popo the 1950's neighborhood activist speaking.

I've adopted a policy of "three don'ts" to deal with her scolding: don't argue, don't push the point and don't care. I made good use of the time by calculating the day's food expenses on a small abacus.

Had we not been engaged in that silent stand-off, the men would have never allowed Popo to take the stage and air her views. Pleased to note the silence around her, Popo turned to me and said in a pleasant voice, "When your husband was labeled a Rightist, you took good care of him. Now that he's a government official, you should do even more. The higher up he moves, the more prestige you have. That's called— '' She forgot how the saying went and turned to Yimin, "What's that called?"

Yimin had been struggling to keep quiet. He seized this chance to speak and enunciated each word: "A man's success is his wife's honor."

Blind to my furious glance, he proudly continued, "When I get married, I want my wife to take care of my home and serve me, so I can concentrate on my career. A virtuous wife is like heaven on earth."

"BAM!" I hurled the abacus to the floor. The wooden frame split in two, and beads rolled in all directions.

"Don't you ever speak like that to your mother!" I shouted.

"Why? What'd I do?" Yimin asked in a bewildered voice.

"I slave for old and young alike in this house. You're over twenty years old but think you can sit there on the couch with your legs crossed, listening to your music and reading your books, expecting me to wait on you. Sure, you all like your books, your debates and essays. That's all you want to think about. Get some wife to sacrifice for your comfort. You think you're all so enlightened — enlightened my ass!" I stood there shrieking, my voice and hands trembling.

Popo turned crimson. She screeched back harshly, "Who are you really yelling at? We've only been here a few days, and you already want to throw us out!"

Old Liu rushed to interject, "She's not talking about you!" Linlin jumped up to console her. But her rage grew.

"It's even worse if she's yelling at Yimin! I raised that boy. If she criticizes him, it's a slap in my face! I can yell at him and hit him, but nobody else has the right!"

The old woman survived the Allied Forces and Japanese invasions. She followed her husband through the dark years of the Kuomintang era, six sons in tow. Her husband had been a kindly, honest man; Popo was the one who'd fought for the whole crew. She's always been the champion, the heroine of the family.

Swallowing down a lump of bitterness, I gave up the fight.

Yimin broke the insufferable silence in an injured, challenging tone, "How come Ma got so mad when I talked about getting a wife?"

"I have spent— " I glanced at my watch, " — four hours on your dinner, from five o'clock till...."

"Even if you don't cook for me," Yimin interrupted, "I can always eat somewhere else."

I felt like I'd been clubbed over the head.

Four hours in the evening, two and a half at noon, and half an hour in the morning — seven hours I'd wasted on their meals. Class preparation? I'd neglected it entirely. All that housework, that running around, that frustration.... And for what? "Even if you don't cook for me, I can always eat somewhere else." Anyone can eat for a couple *yuan* at a restaurant. The school cafeteria is even cheaper, and if you're tight for money, you can go to a friend's house or buy some bread. Who was I trying to intimidate?

My work had all been for nothing, a big zero.

Oh, God! Why was I born a woman?

I crumbled, bursting into tears and laughing uproariously in the same breath. I wished I could scream like the little boy in *The Tin Drum*. I wanted to shatter windows, the glass face on the town clock, the old ladies' teacups....

I wanted to light a match and set that room on fire.

IV

The next morning when my husband left for work, I bolted the door to our room behind him and set to work on my lecture. At three I descended the twelve flights, ravenous, to buy bread and a bottle of soda. Back upstairs I continued my flight through the academic kingdom. My mind soared, swooped to the attack, ignited into sparkling flames. Tasting a dazzling, dizzying happiness, I recalled a passage I'd once read: "He locked the door, laughing with a fully contented heart. He'd finally found himself. How long had he been astray?''

How much better it was to forget them and do what I wanted! If every day could be like that, I'd win back my freedom. I'd make myself whole again.

But a dark shadow hung over me. Like a small animal escaped from its cage, I gazed up at the great blue sky, breathing in fresh, new air. It was only a matter of time before they recaptured me and locked me up again.

In all of Beijing, there aren't six square meters I can call my own. If I had my own apartment, I could've hidden out until, lecture complete, I'd emerge to face, in my colleague's words, the "critical'' first class.

I stretched out on the bed, cradling my head in my hands.

I heard a key slip into the lock.

Old Liu and Yimin walked in, eyes averted to the stack of books against the wall.

From where I lay on the bed, they looked larger-than-life. They searched through the stack, ignoring me, and walked back out again.

I'd done my duty, I thought. Hard times for my husband were over. Linlin was grown up. I'd carried them safely through hardship and fatigue to the other shore. No unfinished business remained. Death waited seductively.

I longed for that unknown and unknowable place.

I drifted into semi-consciousness, floating, it seemed, toward some kind of dream-scape. No, I was floating somewhere between life and death. How relaxing — that world of death.

No sorrow or worry, no dispute or disruption. No forced household labor.

That evening the mediators arrived in full force.

First came my older brother. He's the type who, no

matter how frenzied others may get, can maintain his placid, easy-going manner. Wearing his politely condescending smile, he seated himself on the chair next to my table. Linlin carried in two cups of hot tea — just what I needed to soothe my parched throat.

"What's the matter? Another fight?" My brother's voice oozed sweetly, coating me in syrupy goo.

I didn't need that. I needed black and white, yes or no. I needed a road clear of the trees. I'd rather they came to pound their fists on the table and fight over right and wrong.

I said nothing.

He smiled his condescending smile. Was that the man labeled a Rightist in 1957 — a tumultuous, terrifying time for the country — the same who'd struggled to uphold the truth and refused to be cowed? The victim of "class struggle"[12] and "mass criticism"[13] who'd persisted in analyzing his own behavior and dissecting his own thoughts? His refusal to accept the label of Bourgeois Rightist had brought a string of punishments culminating in "promotion" to hard labor on the Qing River Farm.[14] He was so terrified when they announced his punishment he wet his pants. But he never stopped searching for the truth. His new wife left him, and he drifted homeless for over twenty years, twenty years of bare survival. He'd been rectified in 1978 with the distinction of having "dared to uphold the truth."

Spongy passivity must be residue from his suffering as a Rightist. I can't stand it.

"I'm an old woman with nothing left to say. If my husband were too busy or Linlin still a child, you could argue that it's my duty to take care of them. But why should Yimin, a grown boy of twenty, come home and sit there with his legs crossed, waiting for me to serve him?"

"He's your son," my brother replied without a thought, as if reminding me of a law of nature.

His impartial, matter-of-fact statement exploded on my ears like a thunderclap. Thousands of years of Chinese culture came pouring down, not only from his kind lips, but from my husband's family, my family, friends, colleagues.....

My brother took his condescending smile and went

away, confident that, as my older brother, he'd taught me how to behave.

Next came my sister. She introduced Old Liu to me thirty years ago; whenever I "break down" or malfunction, he goes to her to lodge a complaint.

My sister has a rapid-fire tongue, an immense heart and a body to match. Lowering her abundance into the chair vacated by my brother, she settled in for a good talk.

Still smarting from my brother's interview, I wanted to spit out a bellyful of grievances. "What have I done to deserve this frustration? What have I ever done to anyone — "

"NOT *this* again!" she snapped, impatiently cutting off my old complaints.

I was stunned into silence. I could hear the voice of Xianglin's Wife: "I was really stupid, really. I only knew that when it snows the wild beasts in the glen have nothing to eat and sometimes come into the villages. I didn't know they came in the spring too...." [15] The villagers, fed up with the old story, would scatter when she opened her mouth, afraid to be caught at her side.

There I was, a modern-day Xianglin's Wife. Touch my housework nerve, and I'd set off. Give me a listening ear, and I'd launch into my tirade.

On the commuter bus to work one day, I'd grumbled about the nuisance of housework to the professor at my side, drawing in eyes and ears all around. "Women have to work just like men," I complained, "but men don't have to do the housework. They just lie on top and let us carry them around."

One woman marched right over after we got off to put me in my place. "How can you talk about Old Liu like that on the bus?!" She hissed.

What she really meant was: "We must protect the good name of government officials and celebrities."

A product of the 1950s, I'm a typical introspective intellectual. I was seized by guilt. What had I been doing, taking center stage, airing my views for all the world to hear? I'd even said, "Men just lie on top...." What if my words were misconstrued? I sank with embarrassment.

Later, I remember whispering the names of two old colleagues to myself. "Li Wei." "Zhang Mu." These two have never been spiritual saviors of any kind, but for some reason, when depression or disappointment takes me, I've gotten in the habit of whispering their names. I wonder why I do it — if my husband were to hear, he'd never understand. Why not just "Mama," if anything at all? I've tried, but though the image of my dead mother evokes great tenderness, the feeling isn't the same. The names of those two work better.

An enormous sense of loss, a hollowness in my heart, had grown from the lapse of decades and cut off all roads to success. A giant pump had sucked away my confidence. I was empty. I craved work, needed it, but before me stretched a horizon of housework, competing for my time, pushing me, driving me to the brink of insanity....

Linlin came in to tell me I had a phone call. I recognized the voice of a well-known writer on the line.

"Hello, Maomei?... Old Liu has a lot of responsibility these days. You should help him with his work."

"Everybody has to do their own job," I replied curtly.

"That's right," he laughed. "But, ha, ha.... You should at least make sure he doesn't have to worry about all those little daily hassles. When he comes home at night, he should have a hot meal waiting for him. In any marriage, one of the partners has to make sacrifices to pave the way for the other."

"Do you think," I hurled back, "my ego is as negligible as my social status... as insignificant?"

For a moment he was confused into muttering, "But ... but ... see here now...."

Then, ever the well-known writer, never at a loss for words, he quickly found them: "Make this sacrifice for him now, and we writers will owe you a huge debt of gratitude."

Why was it me that had to make the sacrifice? What did I care about their "debt of gratitude?" I slammed down the receiver. You writers can go to hell.

The next morning a good friend arrived unannounced. She listened to my tale of woe and wiped away her tears. It wasn't the first time she'd heard me get so worked up, but she was always willing to share my frustration.

There's no way out, I told her. All I have left is to die.

My friend is a university teacher, smart and talented, and full of good ideas.

"That's how people always think," she said. "Run up against a hurdle and opt for death. All you have to do is hire a maid and your problems are solved. You shouldn't give a damn about whether they like it or not."

She took me out to find a maid, and flying in the face of convention, I actually did hire a young housekeeper.

Nobody said a word at home; my obstinacy could only be met with silence. I don't like to run up against my husband and usually take his opinion into consideration, but that time, for all to see, I'd acted boldly against his wishes. I'd found within myself a new independent kind of beauty.

Later, when I was in my room preparing for class, I could hear the maid outside sweeping, mopping, cooking ... and I felt a surge of compassion for all women. The problem hadn't been solved; I'd just found a scapegoat for a while.

V

In Sichuan Province, where I grew up, a girl with an impervious spirit was called "Twisted Little Sister." That was my nickname as a child.

"Twisted Little Sister." I stopped thinking about the housework altogether. Whatever the maid cooked, we ate. However she cooked it, well, that's how it was. I had better things to do than waste my time in the kitchen, and if the food wasn't to taste, too bad.

I shut myself in from early morning until late at night. Interrupted every evening by the dinner crowd, I simply moved the table to the boys' room next door and used the bed as my desk.

Then came the day when I looked at my lecture and knew it was ready. Complete, precise, thorough. No longer did that famous professor seem so far out of reach.

Delivery was less of a problem. As a former actress, I knew how to use personal experience and expression to bring out the most in my lecture. I knew how to vary pronunciation, tone and rhythm. I knew where to speed up and lightly trip over, where to slow down and pound home the point. I knew how to make a surprise attack....

In all my ten years of acting, I'd never had to recite so many lines. I practiced tirelessly, analyzing every detail, pulling everything I had from deep inside my "impervious spirit." I could feel my skin peeling away.

Every night after dinner I threw down my chopsticks and ran to the other room to practice. Old Liu had read my lecture and was familiar with segments of my rehearsal. He thought I was taking it too seriously.

"Where are you going?"

"To prepare for class."

"You've prepared well enough, believe me. Would I say it if it weren't true?"

But I raced along like a lunatic. I thought back to my years in the countryside and remembered the women. I remembered how they shouldered the farm work, housework and child care with spirit and energy. Marx and Lenin wrote that women live under both the oppression of class and that of clan and patriarchal authority. Awakened from our ignorant slumber, we women ought to possess extraordinary revolutionary zeal.

An old folk song I learned back then came to mind:

"Pitch black dry well,
   a thousand *zhang* deep;
Oh, woman,
   she lies at the bot-tom...."

The chains of my oppression fed my determination to keep struggling, no matter what the cost. I couldn't do just a passing job. Only with a clear, uncontested victory could I throw off the thousand-year-old millstone around my neck.

I finally stood before my class.

The faculty director had escorted me in, as is the custom with new teachers. After an introduction, she would go sit in the back to assess my political awareness and professional ability.

"All rise!" the class monitor called. A hundred pairs of eyes turned in my direction.

"Good day, teacher!" they responded in unison.

I stood locked to the lectern, gazing out at them.

The director whispered something in my ear, but without a clue as to what she'd said, I held my stance in silence.

She cupped her hands around my ear and whispered, "You have to say, 'Good day, students' before they can sit down."

So that's what it was.

"Good day, students!" The words fell from my lips.

The happy explosion of laughter that followed charged the room with energy and excitement.

Word by word, I pulled the lecture imprinted on my brain into the waiting classroom.

Students from every department — fine arts, lighting, recording, acting — gazed up at me with lively, intelligent eyes. My time preparing for them had been well spent; we quickly established a highly energized rapport. Looking out on their curious, attractive faces, I was transported to the youthful simplicity of thirty years ago when I had sat in such a chair, a vital force pulsing through the room and my mind.

After a while I received a note from the director. It read: "You're doing a good job, but don't use the word 'damn'." I couldn't help but chuckle. With the latest concern on campus for "clean speech," I was standing at the podium crying "damn it!" I smiled at the director and continued, but before I knew it, my blood got pumping and another "damn it" slipped out. "Excuse me," I apologized, "I said 'damn it' again." The class rolled with laughter.

I brought my lecture to a close with an indictment of the age-old specter of feudalism that haunts China to this day. The class exploded in a wild round of applause. Shuffling my papers together, I tried to leave, but the students rushed in from all sides.

Where were you before you came here? What did you do? Will you be our class supervisor? A beautiful acting student, her face covered in tears, asked if I had time to talk later. The bell for the next period rang, and we had to move into the hallway, where the horde finally bid me a reluctant farewell.

Walking back with me along the shady campus lane, the faculty director exclaimed emotionally, "In all these years, I've never witnessed such a scene as today!"

I found the whole family waiting for me at home. They'd lived with my anxiety for weeks and knew it was my big day. Eight eyes turned inquisitively upon me.

"Well, how'd it go?" Old Liu broke the silence.

"Quite well."

The room heaved a great sigh of relief.

Putting down my papers, I suddenly blurted out, "I despise you all. For twenty years you've treated me like your maid."

No one, surprisingly, was the slightest bit angered. They laughed happily, savoring my success as their own. I turned my back on them and ran downstairs into the night.

My class was all the rage at school, each lecture a work of art. In my acting days, when I'd worked under a screenwriter or director, I'd maintained an identity apart from my role. But as a teacher, I wrote and directed and acted. I *was* my role.

One student made tapes of my lectures to listen to in his free time. Another came up with a short skit: Glasses perched on his nose, stack of papers gripped under his arm, he'd step solemnly up to the podium. Off would come the glasses, then the jacket, and a loud passionate "damn it!" would fill the room. He'd close with an apology to the audience.

Despite my victory, I felt no wild joy. Just a deep inner peace. It was just what I needed and desired most, what I hadn't had in years.

VI

My inner peace was abruptly shattered. It was announced at a faculty meeting that every teacher must take on several new classes. We were to teach *The Dream of Red Mansions*,[16] *The West Chamber*,[17] Lu Xun, Xu Zhimo, Shen Congwen and many contemporary writers as well. We had to cover Beckett, Heller, the *nouveau roman*, "Absurdist Literature" and "black humor."

The way I prepared for class, I'd have to mash my brain to a pulp and replace it with a new one.

Our faculty director asked us to choose from the list. Experienced teachers easily pick up a new class, and recent graduates can use notes from college literature courses as teaching material. Afraid to show my ignorance, I picked two relatively familiar and enjoyable drama topics. Familiarity and enjoyment are one thing, explicating clearly and thoroughly another. I'd have to throw myself back into a pile of books. I'd have to pour over stacks of material. I'd have to work for hours to compose original arguments.

I trudged back to the library with my bags and a heavy heart.

At home I was dealt a devastating blow. My scapegoat, the housekeeper, had gone. A private business, offering wages double what I could afford, had hired her away. Popo made such a to-do telling me this, I knew she wanted me to feel presumptuous for having hired someone in the first place. But how could my wallet compete with private enterprise?

I looked around the room. Cigarette butts and pumpkin seed shells spilled from the ashtray; scraps of paper littered the floor; nylon thread spiraled from the desk drawer; Linlin's shirt and dirty socks lay crumpled on the bed. The stone-cold stove waited in the kitchen with open jaws to chew me up, flesh and bones, and swallow me down.

Then came Popo again. It's five o'clock already, everyone will be home soon. There's no oil or ginger in the house, and what about fresh vegetables.... I pulled my books from the bags. My nerve endings felt like they were on fire. I wanted to fall apart, scream out loud, sob myself dry.

But I didn't make a noise. I felt like I was covered in glass, bound in rubber; I hadn't to breathe, hadn't to feel anything, hadn't to hold onto myself. I walked silently into the kitchen, took up the vegetable basket and oil bottle and walked silently to that ancient gathering place of women, the market. Tears from my stinging eyes streaked down my throat, my chest, into my heart.

Wise sages who see things in perspective live to a ripe old age. "If I could live my life over again," they say, "I'd invite my friends over to eat and not care about the stained rug or faded sofa. I'd listen quietly to grandpa talk about his youth and not get annoyed every time he opened his mouth. I'd enjoy the children's wild kisses and never coolly say, 'Calm down. Go wash your hands for dinner.' If I got sick, I'd lie down and not worry that everything would fall apart without me. If I could live my life over again, I'd seize every second to carefully, honestly look. I'd experience deeply every moment and engrave it on my heart forever."

But I can't.

If I could live my life over again, I'd be a wolf and not a sheep.

Everybody has a sign in the Chinese zodiac.[18] It's not supposed to mean anything in real life, but when I think about how wretched mine's been, it's fitting that I'm a sheep. I submit docilely to my own slaughter. I detest my sign, and so desperately do I want to bite someone, I wish I were a wolf.

I don't have the carefree, easy-going nature of a sage. I can't.

"Sss.... Saa, Sss.... Saa" Shallow fry, deep fry, stir fry, boil, steam, scald, brew.... That's the tune I'm forced to dance to. Fry, boil, steam.... But not only chicken, fish, meat and vegetables fill the pot. My hands, arms and chest are stirred in as well.

"Pat-a-tat," "Crack-crack," "Boom-boom," sounds my war drum as I pound the cutting board, chopping my own meat and bones to shreds.

And to scrub the clothes in the wash tub.

And to push the needle, pull the thread....

Put this down, pick that up, around and around.

The tune of my life, the waltzing melody and pounding drum beat will follow me to the grave. I've been sentenced for life.

Like a caged wild animal, I roar and bellow. I whimper. I become crazed, rabid. But to no avail.

Dancing around the kitchen, thick with the stink of oil, the stench of meat, the reek of gas, I whisper to myself, "Li Wei," "Zhang Mu." "What's the matter?" "Please come in."

That braised fish on the platter. It looks like my hand. Braised hand? I look again. My other hand, bloodless and ugly, lies on its side in the sink.

Growing from my wrists I see not a pair of hands, but a pair of fish, two live fish.

I shake my head.

What's wrong with me? No, No! I can't go crazy! I run for the tap and let the cool water splash over my face.

I have to get out of this kitchen, fast!

My head aches terribly.

I pick up the plate of fish, but before I can reach the door, it opens, and I am met by a grinning Popo and her jubilant crowd of men.

"Maomei! Congratulations! You're going to be a mother-in-law!" Popo announced. "Tomorrow Yimin's fiancee and her parents are coming over for dinner." She held out a fistful of bills. "Here's fifty *yuan*. My treat."

Old Liu and Linlin smiled benignly from behind.

"Grandma's putting out so much money, we'll really have a feast!" Yimin hooted excitedly.

"Stay calm," I warn myself. But my hands have already slammed the plate of fish to the floor, and my foot, with a furious kick, sends the fish flying across the room, splattering sauce everywhere.

"You can eat that, goddamnit!" I scream. I throw open the door, tear past the elevator and fly down the pitch black stairwell.

The stairs are swirling.

The world is swirling.
Ah, I am a wolf.
A vast golden plain stretches before me....

Slowly, slowly, I am aware of my shaking hands. Gradually, I can focus on what's before me. That plate of fish, placed safely on the table.

Notes

1. The Great Proletarian Cultural Revolution (See Note 4 of the Introduction for more on the Cultural Revolution.)
2. "Old" is customarily used before a last name to indicate respect when addressing those older than oneself. In this case, the narrator calls her husband by the name he is known in public: "Old Liu." "Little," by the same token, as in "Little Zhang," is a term of endearment usually reserved for those of younger age or lower status.
3. Housing in Beijing and most other large cities in China is extremely tight. Two rooms of this size is considered spacious for many families.
4. In reference to the hard years she spent in the countryside after her husband was labeled a Rightist in 1957.
5. As referred to in China, "liberation" is the victory won by the People's Liberation Army (PLA) under the leadership of the Communist Party of China, which overthrew the Nationalist government and made possible the founding of the People's Republic of China in 1949.
6. In 1957 the Anti-Rightist campaign was launched in reaction to an outpouring of criticism of the Communist Party by intellectuals (academics, scientists, artists, writers, professionals, etc.). According to Chinese figures, some 400,000 "enemies" of the Party were stigmatized; thousands were executed and tens of thousands sent to the countryside to do manual labor. The term "Rightist" has been applied to fit a number of offenses against the Party.
7. There are ten *mao* to the *yuan*.
8. The Japanese occupied northern China from 1937 to 1945.
9. A term commonly used for household chores.
10. Zhu Ziqing (1898-1948), poet and essayist, is acknowledged as one of the most outstanding prose writers of modern Chinese literature.
11. From Mao Zedong's phrase "Serve the People."
12. The concept of class struggle was based on Mao Zedong's theory that permanent, sometimes violent, struggle between the working and capitalist classes was necessary to combat the rise of a new bourgeoisie. In

practice, class struggle meant, through various campaigns and movements over a thirty-year period, loss of jobs, homes, land and dignity for millions of intellectual and landholding Chinese.

13. Community meetings, in which accused offenders were publicly criticized and heard, were the most popular form of mass criticism employed in the struggle between the classes.

14. A maximum security labor reform prison located in the northern suburbs of Beijing.

15. Xianglin's Wife is the unfortunate protagonist in Lu Xun's short story "New Year's Sacrifice," written in 1924. When her only son is killed by wolves shortly after her husband's death, her sole topic of conversation turns around remorse over the incident.

16. One of the great Chinese classics, written in the mid-18th century by Cao Xueqin.

17. A 14th century novel by Wang Shifu, also a classic.

18. The Chinese zodiac, based on the lunar calendar, runs on a sixty-year cycle with a different animal representing each of twelve years. The narrator was born in the year of the sheep.

Octday

Tie Ning

Monday (Weekday One)[1]

An extravagance of sunshine bathed the street where a young boy with a book bag squirted water at the passing cyclists from a rubber ball. Smells, the face powder of women and tobacco of men, enveloped the long stream of bikes like a cloud. The women's faces glowed white above yellow necks. Their red lips were parted; fierce, black streaks arched a thin line between eye and brow. Zhu Xiaofen brushed past thinking, there's really nothing wrong with that. You can't let cosmetic companies go out of business just so women can look natural.

Zhu Xiaofen was above all that.

Zhu Xiaofen hadn't felt this happy, this at ease with herself in a long time, ever since the day she'd been married. But now she was divorced, once and for all and in good time — she'd just turned thirty-four. Every time she thought about her age and her divorce, she felt so happy she wanted to jump rope, do the "double twist" she'd loved as a child. JUST-JUMP-THAT-ROPE! She pushed down hard on the pedals, tensing her thighs and tightening her hamstrings right up to the buttock. Her butt had rounded out after the baby, but what did that matter? She could jump, and jumping could work every part of her body — strengthen her nervous system and improve blood circulation and expand lung capacity and improve digestion and raise metabolism.... She had to jump. Jumping was the prelude to flying, and anybody who wanted to fly had to jump and jump and jump.

Zhu Xiaofen had a child, as already mentioned. She

49

may have divorced the father, but she had to keep that ten-month-old baby, loving it even more after her marriage had broken up. Her parents had taken over child care for her. They'd initially talked about the baby as a reason to keep the marriage together. "For the child's sake," they'd said. "But it is for the child's sake," she'd responded. They knew whose child she meant.

Zhu Xiaofen wasn't always so clever with words. In fact, she and her husband had almost never argued. She regretted agreeing to marry him the minute the words were out of her mouth, and having eventually lost all interest in him, didn't care enough to fight.

She worked as a fiction editor for a regional literary magazine, and after marriage, spent all her time away from home, scouting the country for new manuscripts. She had to watch what the writers were thinking and attune herself to their moods and to the moods of their husbands and wives and call upon new brassy stars and encourage eager, embarrassed first-timers quietly budding in the corners. She loved her work, loved it so much she stopped breast-feeding after only two months to attend a writers' conference in Xinjiang.[2] Dark wet stains blazoned across the front of her bulging blouse declared her oblivious spirit of selflessness. She was always pulling in at least second-rate manuscripts — people liked her sincerity — and then, out of the blue, a story by one of her new discoveries published in her magazine won a national award. Perfect timing. When they got around to reviewing jobs, everybody in the editorial department agreed an exception should be made to give her a promotion — she was later named Associate Senior Editor.

Her husband was the last to hear the good news. Zhu Xiaofen liked to tell him bad news, never the good — hard to say whether it was to make him angry or depressed. At home all he could do was dust off invisible bits of dirt from his clothes with his little finger. Watching him made her dizzy.

At last came the day when she returned from a month on the road to a locked door. Locked from the inside. She knew it then, standing on the door mat, knew she was about to break away, be freed, and all she could think was to thank the door for its rebuff. When her husband finally swung it open, she saw one of those white-faced yellow-necked women in the shadows.

They parted peacefully, though her husband did have his say: "I knew you were waiting all along for the day you couldn't get the door unlocked." She only smiled and thought that he might have had her figured out after all. He was good for more than just picking off lint with his little finger. But understanding doesn't imply love. It may be the more you understand someone, the more you feel disgusted by them.

Zhu Xiaofen raced along, propelled, it seemed, by a thrust from behind. Or perhaps it was the force of her elation that pushed her on, the morning wind whistling past her ears and stroking the fine golden hair on her tanned calves. She parked her bike in the shed and skipped upstairs to the editorial department, where she found her colleagues gathered in her office, either by coincidence or to respectfully await her arrival. The air hung with unspoken distress.

Tuesday (Weekday Two)

"Utterly despicable!"

Those were Editor-in-chief Zou's words. Yesterday everybody in the department had taken their turn sympathizing with Zhu Xiaofen; today Big Sister Zou's "despicable" set off a round of public criticism directed indiscriminately at her husband.

The sympathy was naturally for her divorce. She managed to endure their pity, though she wasn't at all prepared for it, reasoning that it was normal for her colleagues to show their concern at a critical juncture like this, at a time when she was making important life changes. But she thought, considering her own high spirits, they didn't need to feel that miserable. Besides, their group sorrow was so well enacted, she wondered if they hadn't been rehearsing behind her back.

"Utterly despicable!" Big Sister Zou narrowed her attack. "His baby's only ten months old, and he's willing to give it all up."

"That's what I call in-hu-mane," another voice chimed in.

Zhu Xiaofen tried to explain. Her husband wasn't to blame; she was the one who'd asked for a divorce. Big Sister Zou interrupted her, saying women of the eighties had stooped so low they felt they had to save face while shouldering incredible injustice, and without pausing for a breath, asked Zhu Xiaofen if she'd had her breakfast, as if divorce meant she couldn't get a decent thing to eat in the morning. Zhu Xiaofen said thank you, she'd eaten, whereupon Big Sister Zou told department clerk "Crackerjack" to make her a cup of tea. Zhu Xiaofen wasn't in the habit of morning tea, but Crackerjack had already presented her the steaming cup and was explaining how she'd bought this new health drink made from Yunnan *Maifanshi* [3] black tea on last month's business trip to Liaoning Province. [4] Whereupon everybody in the room gazed down at Zhu Xiaofen and the cup, reminding her of the scene in *Thunderstorm* where Zhou Puyuan forces Fan Yi to drink her medicine. [5] She wondered for the longest time who could be the German doctor, considering first Big Sister Zou, then Crackerjack, then the Yunnan *Maifanshi* black tea company. Finally puckering her lips, she took a sip, afraid if she waited much longer, someone would kneel down and beg her to drink. The warm liquid in her belly, she wanted to laugh. She wanted to tell them all, calmly, sedately, there was nothing to worry about. She was fine. In fact, she felt great. She felt young and happy and ready to jump the "double twist" with the rope she had in her bag that very moment. But they didn't give her the chance. Big Sister Zou patted her shoulder, indicating there was no need to say anything. They understood everything.

Big Sister Zou's husband had died when she was young; she knew the hardship of rearing five children alone. One of her favorite stories was the sad plight of those five during her "cowshed" [6] days in the Cultural Revolution. As the tale went, the oldest put some ribs on to boil, but all five cleaned out the pot, leaving only the bones and a thin broth, before the meat was even half-cooked. Everybody knew Big Sister Zou's pork rib story. It was a regular in the editorial department repertoire. She'd won their respect alright — one mention of her would inevitably call up a chorus of "sure hasn't been easy." That phrase cut two ways; in its admiration, Big Sister Zou gained consolation, in its superiority, she knew alienation. Now that Zhu Xiaofen was divorced — not widowed — but a single woman nonetheless, Big Sister Zou didn't feel so all alone. She'd have someone to share "sure hasn't been easy" with. People need a common language, Big Sister Zou thought. Why should I have a patent right to that phrase?

Berating Zhu Xiaofen's husband, she thought of how she could help her through the lonely days ahead. She would buy milk powder and fruit for the baby and she could....

"Drink up." She pointed at the big cup of tea in Zhu Xiaofen's hands.

Wednesday (Weekday Three)

Two days of gifts later — melons, coca-cola, dried fruit, honey — and Zhu Xiaofen was beginning to hate the parcel-laden who came knocking at her parents' door. Busybodies like that disrupted the whole family.

It seemed like it would be a quiet evening. But just as Zhu Xiaofen was stepping from the bath, her old "troop friend"[7] Yu Zhen charged in. College classmates, they'd gone their separate ways after graduation, Yu Zhen taking a teaching job at the school and Zhu Xiaofen moving on to become an editor.

Yu Zhen had a beak for a mouth, a sharp, pointed thing from which emitted a long stream of her favorite word: "why, why, why, why." If you asked her if she'd eaten dinner, she had to first "why, why, why" before she could answer "yes" or "of course not." Rear end poised mid-air above the couch, she stared in amazement at Zhu Xiaofen, as if a worm were crawling over her face.

"Why, why, why, why!" she chirped. "It's been only a week since I last saw you. Why do you look so terrible? Your face is yellow; your lips are dry; your neck's wrinkled; your hair's thinning. You can't go on like this.

53

What'll become of you? There are nutritional supplements, you know — ginseng root, donkey-hide gelatin, longan fruit. If you don't take better care of yourself, in another week I won't even be able to recognize you. Why aren't you using skin tightening lotion, wrinkle disappearing creme, foundation, eyeliner, mascara, all that? And a girdle. There's a new Japanese girdle for thirty-eight *yuan* you must buy. You've got to change your hairstyle and do something about your wardrobe. You need bright colors. Those plain, simple clothes you wear look good on a teen-ager, but you're way over thirty now. The older you get, the more you've got to make a statement with color. You've got to open up a bit, think of your future."

Eyes glued to her pecking beak, Zhu Xiaofen thought how the only thing she'd left out was a two hundred *yuan* bottle of "101 Hair Formula."[8] The way she talks, you'd think I'm already over the hill, about to die of an incurable disease, too far gone to ask about! "Why, why, why!" Zhu Xiaofen tried out Yu Zhen's word under her breath.

Yu Zhen knew all about Zhu Xiaofen's divorce. In fact, she was trying to get a divorce herself, but her husband wouldn't let go. He said it was her mouth. He loved that beak and wanted to keep the marriage together for its sake. Zhu Xiaofen was free, but Yu Zhen's beak was still held by her husband. That didn't seem fair to her. She felt like she'd been left behind. Why can't I get a divorce and you can? She thought. Besides, who's to say your divorce is a good thing? Don't you know women over thirty have a hard time getting remarried? And look at you — with your horrible complexion, dry lips and wrinkled neck.

Zhu Xiaofen's complexion was fine, her lips pink and healthy, her hair strong and shiny, but to hear Yu Zhen go on.... She knew Yu Zhen was making things seem much worse than they really were. Those weren't all good intentions lurking behind her concern. "You've got to think of your future. What'll become of you?" she was saying. What do you care what happens to me? And why are you getting so excited about it anyway....

It may have been that Yu Zhen didn't mean to viciously malign Zhu Xiaofen. It may have been she actually did see a sallow complexion, chapped lips and thinning hair. Or she thought she *ought* to see those things. Since she ought to have seen those things, perhaps they were really there for her to see. Existence determines consciousness. You stub your toe on a rock, but if the rock doesn't exist, then how could you have stubbed your toe? Ah, Yu Zhen, you pure materialist. Maybe you don't mean to slander me after all.

Zhu Xiaofen made up an excuse to get rid of her friend and yawning, walked back into the bathroom. Peering at her reflection in the mirror, she patted her face and thought, if there's one thing I've got to do tomorrow, it's jump rope.

Thursday (Weekday Four)

The editorial department took a morning break at ten. Some did calisthenics, others practiced *Qigong*,[9] and the rest stood around to chat. Zhu Xiaofen went out into the courtyard to jump rope under the walnut tree. At first she couldn't get it right. The rope caught at her ankles, twisted around her neck —what an awkward mess! But then she caught the rhythm and slipped into its natural easy beat. Why hadn't she done this sooner? She should have come out to jump on Monday. She should have jumped to let that crowd upstairs know how happy she was, how relaxed she felt. They might have then been able to avoid the scene of a few days before. She had to jump her best now, jump for all she was worth, as if to do right by that flurry of consolation touched off by Big Sister Zou. She was obviously fine. Look, there she goes with the "double twist," her bounce as springy as ever. Those large, flat walnut leaves look like the eyes of a giant Buddha, their scent faintly bitter.

She saw the calisthenics crowd and the *Qigong* group stop what they were doing to watch her. She saw Big Sister Zou rush out of the building in a sweat, discreetly waving a fat white hand for her to stop. Stop jumping. Those deadpan eyes and that fat white hand — she felt as if they were watching her dance in iron chains, their mood was that deadly somber.

Big Sister Zou swooped in close and cooed soothingly,
"Don't jump, Zhu Xiaofen. Why are you still so upset?
What's past is past. You've got to let go. There's no need
to come out here in front of us all and jump rope. We feel
terrible enough for you as it is. Why can't you unwind a little, tell us your troubles? It would do you good. For my
sake, alright?" Big Sister Zou pleaded so earnestly and with
such grave concern, Zhu Xiaofen found it impossible to defend herself. She hung the rope over her shoulder and
reluctantly gave in. What did they know about how she felt?
Since when did jumping rope mean she was upset? What is
relaxed anyway? How was she supposed to act relaxed?
Thursday already and we can't get past this business. It's
true you should "think of others before yourself," [10] but
you've got to let people live their own lives. Tell me how I
should deal with this. Or maybe I'll go on a business trip.
I've got to get away for a few days. I've got to escape this
confounding, smothering appeasement. I can't let them push
me around.

Friday (Weekday Five)

Zhu Xiaofen took a day's train ride to a small,
untarnished resort town on the coast where some writers had
gathered, bringing their work, to pass the sweltering summer
days.

High season meant huge crowds. It took nearly forty
minutes of being squeezed through the human flood for Zhu
Xiaofen to work her way to the station exit. Once there, she
wasn't able to slip out and away — the ticket checker was
an old elementary school classmate. Years later, and she
could still pick out Zhu Xiaofen from the bobbing heads
around her. "Hey! I heard you got divorced," she hollered
across. "They say that good-for-nothing dumped you. Well,
if you're dumped, you're dumped, no big deal. At first I
couldn't believe it, but here you are plain as day. You got
someone to pick you up? Which hotel you staying at? The
Grand? Look, if you haven't got someone to drive you
over, my husband's outside in his cab. He can take you."

Mouth and hands flapping at the same rate, the checker deftly ripped used tickets while Zhu Xiaofen stood to one side like a museum piece to be gawked at by the exiting passengers. Zhu Xiaofen knew her extraordinary volume wasn't deliberate — railroad employees don't know how to speak softly. Working around clanking, chugging trains and mobs of people all day, if you don't speak up, no one will hear you. She could even forgive her classmate for jabbering on about her private life and for the caustic, malicious way she drawled "dumped," but if there was one thing she couldn't stand, it was her assumption that there was no one to pick her up. Why would she, Zhu Xiaofen, Associate Senior Editor at a regional level publication, come all this way if there was no car? Don't tell me once you're divorced you've got to rely on your elementary school classmate's husband to get to a hotel? No, thank you. Don't trouble your husband. There's a car waiting for me, she shouted back. Her driver walked up at that opportune moment to take her bag, shutting up the checker for good.

She knew many of the guests at the hotel, or rather, she knew many of the men. Most of the women had come along with their husbands. They all treated Zhu Xiaofen with special warmth and concern, scrambling to fill her bowl that night at dinner. The cool sea breeze blowing in off the water beyond the restaurant swept clean the heat from Zhu Xiaofen's face. Shrimp and cuttlefish, her two favorites, fresh from the sea and cooked to perfection, were among the dishes that night. Her tablemates picked a few mouthfuls from those plates then left the rest for her, making her feel like a glutton every time she stretched out her chopsticks.

Zhu Xiaofen sensed they knew everything about her divorce and, seized by a bewildering anxiety, couldn't figure out how she was supposed to act. All their comforting made her dizzy. Maybe it was the summer heat. She'd brought along her jump rope but had a hunch if she went skipping around the hotel courtyard, they'd say she was doing it for their benefit, to show them she didn't care. Forget about jumping rope. Tomorrow I'll go swimming, she thought. Everybody here can enjoy the water. It doesn't matter if you're divorced, remarried or single. You can be a bigamist and still go swimming.

Thus decided, she went back to her room for a good night's sleep.

Saturday (Weekday Six)

It was a fine powdery sand beach. Zhu Xiaofen remembered how two years back, when swimming at a reservoir with gravel banks, she'd stumbled over the sharp rocks. Her husband had tried to pick her up, but she'd cried out as if insulted. I couldn't let him carry me around in broad daylight — better a stranger than him, she thought viciously. Her embarrassed husband had brushed himself off and pushed away.

Zhu Xiaofen took a dip in the water and stretched out in the sun alongside two author friends. It suddenly occurred to her that neither of their wives had come. Hadn't they said yesterday they came swimming every day at noon with their husbands? She politely inquired after the two women and was told the wives had specially requested their husbands accompany Zhu Xiaofen that day. They know you're on your own now and are afraid the sight of us couples would be hard on you, they explained. So it's better we split up. You see how well our wives understand you, even though you're not that close.

They'd figured everything out. Zhu Xiaofen couldn't fathom how the waves stirred up by her editorial department had spread this far. Now what was she supposed to do? Thank the wives for their thoughtfulness or laugh at them for their brilliant good deed? Or perhaps shove two fistfuls of sand down the throats of their clever husbands?

She stood up, and leaving them behind, threw herself back into the sea. She'd intended to strike up a light conversation with the two men, knowing professionally she shouldn't let a single opportunity pass her by — even when she most wanted to be alone. Like right now. They'd even started the conversation for her, but she'd tossed it aside and, without a second thought, took to the sea. The sky was dark and gray, the water warm. An old woman over seventy was paddling gracefully all alone way out by the shark barrier. Zhu Xiaofen headed in her direction. She didn't give a thought to who the woman was but admired the oblivious way she stretched out so easily along the waves. Her white seersucker cap bobbed like a lonely bouquet of vibrant flowers.

The two writers visited Zhu Xiaofen in her room that night after dinner. They came to talk business. Their most recent manuscripts, well, they were originally intended for so-and-so from such-and-such major literary publication. So-and-so had been trying to nail them down for eight years, or maybe nine, it's been so long it's hard to keep track, but now Zhu Xiaofen had come and under such difficult circumstances. Ordinary folks could never understand how you feel. Ordinary folks? Not even second-rate writers can enter that realm of secret anguish and solitude. But we understand, you see, and so we've come. You don't need to tell us a thing, Zhu Xiaofen. There isn't a single human emotion we first-rate writers can't comprehend. After much consideration, we've decided to make so-and-so wait another year (it's already been eight, after all, or maybe nine) and give you our latest work, the stories we finished this afternoon just before dinner. What do you say to that? Let's relax and enjoy ourselves for the rest of the week. Don't worry, we won't ask about your you-know-what. And let's not talk about literature, or life, or any of that. Whoever brings it up is a damn sonavabitch, whadaya say?

They really did pull out two thick, heavy manuscripts and "thunk," set them solemnly on the tea table. Their faces shone with the august presence of two knights delivering a declaration.

Zhu Xiaofen, you lucky thing. You didn't have to go out and commission these manuscripts — they walked right into your room on their own. Why are you in such a hurry to leave this cool, breezy place and get back on the hot, crowded train? You had the work of famous authors in your hands.

Sunday (Weekday Seven)

The hard seat[11] compartment steamed with the stench of packed bodies, but the passengers, long accustomed to train ordeals, remained placidly cool. Some perched on the sink in the bathroom. Others stretched out on the floor beneath the seats. Zhu Xiaofen stood in the aisle, her feet and ankles assaulted by the persimmon and watermelon remains of those on the floor.

She didn't mind. If she were down there, she'd do the same. She'd probably even spit on their shoes. Spitting sounded good right then; her mouth was suddenly full of saliva, rolling around under her tongue. Spitting was truly satisfying, a grand sight, the fireworks of human experience. But she had to swallow to clear out her mouth for talking. She saw someone she knew. It was her old high school principal.

The principal had been sitting by the window all along, but it wasn't until she was about to get off the train that she recognized her former student. With her gray hair and kind eyes, she looked like a sweet old grandma, but her voice still rang with severe force.

"Why, if it isn't Zhu Xiaofen! I've heard about your divorce. Plenty of rumors, alright. You're still so young, can't be much more than thirty. You've got to straighten up your life. If you took things seriously, how could he leave you? You know I only mean well. I like to see all my students have a good future. Well, goodbye. I'm getting off at the next stop to see my grandson. Are you going all the way into the city? Here, take my seat."

Zhu Xiaofen sat down, watermelon seeds plastered across her ankles, and waved mechanically to the principal. Today must be Saturday. No, it's already Sunday, she corrected herself. The ancient Romans had an eight-day week. Wouldn't that be nice? An octa-week. Eight days are much better than seven, and tomorrow is Octday. Every week should have a day I can call my own. I need an eighth day.

Zhu Xiaofen determined to stay home and do whatever she liked on her Octday.

Octday (Weekday Eight)

A nasty odor wafted through the corridor. The water had been off for three days already, and the toilets were overflowing.

Trailing behind Zhu Xiaofen up the stairs, Crackerjack was explaining how no one knew when they'd have water again. The closest toilet was against the northern wall of the large courtyard in the sweater factory, a good ten-minute bike ride away. She then apologized for asking Zhu Xiaofen into the office the first day back from her trip, but a woman from "The Marriage and Family Research Center" of the Municipal Women's Federation had come especially to see her.

The woman waiting for her turned out to be an old acquaintance. Years back, she'd tried to get a job in the city, but the magazine had hired Zhu Xiaofen instead. Zhu Xiaofen had later rejected one of her manuscripts. They weren't close, but they weren't exactly strangers either.

The woman from the research center announced she'd come to interview Zhu Xiaofen, then set off on a long discourse, sponging away the sweaty fog on her glasses as she talked with a handkerchief. Those bulging eyes and thick lenses made her look like a big, diligent ant. She'd already been in to see Big Sister Zou, she said, and they both agreed Zhu Xiaofen's biggest problem was her refusal to relax and open up. She may not know Zhu Xiaofen that well, but she could see right through her. Why make such a big deal about who asked for the divorce? According to her research, men often claim it's the woman who initiates divorce in order to preserve her sense of self-respect. Acquiescence on the woman's part is mere vanity, pathetic pride. Zhu Xiaofen, the crux of your problem lies right there. Why can't you admit your husband didn't want you anymore? The Women's Federation stands up for abandoned women like you. But look how you've handled the problem. You've gone out to jump rope. You're obviously just trying to hide your depression....

Zhu Xiaofen had to use the toilet.

Crackerjack held out a cup of her Yunnan *Maifanshi*

61

health drink. How could they make tea with the water off? This tea must be as precious as gold, Zhu Xiaofen thought, taking a sip.

Picking up where she'd left off, the woman from the research center said that everybody, but especially women, should cry when the time comes to cry and laugh when the time comes to laugh. Zhu Xiaofen, you're trying to escape reality. But how can you? You have a ten-month-old baby. You may never find another man who loves you, and even if you do, do you plan to have his child as well? Ninety-nine point nine eight two percent of the men I've surveyed say they want their own child....

Zhu Xiaofen's eyes began to water from the urgent pain in her bladder. Crackerjack immediately reported this development to Big Sister Zou and the rest of the editorial department, who upon hearing the news, let out a long communal sigh of relief — Zhu Xiaofen was finally going to cry. She was finally going to let it out. Their week of comforting and consoling had paid off. They jumped for joy. They sighed. They clasped their hands and paced the room.

No time for polite etiquette. Unable to hold it any longer, Zhu Xiaofen dashed out the door, leapt down the stairs, and grabbing her bike, sprinted toward the sweater factory.

She took a long time to drain herself empty. Reemerging in the sun, she wheeled her bicycle back to the factory gate. Her eyes, now dry, stung in the harsh morning glare. "Pa, pa," she patted the bike seat. That wasn't her bike. Storming down the stairs a moment ago, she hadn't even pulled out her key. Whose bike could it be? Why wasn't it locked? A new, good model like that leaning dubiously against the bike shed made her wonder if the whole thing hadn't been planned.

She patted the seat again, and leaping astride, rode off with no particular direction in mind. Octday was purely her invention, she remembered. Monday has to come after Day Seven, and besides, it's not called Day Seven. It's called Sunday, the day of rest.

Notes

1. The days of the week in Chinese, beginning with Monday, are numbered from one to six, literally translated to "Weekday One, Weekday Two...." Sunday, the exception, is equivalent to its English counterpart.
2. Xinjiang Uygur Autonomous Region is located in the northwest corner of China.
3. *Maifanshi* (Wheat Rice Stone), also known as "magic stone," can absorb metal particles such as cadmium, mercury and lead in water and release various trace elements beneficial to human health. Regular consumption can strengthen resistance to disease.
4. One of China's three northeastern provinces, Liaoning borders on North Korea.
5. *Thunderstorm*, a modern drama set in the home of a wealthy northern industrialist, was written in 1933 by playwright Cao Yu. Fan Yi, the young, beautiful, melancholic wife, suffering from impossible love for her step-son, is compelled to drink a cup of bitter Chinese medicine by her despotic older husband, who orders the step-son to kneel down before her in an act of supplication. He later arranges an appointment with the German psychiatrist, Dr. Kramer, to see about her "mental unbalance."
6. Intellectuals and government officials accused during the Cultural Revolution (1966-1976) of Rightist or "counter-revolutionary" activities were often removed from their homes and secluded to undergo re-education through labor and group study. Their living quarters were sometimes called "cowsheds."
7. During the Cultural Revolution, the Red Guards (comprised of revolutionary students and workers) were split into numerous opposing factions. Borrowing an army term, members of the same faction called each other "troop friend" (*zhanyou*). (See Note 2 of "Rejecting Fate" for more on the Red Guards.)
8. A popular Chinese-brand hair restorative sold domestically and abroad.
9. Traditional Chinese meditation combining body movements and breathing exercises, *Qigong* is often likened to Hindu Yoga.
10. From Mao Zedong's essay "Serve the People."
11. There are four types of train compartments in China: soft sleeper (first class), soft seat (first class), hard sleeper (second class) and hard seat (third class).

Friend on a Rainy Day

(A Play in Four Acts)

Bai Fengxi

A woman is not the moon; she can shine by her own light.

TIME: Present

CHARACTERS:

XIA ZHIXIAN	Woman doctor, 55 years old
PENG YINGE (Dove)	Xia Zhixian's daughter, 26 years old
MO JIN	Woman, 56 years old
CHENG KANG	Mo Jin's son, 28 years old
TIAN QIANGQIANG	Mo Jin's relative, 26 years old
PENG LUN	Peng Yinge's father, 56 years old

ACT ONE

A sunny August day, in the home of Dr. Xia Zhixian.

The moon-gate into the courtyard of the traditional one-story house can be seen on one side. A plane tree shades the yard; two luxuriant potted banana plants sit under the eaves.

There are three rooms: the living room, at center, opens onto the courtyard. An old-fashioned sofa, armchairs and low tea table take up one side of the room; to the other, is a desk piled with books. Though there are few homey touches, some things catch the eye. The wall is lined with baby photos; the glass case below is crowded with dolls from all over the world.

As the curtain rises, Peng Yinge, Dr. Xia's daughter, is walking slowly across the room playing the violin. Her fair skin and fine features are set off by jet-black hair. Pensive eyes

*sparkle beneath thick, arched brows. Her unaffected manner is
that of a natural, quiet beauty. She looks out the window from
time to time, obviously trying to use the music to ward off nervous anticipation. Stopping now and then, she suddenly glances
at her watch and sits down on the sofa in exasperation.*

    *Cheng Kang has quietly entered the room. Tall and well-
built, refined in a masculine way, Cheng appears a quiet, serious young man. He places a tin of candies and gift-wrapped
cake box on the table and tip-toes behind Peng to listen to her
music. When she stops playing, he moves quickly around to face
her.*

CHENG: He whom you await has already arrived!
PENG (*pleasantly surprised*): Cheng Kang! When did you
    get here?
CHENG: Such the mathematician you are—concentrating so
    hard, everything passes you by.
PENG (*gently*): I didn't know you'd be coming so soon.
CHENG: My feet move faster when I think of you. Were
    you worried?
PENG: Very. But sorry, not because of you.
CHENG (*surprised*): Oh!?
PENG (*teasingly*): Are you jealous?
CHENG: So far as our life together is concerned, the word
    "jealous" has been forgotten, right? ... Isn't Dr. Xia
    at home? Oh, that's right, starting today, I should get
    used to calling her "Mother."
PENG (*annoyed*): I really can't forgive Mother. Yesterday I
    told her: Your daughter's getting married. If for once
    in your life, ask for the night off and come home on
    time. That's not asking too much, is it? But she's still
    not back from the hospital.... (*She walks quickly over to
    the telephone.*)
CHENG (*putting his hand on the receiver*): Yinge, don't
    bother her at work. What does it matter anyway? Try
    to understand her.
PENG: Not today. Isn't her own daughter worth one-tenth,
    one one-hundredth the attention she gives to her pa-
    tients? (*dials*) ... Hello. Good morning. May I have the
    obstetrics ward please.... Yes, I'd like to speak to Dr.

Xia.

VOICE: Dr. Xia is in the delivery room at the moment.

PENG: In the delivery room? Alright, could you tell her there's an emergency at home and ask her to come as soon as she's finished. Thank you. (*puts down the receiver*) I don't get it. Can't the hospital do anything without her? Is she afraid the sky's going to fall without her there to hold it up?

CHENG (*with a mixture of disapproval and admiration*): My, what a temper you have, my Dove! Looks like I'm going to have to be careful after we're married.

PENG (*her annoyance subsiding*): Look. (*pointing to a large package on the bureau*) My father sent a wedding present with a long letter to both of us.

CHENG (*excited*): What does he say? Can I read it?

PENG: Of course. Father is so wonderful. His letter is full of love and hope for us.... But he also wants to warn us about something. (*handing the letter to Cheng*) Here, read for yourself.

CHENG (*reading out loud*): ... The two of you are devoted to your work, eager to learn and determined to excel. I applaud you both for having taken the qualifying exam for graduate study in mathematics. As youth of the eighties, working toward your common goals is a premise to shared happiness, but, on the other hand, I hope you will learn from your mother and me. As you begin your new life together, I'd like to present you with the proverb: "Understanding is another word for love." (*tasting the words again*) "Understanding is another word for love." Well said. Really! Dove, I know what he's getting at.

PENG (*morosely*): Understanding? Did he and Mother understand each other back then? I've never heard them get down on themselves, but then again, neither has ever said a bad word against the other. I can't figure it out. Oh, let's drop it. What's the point of talking about it? Today I'll be leaving this home that's not really a home and a mother who needs me as much as I need her.

CHENG: Why make it sound so depressing? Think of the

happiness our marriage will bring your mother. But Yinge, I must confess, I feel a little nervous around her....

PENG: Nervous? A proud person like you?

CHENG: Every time I see her it's so brief. There's no time to talk. Tell me, what does the distinguished doctor think of her son-in-law-to-be?

PENG (*with a sly smile*): No comment.

CHENG: She's very prestigious, but people say she's a little....

PENG (*warily*): A little what? A little odd, right? (*annoyed*) I don't like the way people twist her around. I know who gave you this idea.

CHENG: Who?

PENG: Your mother. She's always calling my mother an "oddball." I hate it when she says that.

CHENG: You shouldn't think about it so much. You're the one who's too proud. They were classmates, remember? I'm sure my mother doesn't mean any harm.

PENG: Odd? I know what that's supposed to mean. Let me tell you one thing: my parents may be divorced, but they're still wonderful people.

CHENG: You're wrong there.

PENG (*taken aback*): What?

CHENG: Well, I should say —not entirely right. Your parents aren't just nice people. They're extraordinary people who've made incredible contributions to society: one's a biologist researching the origin of life; the other delivers life into the world. I respect them both very much. Aren't you being a bit touchy? (*gratified, Peng smiles at him.*)

CHENG (*mildly reproachful*) And as for you ... don't you have something of your mother in you too?

PENG (*naively*): But Cheng Kang, some people say if a woman is too career-minded, her work will engross her so completely she'll have no feeling for anything else. They say it's alright to be friends with such a woman, but not to marry her.

CHENG (*disdainfully*): Prejudice! Ignorance!... Everybody has different values. Those people know absolutely nothing about love!

PENG (*satisfied with Cheng's response, she says jokingly*):
Cheng Kang, if I pass the graduate school entrance
exam, I'll be up to my eyeballs in numbers for the
rest of my life. One-two-three-four-five-six-seven, *do-re-mi-fa-so-la-ti-do*; I'll become a composer of soundless
music, an ascetic oddball who could care less about
creature comforts.

CHENG (*humorously*): Even if you were, I'd still love you.
I could love such an oddball forever.

PENG (*excited*): Really? I don't believe you. Do you really
mean it?

CHENG (*in a serious tone*): What do you think? What is to-day? Don't tell me you want your husband to pledge
his love for you all over again.

PENG (*hugging him happily*): No, I'll never be like that.
I'm not like Mother. I want a career *and* marriage.
I'd hate myself if I couldn't feel anything, if I lost my
natural maternal instincts. Do you believe me?

CHENG: I'm surprised you have to ask.

PENG (*suddenly feeling depressed, pushes him away*): Oh, if
only Father could have understood Mother like you un-derstand me. (*Turning around, she sees the presents he's
brought.*) What're these? (*reprovingly*) Cheng Kang, was
this really necessary?

CHENG: It wasn't me who bought them.

PENG: Then who was it?

CHENG: Mother. I was just about to tell you. Mother says
even though she and Dr. Xia are old classmates, she
wants to follow the custom of inviting the in-laws in per-son to our home on the day of the wedding. She should
be here any minute.

PENG: Any minute?! (*distressed*) Oh dear, why isn't Moth-er back? Look at the house....

CHENG (*trying to calm her*): So what? They're old friends.
My mother won't care.

PENG: It's your fault. Why didn't you tell me sooner?

(*They are interrupted by the toot of a horn and the sound
of a car braking outside. Mo Jin, Cheng Kang's mother, calls
out:* "Yinge! Dove!")

68

Mo Jin is a plump, good-looking woman. Simply yet tasteful-
ly dressed, she's carrying a net bag stuffed with food in one
hand, an expensive handbag in the other.

Peng Yinge and Cheng Kang hurry over to greet her.)

MO: What a maze of lanes out there! It's been such a long
time, I could hardly find the way. (*calling to her driver
outside*) Li, you can go on. Come back for me at two.

PENG (*warmly*): Auntie,[1] sit down, please.

MO (*stroking her arm fondly*): Huh, Auntie, Auntie! Still calling me Auntie on your wedding day? You should call
me by another name, you know.... Go on, what is it?

PENG (a bit bashfully): Mother.

MO (*dramatically*): Yes, dear! (*surprised*) Dove, isn't your
mother at home?

PENG: I'm sorry. I'll call to tell her you've come....

MO: No, no. A doctor's time is for her patients. Don't
bother her at work. Babies get born when they will regardless of the day or what else you've got planned.
She probably couldn't get away. (*taking the food from
her bag*) Dove, bring some plates, will you?

PENG (*embarrassed*): What's all this for? Why didn't you
have Cheng Kang tell us you were coming so Mother
could have gotten something ready.

MO: Oh no, don't think of me as a guest. I know my old
classmate: delivering babies, seeing patients, seeing patients, delivering babies — she's never been able to manage her life. (*with kindly pity*) She denies herself so
much. You know, Kangkang, I got up before six this
morning to come see this dear old classmate of mine. It
took me a full ... (*glances at her watch*) ... a full two
hours to buy these things. Oh, the lines and the
crowds! Phew! And now I've got the smell of fish all
over me as well! Dove, I'm like your mother. I hate
shopping and cooking. If they took a poll and asked:
"What is it you dislike most?" you know what I'd
say? Shopping! (*laughs good-naturedly*)

CHENG: Why didn't you send the maid?

MO: Everybody wants to be with their family on a holiday.
She's got a husband and children and a whole pack of
relatives. So I gave her the day off.

69

PENG: Please make yourself comfortable. I'll go make some tea. (*She turns and exits.*)

MO: Good. Put a lot of tea leaves in mine. I like it strong. (*glancing about the room*) Same as always. (*lowering her voice to a whisper*) Kangkang, how come nothing's ready? A wedding's no small matter. I wonder if she's really that busy. Humph! What an oddball!

CHENG (*in a low voice*): Mother, please don't talk like that. You'll hurt her feelings.

MO (*not without some jealousy*): Oh, you little rascal. How quickly you change sides! Don't you know your own mother? I'm as self-respecting as that mother-in-law of yours. You know, we hardly spoke for years. There was too much we couldn't agree on. If it weren't for you, do you think I'd have come today?

CHENG (*quickly stopping her*): Mother, please. No more, okay?

MO (*straightening up the desk*): Gracious me, can this really be a woman's home? What a mess! Come on, Kangkang, as of today this is your house too. Let's just do it ourselves. (*picking up a vase of plastic flowers*) Here, go wash this off in the sink.

CHENG: Okay. (*He takes the vase and goes out.*)

(*Mo finishes straightening up the books then finds a rag and walks out.*

A few minutes later, Dr. Xia Zhixian hurries in. Slim and attractive, her fair face is etched with light wrinkles; her broad forehead is fringed with gray hair. She is gentle yet dignified, quiet yet resolute. From each hand hangs a nylon net bag stuffed with canned food. She goes behind the door to change into slippers, and turning to hang up her sweater, sees the food on the table.)

XIA: Dove! Dove! How many times have I told you not to accept gifts from patients! (*calling out the window*) Dove, who's been here?

MO (*entering at the sound of her voice*): Who's here? Me!

XIA (*stares in surprise then responds warmly*): Mo Jin! How are you? It's been years!

MO (*grasping Dr. Xia's hand*): Yes, it's been a long time. Fate has brought us together again. Who could have guessed we'd be in-laws one day!

XIA: I'm sorry I was out when you came. Have you been waiting long?

MO: You're a famous doctor now. I know how busy you are. A patient must have kept you.

XIA: Actually, it was the husband of a patient. (*frowning*) Mo Jin, I couldn't believe it. Twenty-seven hours in delivery — we were lucky to save both the mother *and* the child. But when her husband heard it was a girl, he came at me like a crazy man. Oh, he was vicious! (*pointing at her blouse*) Look, he tore off two buttons.

MO (*indignantly*): How barbaric! How stupid! What's wrong with a girl anyway? I love little girls. (*sympathetically*) I must say, Zhixian, you certainly have to put up with a lot at work. Sit down and relax.

(*Peng Yinge enters with the tray of tea things. Cheng Kang puts the vase of plastic flowers back and stands by uneasily.*)

XIA: Have you been keeping well, Mo Jin?

MO: Not as well as you, I'd say. My husband is always going on about you. As for me, I'm forever on the go but never seem to get a thing done. (*amiably*) Zhixian, I know how busy you are — that's why I haven't been around to see you. You're not mad, are you? (*turning to Cheng Kang*) Kangkang, you haven't said hello to your mother-in-law.

(*Cheng Kang looks at her respectfully but appears rather embarrassed.*)

XIA: No, don't force him.

CHENG: Hello, Mother.

(*Xia looks over at Cheng Kang, her face brightening. She then pauses for a moment to scrutinize him.*)

MO: Well, what do you think? Does this son of mine meet the standards of the illustrious Dr. Xia?

XIA (*fondly*): Come here, Cheng Kang. Sit down, will you?

MO: Your daughter is like you, Zhixian, the cream of the crop. Our whole family is proud of her. You know, they wanted to put off the wedding until after the examination scores came out, but I said to them, why wait? It's Mid-autumn Festival; National Day's just around

71

the corner — now's the time to get married. I decided for them!

XIA (*seems preoccupied*): Um ... uh-huh....

MO: I talked it over with my husband, and we agreed to keep it simple, so as not to give a bad impression.[2] Tonight we'd like you to come over for dinner. We'll toast the occasion with a few close friends and relatives and then let the young couple go off on their honeymoon. What do you think?

XIA: Fine, just fine.

MO (*pleased*): See, Kangkang? Your mother-in-law and I are old classmates. I know her inside-and-out. (*laughs heartily*)

(*An attractive young woman appears in the doorway. Tian Qiangqiang, Mo's distant relative, is tall, slender and very pretty. Her voice rings like a silver bell at an octave higher than normal. She brings life and cheer wherever she goes, earning her the nickname "Sweetie."*)[3]

TIAN: Ah, what a festive time! Congratulations, everybody! My best wishes to you all for a happy holiday!

MO (*delighted*): So Qiangqiang has come. Wonderful! What wind has brought our Sweetie here?

TIAN (*as if reciting on stage*): 'Twas the sweet, blissful wind of the east which has borne me on wings and carried me hither. (*pretending to be angry*) Auntie, I just went over to your house to offer my congratulations.... What did I find but a locked gate! Trying to save on wedding sweets and wine,[4] are you? Well you won't get away so easily! (*courteously*) Congratulations, Dr. Xia.

XIA: Thank you, thank you very much. (*with a note of concern*) Qiangqiang, how's your little nephew? Is he gaining weight?

TIAN: He's much better, Dr. Xia. Thank you. (*with feeling, to Mo*) Can you believe my sister's luck? A one in nine chance for a live birth with the placenta contorted like that. Thank God for Dr. Xia. She was with my sister more than fifty hours. If it weren't for her, they'd have both died. (*reaching over to grasp Dr. Xia's hand*) Words can't express my family's gratitude. My mother wanted to send a gift, but then she changed her mind.

For one thing, no gift can be enough, and for another, knowing how you feel about such things, we were afraid you wouldn't accept. Finally, we decided to name the baby ... can you guess? Jingxian. "Jing" for respect, and "Xian" from your name.

CHENG: It's a good idea, but you're not the first. (*pointing to the row of baby photos*) Look, Jingxian — Respect Xian; Yangxian — Revere Xian; Aixian — Love Xian; Muxian — Admire Xian; Nianxian — Cherish Xian.... Even this little African baby is named Zhixian, Junior.

TIAN: So what? They can call their babies whatever they like. We're still going to honor Dr. Xia with this name.

XIA (*deliberately diverting the conversation*): Qiangqiang, what's that shiny thing in your hand?

TIAN: It's a wedding present for Peng Yinge and Cheng Kang. I racked my brains trying to figure out what I should give them. Auntie, I thought about this more than I would have for my own wedding....

PENG (*jokingly*): Stop it, Sweetie. Your words are too sweet even without candy!

TIAN: Yinge, guess what I finally decided on? No vase or tea-set or sheets.... You two great scholars don't need pots and pans or dishes. Dr. Xia, Auntie, I'm sure you'll both like my present.

MO: You little imp! What are you up to now? Don't keep us guessing.

TIAN: With the future in mind, I'm giving them something a little ahead of its time. (*untying the red ribbon on the transparent plastic box*) Look, a cable-stitch baby jacket. I got the pattern out of a fashion magazine and knitted it myself! (*thrusts the jacket into Cheng Kang's hands*)

CHENG (*embarrassed, he pushes it back*): Get out of here! *You* would have thought of this....

TIAN: Don't think you're above it all, my great scholar. Life is life. Sooner or later you two are going to have pots to scour, dishes to wash and a baby to feed — just like any other married couple. (*Mo burst out laughing.*)

MO: She's so practical. That's why I like my Sweetie.

(holding up the jacket to admire it) Zhixian, you've got all these photos on the wall, dolls in the case and babies bawling in the hospital. You see enough of them, don't you? But they're not yours, after all. When it comes to children, none can compare with your own.... Sweetie, your present makes me happier than if you'd given them a car.

TIAN: You've already got that. Besides, I couldn't afford it. Do you like the jacket, Dr. Xia?

XIA: I do, very much. *(apologetically)* I'm sorry — work seems to have gotten to me today. Dove, get the food ready, will you?

CHENG: Everything's set, Mother. Look.

XIA *(surprised at seeing the food on the table)*: Such a big spread! But who....

MO: I know how busy you are, so I brought everything along.

XIA: Thank goodness it's you, Mo Jin. If it were anyone else, I'd be terribly embarrassed. Well then, this lunch is at your expense.

MO: Zhixian, there's an old saying that fits us well: "Though thousands of *li* apart, drawn together by a single thread." Huh.... Just think, in the old days when you, Yinge's father and I were all premed, who would have ever thought we'd one day be in-laws? *(lowering her voice)* When I acted as your go-between, I had no idea you'd break it off. You ... you owe me an apology.

XIA: Aren't you off on a tangent, Mo Jin?

MO *(reproving but kindly)*: Nothing but work on your mind. Work, work, work. You've made a name for yourself alright, but you ... you don't enjoy life — you're a celebrity in the isolation of your own making. You really *are* an "oddball."

CHENG *(hastening to offer a cup of tea to Dr. Xia, he gives his mother a disapproving glance)*: You....

XIA *(gently yet firmly)*: Aren't you exaggerating things a bit, Mo Jin? Perhaps I enjoy life no less than you do.

MO: Alright, let's drop it. Let's not start arguing again the minute we meet. Kangkang, your mother-in-law is an outstanding woman. You know she sets high standards?

CHENG (*bashfully and yet not without humor*): That's why I'm so nervous.

MO: Zhixian, you haven't answered my question yet. Are you pleased with this son of mine?

TIAN (*playfully*): An excellent question. Hear, hear: Dr. Xia will give a short speech on the son-in-law question. Let's all give her a hand.

XIA: Well, I'll say a few words. (*gets up from her seat and paces the room*) Um, I'd ... I'd like to say that before taking something on, we all create an image of what it might be like. That goes for choosing a sweetheart— as well as imagining a future son-in-law. Before you two decided to get married, I had a picture in mind.... (*They watch her with anxious anticipation.*)

XIA (*solemnly*): ... And have felt all along that you fit the bill perfectly.

CHENG (*relieved*): Thank you.

XIA: Cheng Kang, I'm pleased you'll be my son-in-law, very pleased. Now I'd like to hear what you think of Dove.

TIAN: Me too. I'd like to know how this gifted lady of ours won the heart of the great scholar Cheng Kang.

MO (*frowning*): Sweetie, stop teasing. Zhixian, as a doctor, you naturally want to get to the bottom of everything. But love is a private matter, hardly for public discussion. Not to take sides with my son, but aren't you putting him in a corner?

XIA: You're right. It's not an appropriate question. Cheng Kang, what I mean is ... what are your plans for the future?

CHENG (*surprised*): Our plans?

MO: What a question! What are you trying to get at?

PENG (*exasperated*): Mother, this isn't the hospital. You can't interrogate us like your patients.

XIA (*realizing the inappropriateness of her question*): No, of course not. Cheng Kang, don't answer if you don't want to.

CHENG: No, no. I'm perfectly ready to answer. (*He thinks for a moment before beginning to speak.*) We're very much in love, and, what's more, we're confident about the future together. Dove is strong and intelligent. She has great depth of feeling. What attracts me most about her is that, like you, she's dedicated to her work and wants to push ahead. She is, of course, very beautiful too.

XIA: Beautiful? You call her pug nose, thick lips and bushy eyebrows beautiful?

PENG (*with playful coyness*): Well, Mother, who's to blame for that?

MO (*in exasperation*): Zhixian, have I ever pressed questions on your daughter like this?

XIA (*sincerely*): No, Mo Jin, I'm not pressing. You don't know how I feel right now. Really I'm ... quite ... quite worried. (*speaking with difficulty*) Listen to what I have to say....

MO: You're worried? Zhixian, this may sound a bit presumptuous, but ever since my Kangkang turned fourteen, I've had to turn away the matchmakers. I've offended heaven knows how many friends and colleagues in the process. Girls nowadays are so calculating; they think if they marry into our family, they'll have everything — housing, an easy life, a good job. I'd say they're all scheming to get their relatives in on it too. (*She sighs with some degree of superiority.*) Some people are simply too calculating, too smart. Zhixian, what are you worried about? Little Dove is very fortunate indeed.

XIA (*irritated*): What do you mean? That she's marrying above her? Is that what you're trying to say?

MO (*realizing that she's gotten carried away*): Oh no, nothing of the sort. You're the famous doctor — if anyone's marrying up, it's my son.

XIA (*finding this even more obnoxious*): Oh, Mo Jin, why always such commercialism? Better leave the advertising alone.

MO: Advertising? What advertising?

(*The atmosphere becomes tense.*)

TIAN (*quickly intervening*): Really, Auntie! Are you saying that everyone who's been after your Cheng Kang is just trying to marry up?

MO: Silly girl! You think I mean you? You know I like you. And aren't we as close as before?

TIAN: Dr. Xia, to tell the truth, Cheng Kang thinks I'm a nobody, a family-girl. He's been in love with your genius Yinge for a long time. (*jokingly*) It's just as well I knew where I stood, otherwise I'd have been the odd-one out in a love triangle.

CHENG (*embarrassed*): Come on now, Qiangqiang. Aren't you embarrassed to talk like that?

TIAN: Why? Scholars pursue gifted girls; us family-types look for our own kind. To each his own.

MO (*interrupting*): Sweetie, don't butt in. Kangkang, listen to your mother-in-law.... Zhixian, I still don't see what you're worried about.

CHENG (*to Dr. Xia*): Mother, sorry to have interrupted. Please go on.

XIA (*in earnest*): Cheng Kang, this is what I want to tell you: Love isn't a mystery but neither is it easy. Take for example.... Well, I've no example outside my own field, so I'll speak in medical terms. Just as a fetus needs nourishment through gestation, so does the establishment of a home and married life need constant care. In other words, marriage isn't only building a nest after the wedding, but building all the way through life.

MO (*taking up the cue*): Well said. A marriage needs to be built all the way through life. Your mother-in-law is speaking from experience. We Chinese have an old saying: "Everything will thrive with peace in the family."

XIA: In short, I hope you'll love each other and love each other's work and beliefs as well.

CHENG: You couldn't have put it better. I think on this account you can rest assured.

XIA: Good. It makes me happy to hear you say that, Cheng Kang. I'd like to know if ... if something unexpected happened after you and Yinge got married, would you understand her ... support her?

CHENG (*puzzled*): You mean....

XIA: Sorry, my question seems a little out of line.

CHENG: No, no, not at all. It's just that I don't know what you're getting at....

XIA: Let's say ... let's say, for example, that there are going to be contradictions between career and family life. Love without sacrifice can't be regarded as true love. Do you agree?

CHENG: Yes. If it's true love, then it won't seem like a sacrifice when you do something for your beloved. (*uneasily*) Mother, do you mean....

XIA: Well, take for instance....

PENG (*growing impatient*): For instance, for example.... Mother, just how many examples do you intend to give? You have something on your mind, don't you?

XIA (*nodding*): Yes, I do. I do indeed.

PENG: What is it then, Mother?

CHENG (*somewhat tensely*): Yes, what is it?

TIAN (*whispering to Mo Jin*): Auntie, what could it be?

MO (*peering sideways, she says confidently*): Ah, you don't understand, but I do. Nothing's the matter with her, nothing at all.... We have an apt parable: "Bitten by the snake, forever shy of rope." Zhixian, I know what you're thinking. All these years you and Peng Lun have been divorced, you've had your share of heartache and regret. Only you know if I'm right.

XIA (*preoccupied with her thoughts, doesn't seem to take in Mo Jin's words*): Mo Jin, today we celebrate our children's marriage. Cheng Kang and Dove, I hope you're prepared to bear with each other's weaknesses as well as enjoy each other's strengths. We Chinese traditionally place value on lifetime marriage. Don't you agree, Mo Jin?

MO: Of course. I can't stand these easy-come, easy-go divorces. Rest assured, Zhixian. They'll love each other all their lives.... Right, Dove?

(*Peng Yinge and Cheng Kang look at each other and nod. Dr. Xia rises and paces back and forth in agitation.*)

XIA: My little Dove! She may be flying far away.

(*The others watch her in bewilderment.*)

XIA: There is something on my mind; I don't know whether to be happy or worried about it.... It distresses me very much indeed.

CHENG: Does it have to do with the exams?

XIA: Yes.

PENG (*in a disappointed voice*): I've failed; I've been refused admission. Is that it, Mother?

XIA: No, that's not it. You've not only passed, (*pulling a letter from her handbag*) you've far surpassed the requirements for admission to graduate school. The exam board claims you're a genius! (*pause*) Of course she doesn't deserve such praise, but they're recommending her for advanced studies as a Ph.D. candidate at Gottingen University in West Germany.

(*Peng takes the letter from her mother and walks over to Cheng Kang in great excitement.*)

PENG (*surprised and excited*): Oh, I never imagined! Cheng Kang, this is beyond my wildest dreams!

CHENG (*in a grave tone*): I'm ... I'm happy for you, very happy. Congratulations ... Yinge.

TIAN (*in a high, clear voice*): I must say, this really is a happy occasion— "On the nuptial night comes news of passing the imperial examination."

XIA (*heaves a long sigh*): Four years apart is no small matter to newly-weds. Don't you think, Mo Jin?

MO (*manages an awkward smile*): Yes, it's certainly no small matter.

(*The curtain closes on a room of mixed expressions, some happy, others solemn and thoughtful.*)

ACT TWO

A few days later, in the afternoon.

Set in Mo Jin's home, an elegant, well-appointed courtyard house in the traditional style. Carved and painted woodwork, a bit weather-beaten, is still visible. Just outside the living-room door stands a screen of translucent glass that acts as a shelter for rare potted plants and bonsai. Two sofa and armchair sets with chromium arm-rests and wine-colored slips are arranged on either side of the room; the curtains are white. Cookie tins, candy boxes and bottles of quality wine and liquor fill the shining glass case. Elegantly bound books line the shelves of the bookcase.

As the curtain rises, Mo Jin is sitting at the desk looking over some papers with her reading glasses.

MO (*impatiently flinging the papers on the desk*): Humph, what a bunch of garbage! (*She walks around the glass screen and calls to a room on the other side of the courtyard.*) Dove! Kangkang! Your father's been held up tonight, so dinner will be served a little later. If you get hungry, Auntie Liu can make a snack for you.

PENG (*from the other room*): We can wait, Mother. Don't worry about us.

(*As Mo Jin picks up the flower sprinkler, Tian Qiangqiang enters, a sling bag over her shoulder.*)

TIAN: Hello, Auntie. I called your office; they told me you're not feeling well. (*with concern*) What's wrong? Have you been to the doctor's?

Mo: Hello, Sweetie. It's nothing serious — just not feeling myself. The doctor insisted I take a few days off. But I've got so many visitors and the phone ringing off the hook, I do more here than at the office. Come, sit down.

TIAN: Are you home alone? Where are the newly-weds?

MO (*in a low voice*): Shh ... they're in the middle of negotiations.

TIAN: Negotiations? Over what? (*pause*) Auntie, guess why I came.

MO: How should I know? You're too quick for me.

TIAN (*pulling something from her bag*): I've finished your sweater.

MO (*in disbelief*): What? So soon?! It's only been a couple of days!

TIAN: It's getting chilly already. I was afraid you might need it, so I worked every night and during meetings at work. (*holding up the tan sweater*) Here, try it on.

MO (*excitedly*): Oh, my dear Sweetie. Do you know how old I am? It's so stylish! What do you call this stitch? Albanian?

TIAN: That's long gone out of fashion. This is the chain cable stitch. (*helps Mo Jin into the sweater and steps back to admire it*) How chic you look! Auntie, I'm not exaggerating — with this sweater on, you look more elegant than Mrs. Thatcher. Take a look in the mirror and see for yourself.

MO (*delighted*): Not bad, not bad at all. Sweetie, how can I thank you? I'd never be able to knit one myself, even if I spent a lifetime at it.

TIAN: You're too busy. How could you possibly spare time for this sort of thing?

(*Peng Yinge comes out of her room and crosses the courtyard toward the living-room.*)

MO: You know, I've got these two men in the family and no capable girl to help out. My daughter-in-law is even worse than I am. She can't sew a button on properly, let alone embroider or knit. (*stroking Tian's arm fondly, she says meaningfully*) Oh, Sweetie, luck is against me.... But don't worry. Leave everything to me; I'll see to it that you find a good husband. (*Aware that Peng has entered the room, Tian breaks off the conversation.*)

TIAN: Hello, Yinge.

PENG: Oh, Qiangqiang, it's you. Mother complaining about me again?

TIAN: Complaining? Did it sound like she was complaining? Why, she's been praising her gifted daughter-in-law. Yinge, what do you think of the sweater? Doesn't Auntie look chic?

PENG (*appreciatively*): Wonderful! Mother, if I tried, I suppose I could learn to do housework too.

MO: Of course you could. It never hurts to learn how to get on better in life. Alright, next time I'll wear a sweater knitted by Yinge.

TIAN: Knitting is nothing — it's simple manual labor. But I'll never be like Yinge. Everybody has to follow their own calling; each to their own ability.

MO (*studying Peng and sounding her out*): Dove, you seem to be in a good mood. How's the discussion coming along? Well, I hope.

PENG: Yes, I think so.

MO (*gratified, she pats Peng on the shoulder*): Good! That's what I call mutual love and respect.

TIAN: What have you two been negotiating? Most likely your plans to study abroad? (*sympathetically*) It's too bad— just married and to be separated for four long years. That's more than I could bear. Yinge, you've shed a few tears, I suppose? And what about the great scholar? Is he willing to let you go?

(*Peng Yinge shakes her head in grief.*)

TIAN: Of course, that's understandable. If I were him, I wouldn't be able to stand it either. (*jokingly*) Too bad, the great scholar living a bachelor's life right after marriage. My talented lady, are you so cruel as to leave your new husband? You must have a heart of stone.

(*Overcome with grief, Peng Yinge breaks into tears. Hastily drying her eyes, she turns around to pick up the flower sprinkler.*)

MO (*in mild reproach*): Sweetie, see what you've done.

TIAN (*apologetically*): Oh dear, I'm sorry. Yinge, don't take it so hard. Achievement has its price. If you don't pay a little, how can you expect to get your due? Besides, your husband isn't holding you back, and you've got an understanding mother-in-law. You should consider yourself lucky! Go on with your ambitions, Dove. Don't be so sentimental. Don't....

MO (*with a tug at Tian's jacket*): Sweetie, stop it. (*turns to console Peng*) Don't feel bad, Dove. It's alright.

PENG (*laying her head on Mo Jin's shoulder*): Mother, do you know how torn I am? He's such a wonderful husband. I really ... I really don't have the heart to part with him. Mother, I....

MO (*wiping away her tears tenderly*): Don't cry now. Try to be more open-minded about it. Remember: career comes first. Don't let your emotions get in the way. There now, be a good girl and stop crying!

PENG (*controlling herself*): Mother, you're not feeling well. Why aren't you resting? (*turns to water the plants*)

MO: How can I rest when there's so much work to be done? (*breaking off suddenly*) Oh, stop, you foolish girl! You can't water the plant that way. It's a russelia. You'll kill it if you sprinkle water where the shoot is grafted.

PENG: I have to go out and buy some books, Mother.

MO: Go ahead, but don't stay too late. We'll wait dinner for you.

PENG: Bye, Qiangqiang.

TIAN: Bye. Let me know about your farewell party.

(*Peng Yinge exits.*)

MO: Sweetie, you have no idea how things stand, yet you insist on butting in. The matter has taken a turn, a decided turn.

TIAN: What's that?

MO: Listen. (*excitedly*) I got someone to find out about the examination results: Kangkang tested right behind Yinge. There's only one opening to study abroad, and if Yinge backs down, then Kangkang can take her place. Don't you think it's a coincidence the competition should fall between these two? Kangkang would never scramble for this opportunity with anyone else, but seeing as it's a matter between him and his wife, well, that can be easily settled, can't it?

TIAN: You mean to say Kangkang will study abroad instead of Yinge?

MO: Exactly.

TIAN (*not without sarcasm*): Auntie, aren't you being a little selfish?

MO: I'm not interfering; I left it up to them to work out on their own. Didn't you hear her say their talks were a success?

TIAN: My, my, your two scholars are really neck and neck in the race. Tell me, Auntie, how is it you have so many geniuses in the family? Well, I guess I'll be seeing off Kangkang, not Yinge. Auntie, I'll let you get some rest now. (*in a sweet, coy voice as she rises to her feet*) Auntie ... you.... (*stops short*)

MO: What is it?

TIAN: What do you think? You've been so busy with your children, you've neglected your health and probably forgotten the favor I asked of you. Have you talked to Uncle about my job?

MO (*frowning*): Oh dear, Sweetie, to tell the truth, I hate to get involved. It's not like it used to be. We've got people watching us all the time. You know your uncle; he always goes by the book. If I keep at him, he's going to get angry.

TIAN (*in an overly sweet tone*): Uncle angry at you? Doesn't everybody know where he gets his orders? That he's the most.... (*whispering into Mo Jin's ear*) obedient husband around?

MO (*sternly*): You little brat. Try talking like that in front of other people, and you'll get a good hiding.... I'm warning you.

TIAN: Come on. I'll dial for you. (*picks up the receiver and dials*)

MO (*takes the receiver from Tian*): Hello. Cheng? Have you taken your medicine?

VOICE (*Mo's husband*): Oh no, I forgot.

MO (*annoyed*): Didn't they remind you? ... Humph, I've told them time and time again. How can they be so irresponsible? I'll have to talk to them later.

VOICE: No, no. Don't do that. Anything else?

MO: Miss Tian is here again. What about her request?

VOICE: Tell her to follow the proper procedure and wait for their decision.

TIAN (*losing patience*): And wait for heaven knows how long!

MO (*picking up the cue*): And wait for heaven knows how long!

VOICE: You have to give them time. They're always careful when it comes to personnel.

MO (*peeved*): Fine, just fine. Don't trouble yourself about it! (*slams down the receiver*)

TIAN (*disappointed*): Auntie, does this mean the whole thing's off?

MO (*in a stern tone*): Humph. People say I use his influence to get things done. That's a bunch of nonsense! ... Don't worry, Sweetie. I'll have the personnel director over for a talk. I can manage a trivial matter like this.

TIAN: Exactly. That's what everybody told me: you don't need gifts or special deals. Talk it over with your aunt, and it's as good as done.

MO (*guardedly*): What does that mean? I don't do anything

against the rules, I can assure you that.

TIAN: Of course not. That's not what I meant. Everybody says you've got drive and prestige. You're good at handling these things, that's all.

(*Cheng Kang enters.*)

MO: Oh, you! Such sweet words! How can I ever answer that?

TIAN: Well, so long. (*Turning to go, she sees Cheng Kang.*) Oh, it's you, the great scholar. When are we going to see you off?

CHENG (*surprised*): Eh? Uh ... when did you come?

TIAN: What airs! Showing up just when I'm about to leave. Well, bye now.

CHENG (*quietly*): Uh, sorry. Goodbye.

MO: Sweetie, see to it you don't go off at the mouth, or it may be difficult for us to....

(*Mo Jin and Tian exit, talking as they go. Cheng Kang, his brows knit in consternation, opens a drawer and fishes about for something. He pulls out a pack of cigarettes, takes one, lights it and takes several long pulls. Mo Jin returns from outside.*)

MO (*shocked*): Kangkang, when did you start to smoke? Put it out. I just got your father to quit, and now you're starting. Put it out this minute!

CHENG: Relax, Mother. It's just something to do. I won't get addicted. This is what's known as "Sipping tea to kill time, drinking to drive away melancholy, smoking to escape boredom."

MO: Boredom? With all you've got? A fine career, a wife after your own heart.... How many young men are so fortunate?

(*She grabs the cigarette and puts it out.*)

CHENG (*in sullen resignation*): Oh, to live the life of a bachelor once again!

MO (*tenderly*): You find it difficult to part with Yinge, don't you? (*humoring him*) Come on now! A real man has the world at heart. Yinge tells me you had a nice talk together. You did, didn't you?

CHENG: Yes, of course.

MO (*elated*): I was wrong about her. I thought she was am-

85

bitious and headstrong like her mother. I'm glad to see she's so understanding and reasonable.

CHENG (*baffled*): What do you mean, Mother?

MO: She said herself that your talk went well. Hasn't she agreed to let you study abroad?

CHENG: How could she possibly?

MO (*chagrined*): What?! After all that, you're still letting her go?

CHENG: The exam results speak for themselves. Mother, don't worry yourself over this. What right do I have to hold her back?

MO (*agitated*): Oh, you.... (*petulantly*) Kangkang, you've changed; you're not what you used to be. My words mean nothing to you anymore. Do you know how much trouble I've taken on your behalf the last few days? I've cleared the way for you, and you're backing out at a word from your wife.

CHENG: Science requires real talent and honest work; it admits no falsehood.

MO: Falsehood? No principle has been compromised in reconsidering your case. You've yielded simply because Yinge won't give in, haven't you? Answer me.

CHENG: No, that's not it. Dove has been thinking of me all along....

MO (*cutting him off*): And you're still willing to let her go?

CHENG: Yes!

MO: That's not true. You can't fool me. Only a minute ago you were mumbling about "Sipping tea to kill time, drinking to drive away melancholy, smoking to escape boredom." No, I can't leave this up to the two of you; I'll decide for you.

CHENG: Mother, please, leave it alone. We'll decide for ourselves. There's no point arguing over it.

MO: Arguing? You fool! Do you think this is merely a question of studying abroad, of getting an academic degree? It's not that simple, my boy. (*with real earnestness*) What's at stake here is your marriage, peace and harmony in the family. Don't you see? Tell me, you're in love with her, aren't you? Aren't you afraid of losing her?

CHENG (*in scornful disagreement*): What on earth are you talking about? Don't you think I have any confidence in myself? Don't I know how much we love each other? Do you understand Yinge as I do? Mother, I beg you — leave it alone.

MO (*with a sneer*): Alright. I hope you're right. Though there is reason for the old saying: "When the woman's stronger than the man, future happiness can't last long." A woman shouldn't be too strong; if she overpowers her husband at work, there'll be no peace in the family.

CHENG (*unprepared for this outburst, he says jokingly*): Mother, what's come over you? I never thought someone open-minded like you could have such ideas. Where do you come up with your theories?

MO (*seriously*): Theories? You need theories? You have a living example right in front of you. You get what I mean, don't you?

CHENG (*shaking his head in wonderment*): No, I don't.

MO: Answer me this: Your mother-in-law's a good person, isn't she?

CHENG: Of course.

MO: In her devotion to career, she's a strong and competent woman, right?

CHENG: Yes.

MO: An outstanding doctor of gynecology and obstetrics is somebody —

CHENG: Yes, Of course.

MO: Let me ask you another question. What kind of family life does she lead? That you know only too well. Didn't she and Peng Lun vow to love each other till the end of the world? Weren't they once head over heels in love as you and Yinge are now? Well, and what's come of it? Both were ambitious and head-strong; both tried to get the upper hand, only to end up fighting and finally splitting up, leaving behind a broken family. Isn't that a fact?

(*Cheng Kang is obviously shaken. Pondering the question, he nervously takes another cigarette. Mo Jin blows out the match as he tries to light it.*)

CHENG (*hesitantly*): Mother, couldn't there have been other reasons for their split-up?

MO: Other reasons? None at all. Peng Lun is a true scientist with a brilliant mind and great charm. As luck would have it, he met up with an oddball and was made miserable without a family. If he knew Yinge was taking this offer, I'm sure he'd advise against it. He knows how difficult it's been.

CHENG: This ... this may not be the fault of only one side.... Both had a career to think of. Dove's mother is, after all, an extraordinary woman.

MO (*her anger now shifted to Xia Zhixian*): An extraordinary woman?! Is she the only one? I don't mean to brag, but I was an outstanding student in med-school, certainly never inferior to your mother-in-law. In the fifties my name was in the papers. But later, I ... I was less ambitious, and after I married your father, I became quite practical. I put the family first. Do you have any idea? I gave up my career to help your father. I took care of him so he could work. Everything he's done has been possible because of me. A husband and wife should cooperate and support each other. (*scornfully*) I really don't see the point in competing with one's own husband. Humph ... Yinge's just like her mother. For all I know, she'll end up ... an oddball too.

(*Peng Yinge walks in from outside. Hearing their conversation, she stops short.*)

CHENG (*in angry protest*): Mother, what on earth are you raving about?

MO (*taken aback*): What?! Me raving?! ... Alright, I'm raving. I've hurt your pride, haven't I? I'll go apologize to your wife and mother-in-law. Will that do?

CHEN G (*realizing his slip of the tongue*): No, Mother, that's not what I meant.

MO (*earnestly*): My boy, I have more experience than you. Have you thought about what it'll be like four years from now when she has her doctorate — what you'll be beside her? People will introduce you: "This is Cheng Kang, husband of Dr. Peng Yinge." How will you feel then? What man has no pride? Just imagine, when....

(*His pride stung to the quick, Cheng Kang leaps to his feet and begins pacing the floor.*)

MO (*taking advantage of his emotional state*): Kangkang, beside her you'll be nothing, a mere prop. You with your pride! What mother doesn't know her own child?

CHENG (*cutting her off sharply*): Mother! (*in a state of mental turmoil, muttering to himself*) I should let her go ... I should.... Of course I should.

MO (*pressing on*): What worries me is that once her status changes, her attitude will too. She won't be the little dove she is now.... It used to be that men left their wives, but these days women leave their husbands—

CHENG (*exploding*): Stop it! Stop it! Haven't you said enough already?

MO (*alarmed by his sudden outburst*): Eh? But Kangkang....

CHENG (*bereft of reason, seems to be at once arguing with her and talking to himself*): I'm ready to let her go, ready to suffer the consequences. I'll take what I deserve. There, are you satisfied?

MO (*freezes with shock and apprehension, then breaks into sobs*): Alright, alright.... It's me who has to suffer the consequences. It's me who has to take what I deserve.

CHENG: Mother, I beg you—let me think for a minute in peace.

MO: It's me who misjudged her and hustled you into marrying her.... And now she's spoiling everything.

CHENG: I'm going to go get her.

(*Cheng Kang rushes for the door. Peng Yinge, who is still standing outside, quickly moves out of sight.*)

MO (*holding him back*): Kangkang! Wait!

(*Cheng Kang slams the door shut and slumps despondently on the sofa, his head in his hands.*)

MO (*after a short pause*): To tell the truth, I worried when you two started going out. But you wouldn't listen to me. You refused to consider a fine girl like Qiangqiang. She's "the family type," you said, not "the career type." I wonder where you got all those newfangled words.... I don't know whether this is a case of "Lovers separated by a thousand *li* are fated to meet" or "Enemies are bound to collide on a nar-

89

row pathway." Everybody in science has it good these days. Her mother one-upped me, and now the daughter.... (*growing angrier with every word*) No, this won't do. Trees have bark and people have face. (*suddenly seeing a glimmer of hope*) That's it: I'll get her father to come. Kangkang, I've told you before: "Two strong opponents, and one is bound to lose; if the wife is the stronger, there'll be no peace in the family." Just you wait and see.

(*Peng Yinge, still eavesdropping outside, is enraged by what she hears. About to break into the room, she changes her mind and suddenly dashes off. Mo Jin thinks she hears something and goes to the door to look out. She finds the Persian cat there.*)

MO: Oh, it's you, Mimi.... Kangkang, maybe I'm wrong; maybe you've got the self-confidence to handle it. Think it over and see if what I've said makes any sense.

(*Cheng Kang sits in agitated silence. He is quiet for a long time.*)

CHENG: Why me? ... Why these trials so soon? But, Mother, I can't go back on my word. I love her. I can't bring myself to quarrel with her. I'll let her decide. Anyway, I can't imagine life without her; I can't bear to lose her. (*glances at his watch and then the clock*) Why isn't she back yet? It's getting late.

MO (*with a faint sneer*): See how much she cares for this family? She's not even a PhD yet. Just you wait: there's more to come.

(*The Persian cat keeps meowing as the curtain falls.*)

ACT THREE

The evening of the same day, in Dr. Xia Zhixian's house.

It's a quiet autumn night. The moon outside beams soft and silvery; a light wind sighs gently. An occasional leaf from the plane tree flutters to the ground. Dr. Xia is curled on the sofa in the living-room lit by a beam of moonlight from the window. As she tosses and turns in her sleep, a thick photo album drops from the sofa onto the floor with a thump. She wakes with a start, glances at her watch and gets up to pace the room. She then goes to the telephone and dials.

XIA: Hello. Please give me the obstetrics ward.... Hello. Has the patient in Bed Five shown any sign of change?

VOICE: Dr. Xia? No, she's the same as before.

XIA: I believe I asked you to call me once an hour.

VOICE: If I do that, how can you sleep?

XIA (*in mild reproach*): The less you phone, the less I'm able to sleep. Don't let my sleeping bother you. Please call me if there's any change. Thank you. (*hangs up*)
(*Peng Yinge hurries into the room.*)

XIA (*turning on the light and looking at her happily*): Dove, what are you coming at this late hour for? Miss your mother?

PENG (*with forced calmness*): How have you been, Mother?

XIA: Fine, fine. Just fine.... Ah, it seems ages since I last saw you, but it's only been a few days.... Where have you come from?

PENG: Mother ... you're not going to the hospital tonight, are you?

XIA: Hard to say. (*with a shade of melancholy*) Oh, I must be getting old to get so emotional. Frankly, Dove, I find the house too empty when I come home these days. It's the first time in my life I've felt lonely.

PENG (*noticing the photo album on the floor, turns to her mother with a sad look*): Mother, where ... have you been hiding that album?

XIA (*hastening to cover it up*): I miss you, I really do. I'm being selfish, aren't I? To wish my grown-up daughter hadn't married and gone away....

PENG: Married! Married! Why do we have to get married and leave home anyway? Mother, I'll stay here with you. I'm not going back.

XIA (*jokingly*): Oh? Not going back? You want to stay with your mother? Well then, have him come and live here too. Isn't that being encouraged now — men marrying into their wives' families? So long as Cheng Kang and his parents don't object, I'll certainly welcome him with open arms .... I suppose you haven't had dinner yet. I'll fix us something. (*takes two packages out of the cabinet*) But it's not like at your husband's; there's nothing good to eat here. A bowl of instant noodles each — just like before. Dove, can you stay with me for a while?

(*Peng Yinge nods with a wry smile.*)

XIA: Oh no, you better go home early, or they'll worry about you.

PENG (*sits down on the sofa*): I'm not going back.

XIA (*eyeing her daughter with foreboding*): Dove, why hasn't Cheng Kang come along?

(*Peng Yinge remains silent.*)

XIA: Did you have a fight? But I thought you two were getting on so well.

PENG: Oh yeah, really well.

XIA: Why, have you had a disagreement?

PENG: Much more. We've had an earthquake.

XIA (*distressed, slowly sitting down by her daughter*): Now, now, don't exaggerate. It can't be that serious. An earthquake indeed! Why don't you tell me how it started. (*presses her aching legs out of habit*)

PENG (*trying to cover up*): Oh, it's nothing really. Mother, old ailments kick up in the autumn. How are your varicose veins? Are they bothering you again? Let's eat, and then you can go to bed and get some rest.

XIA: No, I can't go to bed tonight.

PENG: Why not?

XIA: We've got a critical case at the hospital; they may call me back any minute. I didn't want to come home, but they forced me. How can I sleep? ... Come on, tell me what happened.

PENG: I'll tell you tomorrow. Why don't you go to bed while I wait by the phone? I'll wake you if they call. (*imploringly*) Please, Mother, go to bed and get some rest.

XIA: Stop harping. You know, there's been something on my mind the last few days. What have you two decided about your going abroad?

PENG (*after a moment's hesitation, speaking with determina-*

tion): Mother, I've decided to go. I must go. There's nothing to discuss. At first I couldn't decide and felt awful about it.... but they've helped me make up my mind. I'm definitely going.

(*Realizing that what she's been dreading all along is actually happening, Xia rises and paces back and forth, deep in thought*.)

PENG: After all, why should my life be decided by others? I can't understand that; I just can't.

XIA: What's so hard to understand? A married couple should be responsible to each other.

PENG (*with feeling*): You once told me I'd have to make a choice between marriage and career, that I couldn't have both. I remember how I argued with you; I couldn't understand what you were talking about. I was so confident, had so many dreams. I never thought it would all become so clear after I got married. You were right, Mother, absolutely right.

XIA (*in anguish*): You ... Dove ... you....

PENG: Yes, you were right. If marriage means getting caught in a net of my own making, then I'd just as soon break free. That's all there is to it.

XIA (*severely*): Don't talk like that!

PENG: You were right about everything: One plus one does not necessarily equal two. It's much easier, much freer to live the single life....

XIA (*angrily*): That's enough, do you hear me! Say no more!

PENG (*stunned by her mother's angry outburst*): Mother, why are you so angry?

XIA (*remorsefully*): The single life easier? Freer? No, what you're talking about is just a kind of ... selfishness.

PENG (*surprised*): Selfishness? Who's selfish? Me?

XIA (*muttering to herself*): Life is tricky. You always run up against whatever it is you're afraid of. (*earnestly*) Dove, don't take what I told you once as the only truth in life, much less some truth you have to abide by. Why should family life get in the way of work? You can have a successful career *and* a family. (*growing agitated*) Why follow my example? Haven't you always admired Madame Curie? She was a scientist *and* wife and mother.

How did she do it? She had both strength of mind and heart.

PENG (*at a loss*): I used to think like that. But now, I don't get it — what is it you want me to do? Give up my career and resign myself to being a dutiful wife; give up this chance to study abroad? Is that what you want?

XIA: Yes, exactly.

PENG (*confused, looks at her mother incredulously and then, as her eyes shift to the album, suddenly realizes something*): You were looking at old photos. Mother, are you feeling ... lonely? Are you afraid of being lonely?

XIA: If that's what you want to call it, of course, you may. But....

PENG: But what other reason could there be?

(*The telephone rings.*)

XIA (*hurriedly picking up the receiver*): Hello. How's Bed Five?

VOICE: What do you mean "Bed Five"? Zhixian, do you know who this is?

XIA: Oh, it's you, Mo Jin!

VOICE: Dove has disappeared. Is she over there?

(*Peng Yinge waves her hand to signal "no" to her mother.*)

XIA: Yes, she's here. What a considerate mother-in-law you are! Don't worry, she's fine. Goodbye now. (*hangs up*)

PENG (*grumbling*): Why did you have to tell her I'm here?

XIA: I have to be honest.

PENG: Is she honest? Mother, a few minutes ago when I was going in the door, I overheard her telling Cheng Kang all kinds of awful things. She was telling him what to do and ridiculing me.... I heard every word of it....

XIA (*shocked*): You were eavesdropping?

PENG: There's more truth in what you get from eavesdropping than what they say to your face. (*indignantly*) She even talked about you; she said I'm just like you because I won't give in to my husband. And she said.... I couldn't stand listening to her any more....

XIA (*morosely*): Oh dear, how has it come to this? Dove, listen to me. If that's how she feels about it, and you insist on going abroad, there's going to be a fight. In the end ... (*painfully*) in the end, it'll lead to another.... Dear, don't you understand?

PENG (*perplexed*): No, Mother, I don't.

XIA (*in a grave tone*): What I want to say is this: Make some concessions or, sacrifices, if you will. You must and you should.

PENG (*astounded*): You mean ... Mother, do you really mean it?

XIA (*in all seriousness*): I've thought it over, and that's how I feel.

PENG: I don't believe it. I can't believe it.

XIA (*pleading earnestly*): Please listen to my advice.

PENG (*frustrated and disappointed*): I never dreamed you'd think this way. It's been hard enough as it is; I thought you'd help me, encourage me. But you ... (*scarcely able to get it out*) ... it's you who's being selfish.

XIA: Selfish?

PENG: Yes, selfish. What did you do? Why did you and Father get divorced? You were so busy with your career, you couldn't be burdened with the family. (*in anguish*) I was even a burden to you. You both only thought of your work; neither of you wanted to be a parent, so you dumped me off on Grandma's in the countryside. You accomplished what you wanted and made big names for yourselves. Now you're asking me to.... Why? I don't understand....

XIA (*in a pained whisper*): It's nothing you can't understand.

PENG (*obstinately*): But I'll never understand! You did it in your day. What age are we living in now? Why can't I be free to follow my own career? Aren't you still working? Put yourself in my place, Mother. You once pushed me off on Grandma. If I had a baby, would you look after it for me? Would you quit your job for that? It's not like it used to be. (*resolutely*) I'm going to listen to Father, not you.

XIA (*taken aback*): What? What are you talking about?

PENG: I called Father the day before yesterday. He supports me a hundred percent. He says a woman who strives for success has to face a lot more than a man does. She needs courage and strength; she shouldn't let the fact that she's a woman get in the way of her plans. He used you as an example. "Why can't a woman have a career?" he said. "Isn't your mother a successful career woman?"

(*Dr. Xia rises abruptly and walks aimlessly about the room before stopping at the window. The curtains billow; her hair is gently ruffled in the night breeze. The room seems to take on the feeling of her disquietude and sorrow. She turns to face Peng Yinge.*)

XIA (*smiling bitterly*): So now he's so cool-headed, so high-minded, is that it? What about before? Couldn't he see the obstacles he put in my way? (*deeply buried emotions begin to surge*) A fine man he was.... He understood me best; he was my closest partner in work. What made him so unreasonable later? ... When I got the chance to study abroad, he had the nerve to say: I want you to be my wife, not some famous doctor....

PENG (*eyes fixed on her mother*): You? Mother....

XIA: Dove, do you think I sent you to Grandma's to get rid of you? Is there any mother who doesn't love her children? I had to give up a lot for my work, but when it came to you, my daughter....I thought about you every free moment; I missed you so much. I used to sneak off to see you, but when I got to your grandmother's, do you know how she treated me? Do you know what she'd say? "How can you call yourself a woman when you've abandoned your husband and neglected your child? And you have the gall to come to see her!" She hid you from me and threw me out ... After she died, it was all I could do to get you back. Dove, I've let you have your way the past several years. But this problem now — it's all I've been thinking about. You and Cheng Kang get along well, you love each other. To love and be loved is a happiness hard to come by.... How can I put it? I don't want you to repeat my

96

my mistakes....

(*Seeing the tears streaming down her mother's cheeks, Peng Yinge can't hold back her own. The room is silent but for the clock ticking on the desk.*)

PENG (*quietly bringing a bowl of noodles to her mother*): Mother, the noodles are getting cold.

(*The toot of a car horn is heard off-stage.*)

XIA: Dove, that must be the car to take me to the hospital. If you don't want to go back to the Chengs', go to bed, and we'll talk about it tomorrow.

(*Peng Yinge hands her mother her jacket and handbag. Mo Jin and Cheng Kang enter from the courtyard. For a moment, Peng Yinge seems ready to dodge them, but then changes her mind and greets them calmly.*)

PENG: Mother, why have you come out so late?

MO (*casually*): Zhixian, I'm sorry. You probably didn't expect us.

CHENG (*courteously*): Hello, Mother. Are you going to the hospital?

XIA: No, no. (*in jest*) Cheng Kang, what scene is this? Don't tell me it's *Lin Chong Flees by Night* [5] (*turning to her daughter in reproach*) Dove, look what you've done, making everybody chase around after you. Why, even the Grand Dame of Daguanyuan [6] is out on an inspection tour. (*to Mo Jin*) My dear, didn't I tell you she was here? Were you still worried?

MO (*amicably*): I've come to make sure she's alright. Dove, it's quite late. (*testily*) Why didn't you come home? Why didn't you tell us you were coming to see your mother? We looked everywhere for you.

XIA: Mo Jin, please sit down. Dove, go boil some water for tea.

MO: No, don't trouble yourself. I don't drink tea at night. Thank you anyway.

CHENG (*goes up to Peng, hands her a woolen vest and whispers*): I was worried sick. Didn't you say you'd be back soon? Here, put this on.

PENG (*frostily*): Thanks.

(*Cheng Kang, his heart heavy, sits down without a word. Peng Yinge stands by, hanging her head and looking miserable.*)

XIA (*in an attempt to ease the tension*): Well, everybody seems to have something on their minds. Mo Jin, is anything the matter?

MO (*after a moment of silence*): Very well. As in-laws, we ought to be frank with one another. And so long as you're home tonight, we might as well use the opportunity to discuss a problem that concerns us all. (*adopting a well-devised plan of attack*) Dove is an outstanding, gifted girl. Her exam score far exceeded our highest expectations, and the board has chosen her to study abroad. It's a great honor for both families, and we, of course, would like to see her continue her studies. Women must work hard too, for the future of China—

PENG (*affected*): Thank you for being so supportive, Mother.

MO (*somewhat ill at ease but trying to appear calm*): We recently found out something Dove might have told you about. Cheng Kang scored just a few points behind Dove on the exam. Ha, ha! What a coincidence! Of all people, these two would be top competitors! (*earnestly*) Zhixian, after a lot of careful thought, I've come to the conclusion that, Dove being a girl and all, as her parents, we're bound to feel uneasy about her living alone in a foreign country for four long years. Besides, there's no one to keep you company now, and with her gone, you'd be lonelier than ever. I'm worried about both of you. Zhixian, you understand, don't you?

PENG: Well, we can make allowances for personal feelings, but exam scores don't. So, (*with a quick smile*) dear folks, it's good bye for now. I'll see you again in a few years.

MO (*in an affectionate tone*): You mustn't be so headstrong, my dear. Zhixian, let me make myself clear: This question concerns both our families. As I've said, Dove is a girl. The opportunity is open to both of them; if she gives it up, Cheng Kang can go. No one else will reap the windfall.

PENG: Windfall? Mother is certainly good at cost accounting. But what we're talking about has nothing to do with business.

(*Mo Jin is too affronted to speak.*)

XIA (*sternly*): Behave yourself, Dove!

MO: A married couple ought to cooperate and support each other. Why fight to see who can get the upper hand? It's simply unnecessary. If Cheng Kang becomes a scientist, you'll be the wife of a scientist; you'll receive due credit and enjoy the same prestige.

PENG (*ingenuously yet obstinately*): But I don't want to be the wife of a scientist; I want to be a scientist in my own right.

MO (*mockingly*): Ha! How ambitious! You want to be a woman Chen Jingrun,[7] is that it? I don't know much about science, but there aren't many women who've made it to the top in mathematicians, now are there?

PENG (*mildly but unyielding*): And so, as a woman, I value the opportunity all that much more.

MO (*with a note of sarcasm*): Your spirit is admirable, dear. But wait and see: no matter how ambitious and determined you are now, after a certain age, you'll find the load too heavy, the odds too great. It's a question of physiology, of division of labor. Practically speaking, women are women, no matter what you say.

PENG (*greatly offended*): Women? What about women? Can't we ever forget that we're women? ... Anyway, I refuse to let my fate be tied to a man!

MO (*shifting her anger*): Zhixian, listen to her. Every bit your daughter — the way she goes on.... What do you think about all this?

XIA (*smiling faintly*): Me? Mo Jin, you and I play the supporting roles. Let's hear what the children have to say. Cheng Kang, what do you think?

CHENG (*frowning*): Mother, honestly, I'm too confused to know what's what anymore.

XIA (*affectionately*): Oh?! What are you confused about?

CHENG: I really don't know what to think. I'm torn in both directions.

PENG: Oh, come off it. If I got my PhD, you'd be mortified to be introduced (*mimicking Mo Jin*) "This is Cheng Kang, husband of Dr. Peng Yinge." How could you stand it? With your pride!

(*Mo Jin and Cheng Kang glance at each other dumbfoundedly*.)

PENG (*unrelenting*): "Two strong opponents, and one is bound to lose; if the wife is the stronger, there'll be no peace in the family." (*with disgust*) Huh, the great moralist!

(*Mo Jin and son exchange awkward glances*.)

CHENG (*hastens to explain to Dr. Xia*): Mother, do you believe that? I'm not as calculating as she makes me out to be. (*in earnest*) I've always despised social convention; there's no room for out-dated ideas between us. Yinge knows that. (*to Peng Yinge*) Calm down, will you? Remember how I encouraged you this afternoon. (*to Dr. Xia*) Mother, we've always supported each other's plans for the future.... It was her drive that attracted me in the first place.

PENG: So what? It attracted you before, but now you're sick of me.

CHENG (*muttering*): My god, you're touchy!

PENG (*retorting*): And you're neurotic!

MO (*unable to hold back her anger*): That's enough from you, Dove. Shouldn't you ... shouldn't you show some discretion? (*Tension permeates the room.*) Zhixian, see for yourself. Doesn't this remind you of when you and Peng Lun.... As mothers, we can't help but worrying. Why won't you speak your mind?

XIA: Dove already knows what I think.

PENG (*in an agitated, plaintive voice*): Please, everybody! (*to Dr. Xia*) Mother! (*to Mo Jin*) Mother, I beg you. Cheng Kang, please. Please believe me: my feelings for you haven't changed. But don't try to hold me back. Can't you see how torn I am? I don't want ... to leave Mother, or you, Cheng Kang. Do you really think I have no heart? (*cries in anguish*) I feel so guilty about leaving you, but ... I'm already twenty-six. I'll be thirty by the time I get back—then there'll be other things to consider. Do you think I haven't thought about that? All I ask is for your understanding and forgiveness. This is the age of scientific discovery. Specializing in one field isn't enough; overall perspective and expertise are needed. Marx said that science can't attain perfection without mathematics. It wasn't easy to get this chance to study abroad—and in mathematics! Mathematics is the queen of all the sciences!

MO (*bursting out in a shrill taunting sneer*): Ha! Listen to her! What ambition! Now she wants to be a queen!

(*Dr. Xia, shocked and enraged, springs to her feet, but then checks herself, though not without considerable effort.*)

PENG (*erupting with fury after a moment of shock*): Queen?! What's so great about being a queen? A queen's just a freeloader who lives off her husband's position and abuses his authority. If he's an official, then she's the official in charge of the official; if he's a commander, then she's commander of the commander. She runs everything — whether it's her place or not…. Women like that ought to wonder what they're really doing for society. So don't … don't judge others by yourself. Don't….

MO (*furious, bangs the table and leaps to her feet*): Kangkang, did you hear that? Did you hear the way she insulted me?!

CHENG (*excitedly*): Yinge, you should show more respect for others … and for yourself too.

PENG: If I'm going to respect myself, I can't let anybody else run my life.

CHENG: The same goes for me. I can't let you run *my life*.

PENG: Who's trying to run your life? I just won't be someone's tag-along, that's all.

CHENG: I don't want you to be my tag-along, but I won't be yours either. (*agitated*) Yinge, listen to me: I don't need you to be some great woman scientist. All I want is a loyal wife. I….

PENG: A-ha! The truth comes out! Well, you're free to go look for your perfect wife. Goodbye! (*wheels around and heads for the inner room*)

CHENG (*sharply*): Come back here!

PENG (*unyielding*): What for? You know, it's very easy. You have the perfect wife waiting for you right now….

CHENG (*urgently*): Yinge, what are you talking about? Do you really believe that nonsense? Stop trying to hurt

101

other people, will you?

MO (*cutting him off*): Let her be jealous. What do you have to lose? That other one is generous and open-minded, not petty like this one.... Yinge, get off your high horse! You're no better than the rest of us.

PENG (*steadying herself with great effort*): I never said I was. I admit I might not achieve a blessed thing. (*to Mo Jin*) Mother, you're probably right that I'll never be a mathematician. I can handle that. Some people may be better than me at housekeeping, but that's not how I want to live. It's just not me. I don't think I'm better than anyone else. I don't want to interfere with anyone's life, and no one has the right to interfere with mine. (*brokenheartedly*) Cheng Kang, you ... you do whatever you like.

CHENG (*recovering from shock*): You ... Dove, listen to me. I was wrong to talk like that. Believe me, I'll never go back on my word. I want to support you. But can't you see how terrible I feel? I'm worried. I ... I.... (*in agony*) I can't stand it!

PENG (*in a quavering voice*): You feel terrible?! You can't stand it?! Cheng Kang, you used to say you wanted a wife with a career, but I can see now what you liked about the idea: it was just an ego trip. The minute it seems your wife is going to do better than you, you feel threatened. Your sense of self-respect can't handle it. (*sobs*)

CHENG (*hastening to justify himself*): No, that's not what I meant. Not at all. Can't you see? What I meant is....

PENG (*unyielding*): I don't want to hear anymore.

CHENG (*shocked*): Yinge, what is it? What's come over you? Why are you acting like this?

MO: Humph! What did I tell you, Kangkang? Didn't I say it would come to this? She hasn't even got her PhD, and she's too good for us. I'm afraid our courtyard house will be too small for the great scientist. Very well, we won't hold you back, Dove. Do what you like. Kangkang, I told you, didn't I? Like mother, like....

PENG (*quivering with rage*): How ... how dare you talk like

102

that about my mother! And to her face! ... Don't you....

XIA (*venting repressed anger, cries out*): Shut up, Dove!

MO (*taken aback*): No need to lose your temper. As the old saying goes: "Everything thrives if there's peace and harmony in the family." We are a self-respecting and loving family. I'm afraid there's no room for the great lady....

CHENG (*in angry exasperation*): Mother, what are you talking about?

(*Mo Jin gestures for him to be quiet. Cheng glares at her and turns away. The tension mounts; silence falls over the room. Leaves outside rustle in the autumn wind; lightning flashes across the sky. Wringing her hands, Dr. Xia struggles to regain composure.*)

XIA: Mo Jin, we've known each other for years. There's no need to dig up my past. You know why Peng Lun and I separated — we couldn't appreciate each other's devotion to work; neither of us was willing to give in. Family life became a burden. We were too young, too headstrong; there were some things we just didn't understand.... Don't you think it's hard on a woman who wants to develop her professional skills but in doing so has to give up the pleasure of a family? Is that supposed to prove that she's strong? Of course not! Dove's situation worries me.... I don't want to see her make the same mistakes. You have no idea how I've tried to talk her around.... I even asked her, to avoid this very fight, to give in and make the sacrifice.

MO (*nodding*): Yes, that's it. A lesson from the past. Yinge, if you think we're being selfish, you should at least listen to your mother. Think of the selfless, unconditional love of your parents. (*trying to make amends*) Zhixian, I hope I haven't offended you. A person's liable to say almost anything in a fit of anger— you know me. Who threw us into this together anyway?

XIA (*with stern dignity*): Mo Jin, I disagree with everything you said just now. I can't accept your reasoning. I can't endorse your views on the role of women or your

103

evaluation of women's worth. I think you're entirely wrong!

(*Mo Jin looks at her in amazement.*)

XIA: Everything you just said, in the last analysis, can be summed up with one simple cliche.

MO (*perplexed*): Which one is that?

XIA (*enunciating clearly*): "A woman's virtue is her ignorance."

MO: What do you mean?

XIA: Just what I said. I've been trying all along to think of what's best for your family, but now I've changed my mind. An individual's talent is for him or her to develop, regardless of sex. (*unequivocally*) Dove, the moon's brilliance is a reflection of the sun. But a woman is not the moon; she can shine by her own light. So go shine; create your own brilliance. You may never become a famous scientist, but remember, the purpose of study is not an academic degree but excellence of scholarship.

MO (*boiling with rage*): Huh! People never change. Zhixian, you destroyed your own family and made life impossible for your husband. Now you want to destroy mine and make my Kangkang suffer. You ... you oddball!

XIA (*disdainfully*): Odd? There's no such thing as odd. Other people seem strange when you can't understand them, that's all.

(*The telephone rings.*)

XIA (*picking up the receiver*): Hello. Bed Five....

VOICE: Dr. Xia, please come quickly. The car is on its way.

XIA: I'll be right there. Goodbye. (*hangs up the phone and picks up her handbag and jacket*)

MO: Bed Five indeed! How can you think about Bed Five when there's a fire in your own backyard? Zhixian, you can't leave yet; you've got to explain yourself. Wait a minute....

(*A car honks off-stage.*)

XIA (*speaking calmly*): Nine months of gestation; one moment for delivery. In this moment, the lives of mother and child are in the doctor's hands. (*resolutely*) I'm sorry, this comes first. Our little family matter can wait. (*turns and leaves*)

104

(Cheng Kang looks on helplessly. Mo Jin glares angrily. Peng Yinge watches morosely as her mother departs.)

ACT FOUR

Ten days later, in Dr. Xia's living-room.

The sky is overcast and dreary; a light autumn rain is falling. The plane tree in the courtyard sways in the wind; the banana plants glisten with raindrops.

Peng Yinge is standing alone at the window playing Dream of the Butterflies,[8] *a plaintive violin solo. The phone rings, but she is too immersed to hear. At a pause in the music she finally takes notice.*

PENG *(picking up the receiver)*: Hello.

VOICE: May I ask who's speaking?

PENG: This is Yinge, Dr. Xia's daughter.

VOICE *(excitedly)*: Dove! My dear Dove! Can't you tell who this is? It's me, your father.

PENG *(crying out happily)*: Father! Father! ... Where are you?

VOICE: I'm at the airport. I just got in.

PENG: What ... what brings you here? How did you know.... Did Mother tell you?

VOICE: No. Your mother-in-law Mo Jin told me....

PENG: She did?!

VOICE: I think she wants to get my help. But ... I'd have come even if she didn't call. My girl, I'd have come anyway.

PENG: Please come quickly, Father. Come ... home, please. *(Tears begin to roll down her cheeks.)*

VOICE *(with a lump in his throat)*: Don't cry, Dove. Don't cry. I'm just afraid I won't be welcome there.

PENG *(urgently)*: Oh, no. Don't think like that. Mother won't make it difficult for you. I know. Really....

VOICE: Well, I'd like to see her too ... see how she's doing.

PENG: Father, I'll let Mother know you're here. I know what to say. Oh, please come quickly. Father, I really … I really miss you. I can hardly wait! Do you want me to go meet you?

VOICE: No, I can make it. Do you still live in the same house?

PENG: Yes. But Father, let me go meet you.

VOICE: No, that's alright. So long as you haven't moved, I can find my way. We'll talk when I get there, okay?

PENG: Okay!

(*She stands holding the receiver for several seconds then reluctantly hangs up. At a loss what to do next, she suddenly opens a drawer and takes out the old photo album. Sitting down on the sofa, she begins to study the photos. Tian Qiangqiang steps under the eaves, folds her umbrella and walks lightly into the room.*)

TIAN: Hello … Hello, Yinge.

(*Peng Yinge is oblivious to her call.*)

TIAN: Yinge, HELLO!

PENG (*looking up in surprise*): Hello, Qiangqiang. What brings you here?

TIAN: Guess who I am today … liaison officer for Cheng Kang.

PENG (*trying to stay calm*): Qiangqiang, you … I….

TIAN: Why only you and I? What about him? (*mysteriously*) Do you have any idea how he's been these past few days? It's pure agony for him. He can't stand to be away from you for a minute, and now it's been ten whole days. You shouldn't do this to him.

PENG (*peevishly*): What do you mean? What have I done?

TIAN: He's going crazy missing you. I can tell — he won't be able to stand it much longer. Dove, just ask him over so you two can talk it out. How awful for you both, if you leave and nothing's been settled. Why don't you ask him over?

(*Yinge paces back and forth, obviously very upset. The rain patters gently; a light wind stirs. She stops at the window and leans her head against the pane. Tears stream down her cheeks like the water against the glass.*)

PENG: Oh, this drizzle! Why not just pour?

TIAN (*sensitive to Yinge's mood; holding back tears of sympathy*): No, let's stop it altogether! Let's have it clear up

right now. This is too ... too depressing. Yinge, you say
the word, and I'll go get him. What do you think?

PENG: You want us to talk? Talk about what? He feels awful? Do you think he's the only one? ... Qiangqiang,
let's just drop it.

(*Cheng Kang suddenly appears in the doorway, a raincoat
thrown over his shoulders. All pause, momentarily stunned.*)

TIAN: Why, you've come before I brought back her answer. Alright, you two talk it over. Cheng Kang, I'll be
leaving then, okay?

CHENG (*nodding*): Okay, thanks.

PENG (*quickly interposes*): No, Qiangqiang, don't go.

(*A moment of silence; Cheng Kang and Peng Yinge seem
about to start talking, but then both abruptly change their
minds.*)

TIAN: My god, Cheng Kang, get on with it. If you think
you're wrong, then admit it.

CHENG (*stubbornly*): What is there to admit?

PENG (*the hope in her eyes dying out*): Since that's the way
you feel about it, then there's nothing to discuss, is
there?

CHENG: But there is. Yinge, I've been wanting so badly to
talk with you about my new idea.

TIAN: Whatever new idea it is, you can't hold her back.
Yinge, do you know what I think about this whole
thing?

PENG: What?

TIAN: I'll tell you: I've butt heads with my aunt over it.
Daring to offend the Emperor, as it were, I've argued
with her in your favor. "Why always go on about
women?" I asked her. "Aren't you a woman yourself?
We women today can stand on our own; we're entitled
to our own opinions; we can tell our husbands what to
do. Who has won these rights for us, do you think?
Strong, capable women, of course." Cheng Kang,
admit I'm right. Or maybe you're afraid to say how
you really feel?

CHENG: Why should I be afraid? I've always thought that.
It takes a strong spirit for women to enjoy equal rights
with men. That's what the women's movement is all about.

107

TIAN: Exactly. But not all women are out to achieve, and neither are all men. The few who can do something are valuable assets to society. I'm not one of them, but Dove, you've got to go all the way. No one can stop you!

PENG (*deeply touched*): Thank you, Qiangqiang.

TIAN (*pulling a long face*): Yinge, to be honest, I'm still a little mad at you. I think you owe me an apology.

PENG (*baffled*): Why? What have I done?

TIAN: You talked behind my back, and you've clean forgotten about it. I have a sense of self-respect too, you know. Why drag me into your fight? I hope you don't do it again.

PENG (*suddenly remembering*): Oh, Sweetie, I'm sorry. I said those things when I was angry. I didn't really mean it like that. Oh, dear ... Let me explain....

TIAN: Forget about it; it's done with. I'd better get going now.

PENG: Why the hurry?

TIAN (*shyly*): I have a date.

PENG (*pleasantly surprised*): A date? You? ... That's great! Who's the lucky man? He must be a good one!

TIAN: He is. As you once said, I've at last found....

PENG: Love and compatibility!

TIAN (*excitedly*): Yes! He's very handsome. But not only handsome; he's also extremely talented.

PENG: He feels the same way about you, I hope?

TIAN: Yes. But he expects a lot — four jobs, in fact.

PENG: Four jobs? What do you mean?

TIAN: He wants me to be his friend, sister, mother and maid. I expect even more of him though — two words: Obey orders!

PENG: Well, congratulations, Qiangqiang! I'm happy for you!

TIAN (*to Cheng Kang*): My great scholar, if you'll excuse me, I must be running along now. Have a good talk, you two. Bye.

(*Peng Yinge sees Tian Qiangqiang out. The two walk arm in arm, whispering together. Left alone in the room which holds so many fond memories, Cheng Kang sentimentally picks up the violin and plucks the strings lightly. Peng Yinge returns shortly.*)

CHENG (*after a moment of silence*): Yinge, you don't look so well. (*taking a jacket off the coat rack*) It's cold today. Why don't you put this on.

PENG (*full of conflicting emotions, lets him help her into the jacket*): Cheng Kang, I can't figure it out. I can't figure out how the Cheng Kang I knew before could have changed so suddenly into.... I just don't understand.

CHENG: Me changed? But I haven't changed, not one single bit. Maybe in the last few days I've come to know myself better. I know I love you more, much more than ever before.

(*Peng Yinge gazes at him lovingly. Tears well up in both their eyes.*)

CHENG (*holding her hands tightly*): Dove, what is it? You're an intelligent woman; you can solve all kinds of math problems — why is it you can't see what's wrong with me?

PENG: I don't know what the problem is.

CHENG: But it's so simple — it's all because I love you. I can't live without you.... Do you know what it's been like for me these last few days? Heaven knows how many times I've paced back and forth outside this house; I wanted to come in so badly but didn't have the courage — my pride always got the better of me. At home, every time the phone rang, I'd get my hopes up, just to have them dashed again.... Oh, it's been hell!

PENG (*gazes at him, deeply moved*): "If love knows time, days apart won't undermine." Cheng Kang, wasn't that one of your favorite lines?

CHENG: But I see now how life doesn't always work out the way we've planned. Not only with other people, even with ourselves — there's just so much that can happen. I think I have reason enough to worry. Dove, as far as our family is concerned....

PENG (*cutting him short*): Don't say any more! (*Suddenly remembering her father is coming, she glances at her watch.*) Did you say you have a new idea? Well, what is it?

CHENG (*plucking up his courage*): I got Mother to agree....

109

PENG (*with disgust*): Your mother?!

CHENG: Yes. (*firmly*) My idea is that neither of us will go abroad. After all, achievement depends largely on individual effort; where we work is of less importance. So....

PENG (*astonished and disappointed*): So this is your wonderful new idea?

CHENG: Let me finish.

PENG (*resentfully*): There's no need.

(*Once again, tension fills the room.*)

CHENG (*surprised and disappointed*): What?! After all I've conceded, you still refuse to reconsider?

PENG: All you've conceded? What have you conceded? I got this chance to study abroad on my own. I don't need anyone to make concessions on my account. (*resolutely*) I shall go all the same, and that's final.

CHENG (*in a frenzy of despair*): No! Think about me; think about us! If you insist on having your way, I don't know if I'll be able to work or study! (*frantically*) Yinge, don't forget about your responsibility to the two of us!

PENG: Don't you have any ideas of your own? You're going on just like your mother. But tell me: How would I not be living up to my responsibilities? When your mother wanted me to let you go in my place, did she remind you of your duties to me? Don't try to dress up the villain as the hero, alright? You know, you're just repeating your mother: "If the wife is the stronger, there'll be no peace in the family." What a bunch of nonsense! (*stops abruptly to glance at her watch*)

CHENG: Why are you always looking at your watch? Do you have something to do?

PENG: In a little while I'm going to have an important ... an important visitor. I have to go meet him.

CHENG (*dubiously*): I don't believe it. Who is it you have to meet?

PENG: Really, I have to go now. (*She opens her umbrella and heads for the door.*)

CHENG (*yelling angrily in frustration*): Then ... there's nothing to stop you. From now on ... you can do whatever you want!

(*Left alone, Cheng Kang paces around the room, fidgety and irresolute. He's suddenly struck by an idea, and walking over to the desk, takes a pen and paper from a drawer. He begins to write, his hand moving quickly over the paper. Dr. Xia enters from the front door.*)

XIA (*surprised*): Hello, Cheng Kang. When did you get here?

CHENG (*hastily putting away the pen and paper; speaking politely*): Mother, how ... have you been? Fine, I hope.

XIA (*studying his expression*): Physically, I'm fine, but emotionally, you two and your ... Oh dear!

CHENG (*apologetically*): I'm sorry, Mother. I know it's hard on you too. I've been feeling terrible ever since that night for the way I acted. I really can't explain....

XIA: Cheng Kang, I'm a doctor; I diagnose patients. It didn't take me long to see what was ailing you that evening. Your sensitivity was like catching a cold, and when your temperature went up, your resistance was weakened. If it had been kept between the two of you, it never would have boiled over like that. The problem is, some things in life are bound to drag in others, and everybody's got their own idea about things. Then it gets very complicated indeed!

CHENG (*embarrassed*): But....

XIA: Have you seen Dove?

CHENG: Yes. She just went out. She said she had to meet someone.

(*Just then, a middle-aged man appears in the courtyard, a black collapsible umbrella in one hand, a traveling bag in the other. He glances about curiously, yet appears to know the place. Peng Lun is tall and well-built; the hair around his temples is beginning to gray, giving him a dignified, good-natured look. He hesitates before knocking lightly on the door. Cheng Kang goes out to meet him.*)

PENG LUN: This is Dr. Xia's house, I believe? Is Peng Yinge in? (*Dr. Xia listens attentively from inside.*)

CHENG (*studying the stranger carefully, suddenly seems to understand*): Uh ... um.... She's gone out to meet you. (*calling into the room*) Mother! (*to Peng Lun*) Please

111

come in, sir. I'll go find her.

PENG LUN: Thank you, young man. Here, take my umbrella.

CHENG: No, thanks. I don't need it. (*rushes out into the drizzle*)

(*Dr. Xia comes to the door. She and Peng Lun turn to stone at the sight of each other. Both are at a loss for words.*)

PENG LUN: I'm afraid I've caught you off guard.

XIA (*trying to keep calm*): Oh, no. Please come in.

PENG LUN (*the room bringing back memories*): How have you been, Zhixian? I've come to see about Dove. There wasn't time to let you know beforehand—I'm sorry to intrude like this.

XIA: No, no, you're not intruding. Did Dove write to you about what's been happening?

PENG LUN: No. It was her mother-in-law. I take it things are fairly tense. My guess is that Mo Jin wants my help.

XIA (*handing him a cup of hot tea*): You're probably right. Here, have some tea.

PENG LUN: Thank you. (*Taking the cup, he pauses in thought then speaks with candor and sincerity.*) Zhixian, isn't it strange how history repeats itself? Dove is in the same predicament we were once in.... It worries me.... I spoke with her over the phone a little while ago. I guess she didn't have time to let you know I was coming.

XIA: No. I just walked in myself.

(*They have regained their composure and appear relaxed in each other's company. They seem to be two old friends meeting after a long time apart.*)

PENG LUN: I often thought of coming to see you. I never made it, but I read about you in the papers. Sometime before the Cultural Revolution — in the fall of 1966 I think   I was in town and wanted to look you up, but you were in trouble then, and they wouldn't let me see you. (*brightening*) Now, thank goodness, everything's back to normal; the nightmare's over.

XIA: How did you make it through those years? I guess you had a hard time too.

PENG LUN: That goes without saying. "Whose courtyard

is not visited by autumn winds? Whose window hears not the pattering of autumn rain?''

XIA (*nodding*): How true! How very true!

PENG LUN (*taking a sip of tea and heaving a great sigh*): Every nation will at times make mistakes ... and suffer the consequences. People are the same. We're bound to go astray from time to time and do some stupid things. When you look back, you can't forgive yourself for that foolishness.... Zhixian, I'm not asking you to forgive me; I'm the last one to deserve forgiveness. But I wish you'd tell me I was wrong.

(*Unable to control her emotions, Dr. Xia goes to the window and, like a child, stretches out her arms in the rain. After awhile, she turns around to face Peng Lun.*)

XIA: No. He who cannot forgive does not deserve forgiveness.

PENG LUN (*reflecting upon her words, yet not fully understanding*): Right. You're absolutely right. I don't deserve forgiveness. You know, I've wanted for so long to sit down and talk with you as a friend.... Zhixian, coming into this house today, I had extremely mixed feelings. Knowing I'm Dove's father is my only happiness. If she's in trouble, I have to see what I can do to help. I think you understand.

XIA: Of course. "What's better than a visit from an old friend on a rainy day?" Neither of us did much for Dove when she was growing up. A few days ago she argued with me. She said I was selfish for putting so much time into my work and so little into being a mother. She's not a child anymore; she has her own mature ideas about life.

PENG LUN (*his eyes lighting up at the favorable comment on their daughter*): Is that so? (*opening the door and looking out*) Where is she anyway? I told her not to go meet me.

XIA (*after a brief pause*): How should I put it? Back in those days, you and I ... perhaps we were too much alike; we thought too much alike. Anything outside of work we considered a burden, an interference....

PENG LUN: That's right! Both trying to be the best! Do

113

you remember what Mo Jin said? She said we were like two bulls, neither willing to give an inch. We were young then; we thought work was everything. We thought if we gave it up, we'd regret it forever.

(Their talk brings them closer and closer; they carry on as if discussing people outside of themselves.)

XIA: Only regret? No. It was either that or nothing.

PENG LUN: True. To this day, I guess neither of us would say we were wrong to have stuck it out. What do you think?

XIA *(nodding)*: I think you're right.

PENG LUN *(gravely)*: But you know, Zhixian, having lived this long, I now know the value of understanding others. As it is, we always expect other people to understand us.... Why couldn't we have tried harder to understand each other? Why couldn't we have found other ways to solve the problem?

XIA *(shaking her head resignedly)*: Why not indeed? There was work and family. Two full-time jobs are enough to grind any woman down.... I used to think one plus one equals two, that the combined effort of two was greater than one, but what came of it? After awhile I began to see the advantages of being single....

PENG LUN: But is that what life's about, Zhixian? The past couple of years I've often asked myself: Is this supposed to be some sort of sacrifice, where I give myself up for my career? No. It's just that I don't know how to live. Admittedly, it's not easy to balance work with everything else in life, but why give up one for the other? *(remorsefully)* The price has been too high, too high.

(Dr. Xia sits silently, deep in thought. Peng Lun looks at her expectantly. Only the sound of wind and rain keep the meditative couple company.)

PENG LUN *(with a faint wry smile)*: Zhixian, it seems that when you have something, you don't value it, but once it's gone, you realize how much it meant to you. You and I are too close, too much ... alike. Ours was no common connection. "Having been to the sea, no lake can compare; Having topped Mount Wushan, other

114

clouds pale to air.'' Ah, to regret the past! Zhixian,
I've often chastised myself for the mistakes I made.

XIA (*sharing his remorse, murmurs to herself*): Sorrow is the
secret we bury deep in our hearts; joy, the public display.

PENG LUN: Yes, that's so true. You're right.... One plus
one equals two — do you mean to tell me you still
don't think this axiom can be applied to life? After
all, we're both over fifty and have been through a
lot.... (*Afraid to embarrass her, he quickly changes the
subject.*) What I mean is, Dove and her husband
shouldn't have to go through all of that.

XIA: That's exactly what I've been thinking.

PENG LUN: Zhixian, what do you think Dove should do?

XIA (*reflecting*): Well, at first I couldn't decide, then I
thought I knew, and now I'm back to square one. You
know, Peng Lun, I've always thought of myself as being
of resolute mind, but for some reason, I don't know
where to turn. I'm glad you've come back.

(*The two are sitting deep in thought when Peng Yinge suddenly bursts into the room. Gasping for breath, she stares
momentarily at her father, then rushes into his arms.*)

PENG: Father!

PENG LUN: Dove, my dear girl! You went to the airport,
didn't you? I guess we missed each other. (*hugging her
affectionately*) My, how you've grown!

PENG: Father, you've also ... you've also aged. How did
you get so tan?

PENG LUN: I do a lot of field work out in the sun. But
I'm in good health. I feel fine.

(*His joy mingled with sorrow, Peng Lun wipes away her
tears, oblivious of the tears rolling down his own cheeks. Dr.
Xia turns her head to dry her eyes.*)

PENG LUN (*quickly changing the subject*): Zhixian, that
young man who was just here— is he Mo Jin's son?
Dove, is he your Cheng Kang?

PENG: Yes.

PENG LUN: He seems like a nice young man. Hmm ... He
doesn't take after his mother much, but he does look
like his father, as I recall.

PENG (*looking closely at each of her parents*): Father, you

115

must be starving. Mother, is there anything for Father
to eat?

XIA (*thinking for a moment*): Oh dear, we've only got instant noodles.

PENG (*somewhat irked*): Instant noodles again! ... Father,
is that alright?

PENG LUN: I don't see why not. Instant noodles are fine.
But don't worry about it yet. Zhixian, I see you're living the same simple life as before.

XIA: Well, no, actually much better.

PENG: Mother's learned to make fried rice.

(*Peng Lun laughs out loud; Xia Zhixian can't help laughing along.*)

PENG (*pulling her father aside and whispering in his ear*):
Didn't I tell you Mother wouldn't make things difficult?

PENG LUN (*whispering back*): You're right. We've been
getting on like old friends.

(*Dr. Xia meanwhile takes a package of instant noodles
from the cabinet and goes out to the kitchen.*)

PENG LUN (*watching her leave the room*): Dove, I'm
afraid you were too young to remember what it was
like. Your mother and I were both busy with work.
Our life at home was, well, quite.... (*chuckling*)
Mildewy rice and sprouted potatoes were the norm.
One time we forgot to give you the birthday cake we'd
bought. Can you guess what happened? An inch of
green mold had taken root by the time we remembered
it. Your mother was extraordinary: she could transform
flora into fauna, inorganic matter into organic!

PENG (*feigning irritation*): Who was to blame? Was it all
Mother's fault?

PENG LUN: Of course not. A person has only so much energy. (*seriously*) My dear, men have always been free
to devote themselves to their jobs; women have always
been burdened with the housework. Every man expects
a good wife and mother, but how many try to be good
husbands and fathers? It's not fair, not fair at all....

PENG: You're right. I'm beginning to understand what
happened between you and mother. I used to blame

116

you both.

PENG LUN (*hastening to divert her*): But let's not dwell on the past. (*solemnly*) Dear, over the years ... well, I'm afraid I haven't been a very good father. (*more cheerfully*) Tell me the whole story, Dove. I've come to help if I can. (*He gets up to pour her a cup of tea.*)

PENG (*in agitation*): Father, there's so much....

PENG LUN: There's no hurry. Take your time. (*brushing wisps of hair from her forehead*) Have some tea first.

(*He's just settled on the sofa and has reached over to hold her hand when Mo Jin calls in a loud voice from outside.*)

MO: Peng Lun! Guess who's here!

(*Mo Jin and Cheng Kang enter. Peng Lun rises and crosses the room to greet them.*)

MO (*cordially*): Hello, my old friend. Do you recognize me?

PENG LUN (*studying her face*): Why hello, Mo Jin! (*shaking hands with her warmly*) We're getting on in years, aren't we? How have you been? Come and sit down.

(*Peng Yinge leaves the room in annoyance. Dr. Xia returns with a steaming bowl of noodles.*)

MO (*glancing quickly at Xia*): I'm my same old self, Peng Lun, as up-front as ever. To be quite honest, I asked you to come so we could talk in private. When Kangkang told me you'd arrived, I dashed over immediately. I didn't want you to think I was putting on airs.

XIA (*graciously*): I guess I'll take the hint. It just so happens I have some shopping to do. Mo Jin, sorry to run out on you like this. (*She changes her shoes and goes out.*)

MO: Kangkang, have you said hello to your uncle? But I think you two have already met.

CHENG (*courteously*): How do you do, sir? I've heard a lot about you, sir.

MO: I suppose you have some idea about what it is I've troubled you to come here for.

PENG LUN (*amicably*): Why Mo Jin, you haven't changed one bit; you haven't even caught your breath and you want to talk business. How is your husband?

MO: He's fine. I just called to tell him you're here. He

117

said to be sure and come by for a visit.

PENG LUN: Thank you. I'll do that.

MO: You've been through a lot, Peng Lun. I've felt badly for you all along. (*sadly*) I thought I was doing you a good turn by bringing you two together. I had no idea it would turn out like it did....

PENG LUN (*cutting her off*): Cheng Kang, did you get wet when you went out just now?

CHENG (*rising to his feet courteously*): It's nothing, sir. Don't worry about it.

MO: I also couldn't have imagined my own son would one day find himself in the same situation. Just married, and your daughter already wants to be done with him....

PENG LUN: Now, now, don't try to scare me, Mo Jin. It can't be that bad.

MO: It can't?! But it's the truth. And all because of this studying abroad business. Kangkang and I came up with some reasonable solutions. We've conceded on many accounts and have done all we can to ensure their happiness and keep peace in the family, but your daughter ... (*lowering her voice and glancing about the room*) is just like your ex-wife. She refuses to listen. (*raising her voice deliberately*) Peng Lun, you were the victim once — you know what it's been like; I guess you can't help but worry too.

(*Peng Lun paces back and forth, deep in thought. He walks over to Cheng Kang and pats him on the shoulder.*)

MO (*sighing*): Ah, you two; different generations, but in the same boat!

PENG LUN (*perplexed*): In the same boat? (*breaking into a hearty laugh*) I see. Yes, there is something to your metaphor.

MO: Put yourself in my place. Could you stand to see the boy suffer so? You must have some sympathy for him?

PENG LUN (*awkwardly*): You mean....

MO: I mean I'm waiting for you to take a stand.

(*The phone rings, saving Peng Lun from this awkward situation.*)

PENG LUN (*picking up the receiver, hesitates*): Cheng Kang, you'd better answer it.

CHENG (*taking the receiver*): Hello. May I ask who's speaking?

VOICE: Who is this?

CHENG (*recognizing the voice*): Hello, Father. This is Kangkang. Mother's here too. She's talking with Uncle Peng Lun.⁹

VOICE: Good. Please put her on.

CHENG: Mother. (*hands the receiver to Mo Jin*)

MO: Lao Cheng, are you free this evening? I've extended the invitation to Peng Lun on your behalf.

VOICE: Mo Jin, let me repeat: I don't like the way you're handling this. Tell Peng Lun I'll see him soon to congratulate him on Yinge's upcoming trip.

MO (*peeved*): You....

VOICE (*firmly*): That's all there is to it. What you're doing is wrong, and you should apologize to Dr. Xia.

MO (*flaring up*): Apologize? Well, it seems you're afraid of offending the great doctor, aren't you? And what about me? Don't forget I gave up everything for your sake, so you could make it big. Now you're the saint, and I'm in the wrong. (*She starts sobbing.*) I know everybody respects Xia Zhixian for what she's done; any respect I get is for being your wife. But I'll tell you this much: I'd give it all up if I could've done something on my own....

VOICE (*in a tone of appeasement*): Now, now, calm down. You're right. (*in earnest*) I know I'm not perfect. But Mo Jin, what about telling your daughter-in-law what you just told me? (*Mo Jin slams down the receiver, cutting short the conversation.*)

PENG LUN (*handing Mo Jin a glass of water*): Take it easy, Mo Jin. You know, (*getting excited*) I was right about Old Cheng. I've always thought of him as a decent and honorable man.¹⁰

MO (*perplexed*): What are you talking about?

PENG LUN: I'll tell you.... (*changing his mind*) But what is there to explain? You're an intelligent person; you understand everything. In fact, you're perfectly clear about it all. What you said over the phone just now

119

goes to prove it.

MO (*resentfully*): Peng Lun, I've not asked you to come so you can flatter me.

PENG LUN: But I mean every word of it.

MO (*harshly*): Looks like you haven't had enough, have you? Let me warn you, Peng Lun: You can't let your daughter make my Kangkang suffer any longer.

CHENG (*exasperated*): Mother, calm down please.

MO: I can't calm down.

PENG LUN (*seriously*): Cheng Kang, you know my work, I believe. I'm a paleobiologist. I study fossils to calculate the age of terrestrial layers. But these ideas up here, (*pointing to his own head*) how many millennia have they passed through before they got to me? China's basically a feudal society, my boy. The roots go deep. If you'd been the one recommended to study abroad instead of Dove, I doubt we'd have this problem right now. You're young; you ought to be more open-minded than I once was. What do you think?

(*Cheng Kang sits silently for a few moments before slowly looking up.*)

CHENG: You're right, sir. I've always been opposed to old ideas and values. I don't think like that. I'm afraid you don't know how I feel right now....

PENG LUN (*in a kindly tone*): I do know, my boy. I know very well indeed. But some things you yourself may not be aware of....

CHENG (*musingly*): You mean to say I ... have feudal ideas? Let me think about that.

PENG LUN: Yes, think it over. In fact, all of us need to do more thinking. If you can see why all of this happened, you'll be glad to see Dove off. (*calling to the other room*) Dove, come out here.

(*Peng Yinge, sorrowful and distant, walks over to her father without looking at the others.*)

PENG LUN: Dove, it's going to be alright. You two need to cool down and talk it over again. Then you can leave with an easy mind.

PENG (*gazing at Cheng Kang in astonishment*): What ... about.... him?

PENG LUN (*patting Cheng Kang affectionately*): Leave him to me. I'll do what I can to help you two work it out.

MO (*no longer able to restrain herself, slams her fist on the table*): Peng Lun, you ... you can't do this! ... You can't let me down like this!

PENG LUN (*sincerely*): Mo Jin, forgive me. Cheng Kang, it's taken me the better part of my life to figure these things out. Why go through the same thing if you can learn from my mistakes?

(*An enraged Mo Jin picks up her bag and turns to storm out the door. Dr. Xia enters just then, her arms full of groceries. Coming face to face, the two pull up short.*)

PENG LUN (*to Peng Yinge and Cheng Kang*): Mutual understanding can create miracles; successful careers will make your life together that much better too.

(*Dr. Xia, Peng Yinge and Cheng Kang look at each other with hope in their eyes; Mo Jin studies their faces. Clouds drift slowly across the sky, which, although not entirely clear and bright, has lost its oppressive gloom. The plane tree and banana plants sway in the breeze.*)

(The End)

Notes

1. "Auntie" is a term of familiarity and respect for women of one's parents' age.
2. Chinese wedding celebrations were traditionally used to gain face in the community by public displays of wealth, expressed by the quantity and quality of the bride's dowry and the size and sumptuousness of the wedding feast. After 1949, the Communist government enforced controls on these lavish displays and wasteful binges. Temperance is still encouraged, which is why Mo Jin is concerned about the impression made by holding a large party.
3. "Sweetie" is homophonic with "Tian," the character's surname.
4. Wine is served at the wedding feast; candy is given away as the guests leave or, nowadays, often presented in lieu of a party.
5. Lin Chong is one of the 108 heroes in the Chinese classic novel *Outlaws of the Marsh*. His wife is insulted by his superior's son, which leads to

a series of events that finally force him to flee by night.

6. The Grand Dame of Daguanyuan is the lady dowager of the Chinese classic novel *The Dream of Red Mansions*. The story is set in a place called Daguanyuan, or Grand View Garden.

7. Chen Jingrun is a well-known contemporary Chinese mathematician who has won international recognition for his work.

8. *Dream of the Butterflies* is the story of two young lovers in ancient China who were torn apart by their families. Rather than marry the man chosen by her parents, the heroine kills herself. The hero then goes to kill himself on her grave, and the two turn into beautiful butterflies. The story has been incorporated into traditional operas and is the theme of the violin solo mentioned here.

9. "Uncle," like "Auntie" above, is a term of familiarity and respect for men of one's parents' age.

10. "A decent and honorable man" is homophonic with the name "Old Cheng."

Women Speak

Xiang Ya

In today's society, are women's ideas about sex changing? If so, how? The liberation of women and transformation of our ideas is perhaps the most convincing illustration of the changes taking place in traditional Chinese society, a society which has recently thrown open its doors to the outside world. These changes now only await greater understanding and deeper investigation.

In presenting the tape-recorded stories of some dozen interviewees,[1] I have attempted to pull back the heavy curtain of obscurity to allow the reader a look into the private worlds of modern day Chinese women. It might seem strange to talk about sex, but don't be alarmed. The women open their hearts and speak honestly; their complex, at times contradictory, experiences help us better understand ourselves, help men better understand us and help us all better understand the age in which we live.

As the writer in this strange and prohibited territory, I do not use names or express my own opinion. All is in the process; all is an exploration. Conclusions are left up to the reader, to this generation and to future generations of readers.

Wives

A. *Her husband had a lover, but it worked out in the end.*

I explained why I'd come. She smiled faintly and gestured for me to sit down.

"People need to understand each other. Sex isn't the only thing between a husband and wife." She spoke openly,

123

her warm, gentle face set in serious concentration. I pulled out my tape-recorder.

"You don't mind, do you?"

"Mind? Why?" She gazed directly into my eyes. "This isn't some juicy story about an affair, and certainly none of us has done anything to be ashamed of!

"I should start from the beginning. My husband and I were sent down to the countryside together during the Cultural Revolution,[2] and when we got back to the city, we were assigned to work in the same hospital. He's two years older, carries himself well and has always excelled in his studies.

"We fell in love and got married. After our daughter was born, he was even more considerate and caring than before. He would say things like 'With you in my life, I have a family. I have everything....' Sometimes men are so silly — as if losing me would mean losing everything.

"One time we weren't careful, and I got pregnant again. The abortion was pretty bloody, and he could hear all the pain I was in from outside the operating room. That night he held me tight, cursing himself over and over again. It was a long time before he made any sexual advances, though I know it's not that he didn't want me." She looked at me full in the face, thoughtfully stroking the lock of hair by her ear.

This was no ordinary woman to talk about sexual desire so openly.

"Do you mind telling me about your sex life?" I ventured.

She laughed. "I know a lot of people think I'm frigid or have some problem with sex if I'm going to let my husband run around with another woman, but that's a really narrow way of thinking. As far as I know, I'm perfectly normal.

"Our first six months of marriage were very intense sexually, and in 1983, when our daughter was five and in full-time child-care, we had, I guess you could say, a second honeymoon. We'd both just graduated from medical school and suddenly felt so free. Life was wonderful — we had new jobs, we had each other. Our second honeymoon was even better than the first. We'd been through a lot together, and sex was nothing new. We merged as two individuals into one.

"That was a wonderful time — a time I'll never forget. Love seemed more than perfect, divine almost. It's made me think that couples who never get there are really missing something." She spoke evenly, mildly, postulating about realms of experience beyond sex as if engaging in scientific inquiry.

"Many people confronted me on this. 'Your life seemed so perfect together,' they said. 'How could this sort of thing happen?' How can you explain an affair if both people really are happy with each other?

"But I don't see the contradiction. A man in love with one woman can easily be loved by another. There's nothing strange about that, especially with a man like my husband who's always had plenty of female attention. It makes sense that if I can love my husband, other women might love him as well. It's a wonderful feeling to love someone. It may cause pain sometimes, but it's always better than hate."

"When did you start to form these ideas?"

"I'm not really sure. I used to get upset when I heard about extramarital affairs, and I'd always cry for the woman in novels or movies who's dumped by her husband, but when it happened to me, for some reason, I didn't feel hurt or insulted. The love in those books and movies is too fragile, too easily destroyed. But the love between my husband and me is deep, like a pool of water. There may be waves on the surface, but below, it's still calm.

"Another important thing is how I feel about myself. I'm confident in my own strength. After eight years together, I knew he couldn't hurt me. I wasn't afraid he'd leave me; I knew I could get through almost anything.

"At first he tried to hide it. I noticed how he was suddenly so polite and careful when he caressed me or told jokes. He'd hug and kiss our daughter as if atoning for a crime. Sometimes I'd catch him in a daze. Even if I spoke softly, he'd jump....

"I'd already heard what was going on, so in retrospect, I can understand why he was like that. He loves

125

me and was afraid I'd be angry and hurt. He was afraid of losing me, so he tried to cover it up. If he wasn't worried about all that, he could have just ignored my feelings and asked for a divorce.

"But I didn't like the way he was dealing with the problem. Open, candid communication is important to me. Our relationship wasn't normal, and that kind of respect meant distance between us, a lack of trust and understanding.

"So one night I asked him, 'If I had a lover, I mean, if I fell in love with someone else while I still love you, would you understand?' He knew exactly what I was getting at, and after a moment of panic, pulled me close and vigorously nodded his head. 'You wouldn't pull away from me?' I asked again. He shook his head. I smiled at him and said, 'The same goes for me. You ought to trust me.' I opened his arms and took him into my own; he closed his eyes like a child and let me stroke his hair. Love and understanding are powerful, cohesive forces. Tagore said that understanding is another word for love. My husband returned my trust and eventually told me the whole story.

"They'd been attracted to each other for some time, but neither was willing to admit it was love. Once, on a trip to the Western Hills, she slipped in her high-heeled shoes, and he caught her in his arms. That was the turning point. Once they'd made physical contact, it was impossible to stop.

"I've met her. She's a nice young woman, bright and studious, and quite beautiful. She's a student at the television university.

"I certainly don't hate her. Love is broad and accepting. Even then I had no problem eating or sleeping. I suppose anyone could find themselves in that kind of situation. And their feeling was genuine; she's not a whore, and he wasn't forcing her to do anything against her will. It was really hard on them though, because they couldn't remove themselves enough to see it that way. They always acted like they were trying to make up for some crime. He'd dive right into the housework when he came home, and she'd duck her head and avoid my eyes when we ran into each other on the street.

"It was all so unnecessary. You can't own anybody with love, and there's no such thing as sin. Real love means letting go, letting whoever or whatever you love go free.

"After a while he told me that she planned to get married. That surprised me — it seemed much too fast. But when I thought over what she must have been going through, I realized, though she was probably grateful, she knew their relationship couldn't go on like that forever. She saw marriage as a way out.

"I went to see her and got straight to the point. 'Do you really love that man?' I asked. 'If you do, I wish you happiness. But if you're just doing this to get out of what's going on, then you're a fool. I want you to know that your relationship with my husband can't hurt me, much less destroy me. But if you go and marry someone you don't love, you'll just be destroying yourself.'

"She let out a sob and threw herself into my arms. Women need to talk to each other. We need to be understood, and we need to be comforted.

"Three years later she married a man she's very much in love with. I'm happy for her. Look, here's a picture of our two families...."

(Thirty-six years old, A is from a family of intellectuals.[3] She was sent to the countryside as an educated youth, spent five years in the army and six years as a nurse. She graduated from medical school in 1983 and is presently a doctor of internal medicine.)

*   *   *

B. *Her husband's rising fame fed her fear.*

I watched her from a distance. She had a slim, graceful figure and the charm of a pretty girl from a common family. But she was obviously the sensitive, melancholic, easily excitable type. She wasn't much over thirty, but definite wrinkles had already been sealed into the corners of her eyes and mouth.

"I'm depressed — I won't hide that from you. I think

127

the purpose of a woman's life is to love a man. We're born to love and will die for that love. I don't care about a career, but I've got to have love! I want the highest, the purest, the most single-minded love. I want to live out my life with the man I love....

"Love has made me crazy. It's made me lose my mind, but nothing's come of it....'' She nervously wrung her hands. I could see her pain was real and very deep.

"I love him so much! He's not very handsome, but he's got a good body and a certain sexual attraction that really turns me on. Most women don't notice him at first, but the minute he says something, they're lost forever!'' Her tone revealed both irritation and depression, her husband's appeal obviously the cause of much worry.

"Friends have told me I live in a closed, feudal world. I won't joke around with other men. If anyone ever tries to mess with me, I'll let him have it. But I've put out so much for him. You have no idea how tough it was to catch him!

"I've heard people say if a woman chases a man, they've both got a problem. A pretty girl like me, they said, shouldn't go for a man like him without any looks. But I never listened. He was smart and I loved him, so I just went for it. I figured if he didn't want me, I'd kill myself in front of him. When I was a little girl, how I dreamed of a love of blood and tears and death!

"I wasn't going to let them tell me what to do. I'm usually pretty easygoing, but with love, it's another thing. Every morning I gave him a big thick letter right in front of everybody. I didn't go to school for that long, so my characters are big and kind of sloppy, but I wrote from my heart. I didn't care if anybody laughed at me!

"He liked my letters, and of course, thought he was pretty great — I had a lot of other guys interested in me then. So that's how I got him. He kept wanting me to go to bed with him, but no way — how could I jump in the sack without being married? What if he dropped me after he got me in bed? Once we were married, he could never run away.

"We got married at the end of the Cultural Revolution. Nobody was really going to work, and even if we did go, we didn't do much. It felt like a long, sweet honeymoon. Every night I'd warm up the quilts before he got in bed. I'd wait for him, wait for his hands, his body, his shining eyes, his breath. He drove me crazy with love!

"You know, it's great to completely possess a man! He used to call me a sex fiend, but I thought: You're my husband. Of course I want to let out my sexual energy with you. Of course I want every bit of you! Any other man can think about me all day long, but he'll never get me.

"I used to make wonderful meals for him. I peeled his apples and pears. At night I washed his feet and clipped his toenails. I gave him everything a man could want from a woman.

"But these past few years I've really gotten scared. His world has grown so large. I don't count so much as before — I'm not all he's got. He's such a big name in literature now, it's like he's forgotten all about me. He's got modern, fashionable women — writers, poets, you name it — around him all the time.... I hate every one of them! The ones who should be married by now are still single; the rest are already divorced! I've looked for stuff they've written — it's enough to make you sick — all they know to talk about is love! No good can come from hanging around them, I tell you.

"Sure, he's got a lot of men friends, but what do I care about them? It's the women who get to me.

"We've grown really far apart. He goes to bed so late now — as soon as he hits the pillow, he's out, without even looking at me.

"I'm losing control. Take his clothes, for instance. I want him to dress so that nobody'll notice him, but he's got to have his own way. He used to wear work clothes when he went out, then it was Sun Yat-sen suits, then Western-style clothes, and now he's gotten into wearing those new jackets. He's like a slippery fish — he writes fiction, poetry, even plays!

"What a waste.... I'd give anything to go back to those days after the wedding! I don't want him to be famous; I don't want him to publish anything. Because I know what fame means — it means women all over him, writing him letters, sending him pictures, all going after him.... I despise them all. If I had a gun, I'd shoot every woman on this earth till I was the only one left!

"He says it's his work. Ha! Those love stories he wrote never happened in my house! He's got to have had other lovers, those damn bitches!

"The idea of him with another woman burns me alive. I shake all over when I think about it. 'Sexual love is exclusive.' I looked that up — it's from Engels. I'll be damned if I'm going to give him up that easy. Of course I want exclusive love; that's all there is. I've got to protect our love — like when I went out to get him in the first place. I've decided I'm not going to have a kid. It would just make me fat and ugly. With that dragging me down, I'd have no way to keep an eye on him.

"I watch him all the time. He can swear at me or beat me, but I'll still open his mail; I'll still follow him around to see where he goes. I didn't care what people think — I want him to make a fool of himself. If he's with men, I won't show up, but if there's a woman around, she better watch out! I may look pretty and gentle, but I can really let loose! I've been a couple times to the office to get his mail and talked to his boss, but he won't tell me anything. Ha! I don't believe a word of it! His boss can care less, but his old lady isn't going to let it go on!

"He said I don't really love him, that I'm just being selfish. I asked him: 'Do you know what Engels said? I've got a theoretical reason for acting like this! Don't think you can get rid of me so easy! We've got potassium cyanide at the factory for gold-plating. Just try it with some woman, and that'll be the end of her! And if you've got any ideas to dump me, just wait till you're asleep; I'll take the scissors to your balls then poison you to death!'

"That was a smart move on my part. He's been keeping his distance from them ever since. I've followed him down the street a couple times; he doesn't even respond to their hellos. I feel a little easier now, but it doesn't mean I can relax completely.

"I know it's only superficial. He's still not mine.

And he's turned cold—when I try to caress him, he pushes me away and says he's lost it. He tries to blame it on me. I hate him—he can't make it with them and wants to get his revenge. That's fine with me. I can't have him, but neither can anyone else!

"Didn't you ask me what I think about sexual love? I think women are born for men and die for men. I belong to my husband, and I'll always be faithful to him. A good woman never marries twice. But my husband also belongs to me; I'll never let him be unfaithful. I've given him everything—naturally I can claim what's mine!"

(*Born into a peasant family, B is thirty-five years old. She worked on a farm for three years after junior middle school and has most recently been employed in a jewelry factory.*)

* * *

C. *She said: "We are two independent planets, both free to come and go."*

She walked out of the manager's office with a small, elegant handbag on her arm. Impeccably dressed and carefully made up, she carried herself with the grace of a woman in her middle years.

"My first husband and I were high school classmates, the perfect match. The whole school knew we were a couple. I've got a good voice—in the Cultural Revolution, I sang in the army ensemble. He was a communications soldier. We got married as soon as he became an officer. When I got out of the army, I was transferred to the provincial song and dance ensemble, and he was discharged the following year.

"Human emotions are such a strange thing. Before marriage, all we could think about was living together; we dreamed of the love we'd share as husband and wife. We started sleeping together back in high school. When my parents found out, there was a huge scene—they said they'd disown me. The school authorities stepped in to write up reports of our misbehavior. They sat us down to talk and got some of our classmates to put pressure on us. But the harder

131

they tried, the more we wanted to be together.

"As soon we got married, things began to fall apart. It was especially obvious after he got out of the army and we started living together. Life was getting comfortable. We had a baby. It should have been a close, happy time, but it seemed we always had to struggle for a bit of conversation. Later, I realized, without any outside pressure, our feelings were diluted to nothing after we'd gotten used to each other.

"I was performing every day and coming home late at night. As for him, well, he was bored and lonely and started going after other women. It's not difficult to imagine — he was young and dashing, very handsome. His father is a high cadre. It was easy for him to get women.

"I threw a big fit at the time, but then I thought: 'Why get so excited? He's no better than I am. If he's going have lovers, why can't I?' I was already a big name in the area; I had plenty of fans to keep me busy for a long time! You want me to drink vinegar, well then, you can wear a green hat![4]

"But to tell the truth, it wasn't right for me. Meeting a lover somewhere, I'd remember those days of passionate high school love. Our kisses then were so pure, our lovemaking driven by a kind of sublime feeling. There I was, doing it just to get him back — I felt like I was destroying some very precious part of myself.

"We went on like that for two years before I asked for a divorce. I'd fallen in love with somebody else. He's a company manager, a young businessman. I'd done commercials for them; our relationship had moved quickly from business to personal.

"With us, it was like love at first sight. He'd never been married and loved me very much. I could tell he and the company had a good future, so I decided to do what I could to help him out.

"My husband refused the divorce. He went to the song and dance company where I worked and made a big scene. He cried and begged me not to leave him. But I didn't feel sorry for him. I happened to know the woman he really loved had just broken up with him in a big fight. When he was having it good, did he feel sorry for me?

132

"He did everything he could to stop me. One time he pretended to go away on a business trip. He came back late at night and found us at home. There was a big fight, of course ... my husband was furious. He was about to start hitting, but I threw myself in front of him. 'Go ahead!' I screamed. 'Do you regret it now? It's too late! It's over! What do you mean by hitting him? All this has happened because we couldn't make it work. If there's a problem, it's between us ... what good does hitting him do?'

"Some people just can't get it straight. They want to blame it all on the lover when they should take responsibility for themselves. Is hitting someone going to settle your marital problems? If you hit him, do you think I'm going to love you? The more you hit, the more I'll hate you!

"Right after that I went to court and filed for a divorce. It was granted almost immediately.

"I spent a lot of time thinking about what I was getting myself into. There I was, planning to marry another handsome young man, an extremely capable, bright young man — another cadre's son — and one four years younger as well. What if he decided to go chasing after women like the first? Wasn't I asking for trouble?

"It's true I'd had a few boyfriends those two years, but it was just sex, meaningless sex that left me feeling empty inside. I knew if I found someone to love, I'd drop the rest and be completely loyal.

"I understand men; they're never satisfied. I decided I'd have to make some changes in our relationship. My first husband didn't value our relationship because he got everything too easily; I was too ready to go along with whatever he wanted.

"So the night of our wedding, I made an announcement in front of the guests. I said: 'We are two independent planets, both free to come and go. We must respect each other; if there comes a day when either of us wants a divorce, the other must not refuse.'

"I've seen over time the wisdom behind what I said that night. First of all, it put us on equal ground. Secondly, it instilled in him a certain fear. He knows I could get up and leave, and that's made him take care about our relationship. I divorced my first husband after all — there's no reason why I can't divorce my second!

"I decided then it was high time I got on with my career. I quit my job with the ensemble and stepped in as assistant manager to the company. My years on the stage had taught me how to play different roles. I also understand something about the way men think. A few of my deals came off successfully, and the company made money — that strengthened my position considerably. I now fly between Beijing, Tianjin, Shanghai, Guangzhou and Shenzhen; I've got contacts everywhere. I can even carry on conversations with foreigners in English.

"I don't feel at all like I did before we got married. I know I'm intelligent and capable, and I've got my own money. I'm not afraid of divorce. He, on the other hand, sometimes looks like he's afraid of losing me. I think love between a woman and man is a unity of opposites.

"We have a good relationship. We love each other and are working toward a common goal. But I still think, if it ever goes bad, we can go our separate ways. I'm always going to live by that idea because it's made me strong and helped me know my own worth. It makes other people respect me and my feelings.

"The more you fear losing something, the more you don't want to be afraid. But when you break through your fear, you become strong. It's then, when you're strong, you can create a positive relationship, and it's then you'll probably never lose the person you love."

(Thirty-nine years old, C is from a military background. She sang in the army for four years during the Cultural Revolution and worked six years as a soloist in the local song and dance ensemble. She's now a company assistant manager.)

Lovers

D. *Conventional love for her is not enough.*

She wore a cream-colored sun dress with a georgette

shawl thrown loosely over her smooth, round shoulders. I noticed the clear pearly sheen on her fingernails when she offered me a cigarette. Her face glowed with lively expression.

"I have no problem with my husband. He's goodhearted and honest. He loves his work and is good at it."

Her husband was a renowned physicist, a thin, middle-aged intellectual in glasses and blue Sun Yat-sen suit.

"But when it comes to sex, he's terrible. He lives in a world of abstract thought and mathematical logic. He's too ordered and conventional — no flair or sense of romance. Sex with him is like eating cabbage all winter long — there's nothing new, nothing fresh. It's like a college student working out a math problem on the board in front of class — everything according to the textbook, finished in ten minutes or less.

"Besides that, he's not well built. But look at me: I'm strong and have lots of energy. I need good sex. I smoke and drink; I jog and play badminton. I want to live like a woman. I like slow, leisurely strolls and good conversation. With my work in literature, I need someone who can appreciate and criticize art, someone I can go to art shows and concerts with....

"I don't blame him. Women shouldn't always be trying to change their husbands. And I understand how from a sexual point of view, men think they have to be stronger — that's what drives them in the competitive world of work. Any hint of impotence, and they lose their self-confidence. When that feeling of inferiority sets in, they may really lose their sexual power.

"We are, after all, husband and wife. We understand each other. I've never made him feel bad about this — I've always let him think I'm satisfied in bed. Through all these years, he's moved up the ladder of success rather quickly. No one can demand perfection, and I don't intend to leave him for this.

"He loves me — even though he doesn't know how to show it, he still loves me. I've given him a home, a son ... he can't do without me. It's funny how he tries to express his feelings. All he knows to do is pat my hand or shoulder ... like a shy virgin. I know his little pat says it

135

all — that's his way of expressing his love. But though I can understand and accept it, for me it's not enough. Women are rational beings, but we've got natural instincts too. I used to wish for a strong, passionate man to share my bed. Then I met him.

"He's a pianist, colorful and flamboyant — a strong personality. He's soft and gentle one minute, cruel and fierce the next. He's eloquent, expressive; he cries as easily as he laughs. He doesn't get along with his wife and says he wants to marry me.

"He could make me happy like no one else. He excites me; there aren't too many people who can do that. He loves me like only a man can love a woman, completely, passionately. He makes me feel like a woman. With him, it's me who lays my head against his shoulder; with my husband, it's the other way around.

"But I don't want to give up my husband, and I certainly don't want to get involved in my lover's family. I've found a way to make up for what my husband can't give me, so what's the use of divorce? Divorce would destroy the life we're used to — that'd be too hard on my husband. Our families and relatives would get involved — you can imagine the mess it would become. We just don't need it.

"So I told him: Get a divorce if you like, but I won't leave my husband. I told him our relationship can never be more than what it is now. After a while, he went along and hasn't brought up the subject since.

"Of course, I have other reasons for maintaining the status quo. Part of our attraction comes from leading separate lives. There's sexual tension when we get together. We're always trying to understand each other and accommodate ourselves — that's what has made our relationship so full and passionate. Also, we can't get together very often, so when we do, it's always exciting — an adventure. Without any pressure, a married couple can never reach that level of excitement. Even if they do, they can't keep it up for long. Sexual feelings over time are bound to lose their fire. For a woman in an unsatisfying relationship, especially if she's with a man like my husband, sex is a distressing experience.

"I've questioned myself a thousand times: Is what I'm doing right? I don't know what the answer is. I'm a person who needs to live, and this affair helps balance me and make me whole. Without the excitement and happiness of our meetings, the longing and anxiety of our times apart, without the pain and joy of our love, my life wouldn't be complete. It may be hard for a woman to express sexual frustration, but I'm sure I'd take it out on my husband. I'd fight with him over little things, give him no peace, as if he owed me something. As it is now, I'm getting what my husband can't give me somewhere else. No one's getting hurt and no one owes anything. I don't blame him; what does he have to blame me for? Isn't this better than divorce?

"Not everyone agrees. A good friend of mine thinks what I'm doing is wrong. She always asks: How can you say you love your husband?

"But I don't think that's a fair question. I know a lot of couples have a terrible sex life, not because of any problem with sex, but because they don't get along. Affairs are quite common now.... Except for prostitutes who do it for money, I think most women want a lover to compensate for what their husbands can't give them. For me it's a good way, a way that's saved my marriage. My intuition and experience tell me I'm doing what's right for me."

(Forty-six years old, D is the daughter of a high-level government functionary. She graduated from the Chinese department of a top university before the Cultural Revolution and is now vice-director of the editorial department in a publishing house.)

* * *

E. *She fell in love with a married man.*

She walked out of the classroom with a pile of books in her arms. Tall and dark-skinned, she looked slightly out-of-date in her gray checked blouse and leather pumps. Her eyes shone big and bright.

"I know what happiness is. I'm in love with a man

137

who loves me. People have called me a home-breaker. My boss put a lot of pressure on me; he said I was a bad example, a corrupter of morals.... He even gave me a disciplinary warning.

"But I've never bent to them! What is it to be immoral? Is it moral to hold on to a husband you don't love to get what you can from him?

"Most people think the lights have to be off to make love, but we keep them on. We're not afraid to see ourselves ... lovemaking is a beautiful thing. I believe that's what's most civilized and moral — the highest kind of love.

"Historically speaking, moral standards have always been changing. What's not sanctioned by society today is not necessarily immoral, and by the same token, what's sanctioned isn't automatically moral. Look at our own history and the moral standards we've gone along with: there was a time when a man could have as many wives as he wanted, or a wife and concubines; he could have his inner and outer bedrooms, his mansion and the brothels. Though few like to admit it, a good many of our past emperors were the sons of royal concubines!

"I don't care about a marriage certificate — what we've got is far more precious. But I do want recognition. I want to be recognized like any couple who loves one another.

"One time we were looking for a place to stay. It was already late, and we'd been turned away by several hotels because we didn't have a marriage license. Around eleven o'clock we found a private place outside of town. For some reason, when he filled out the registration form, he wrote in a fake name for me. He was probably thinking to protect me — but had no idea how I'd react. My love is real. I'm not afraid of risks. I only ask for my love to be recognized — he of all people should face up to that. I turned around without a word and rode away on my bike.

"I once had an officially recognized, certified husband. I spent several perfectly 'moral' years at his side before I left him.

"We were introduced to each other after we both got back to the city[5] and agreed to get married. But sex with him was so forced, so unnatural. At the time I wasn't aware

138

that I didn't love him. He's a good person, but I knew I had to divorce him because of that awful feeling. I felt violated every time he touched me.

"I don't know exactly what it is to not love someone, but I do know that every day I had to touch him or just be around him became more and more difficult. I couldn't stand it when he touched me; I couldn't stand his perfectly legal demands of me. For a woman, I understood that, far worse than having no love, is putting your body in the hands of another against your own heart.

"But I also knew that he'd done nothing wrong. I'd agreed to marry him after all. I just never expected it to turn out like that. It was hard on him too ... he had a wife but no love, no decent sex life. I can't blame him — he had no reason to put up with it any longer— divorce became our only "moral" way out.

"I'm grateful to him. He understood and let me go. I went back to see him a couple times, apologetic and thinking of what I'd given up, but pretty soon I saw how unnecessary that was. His new life was good — he got married again to a pretty young woman, and before I knew it, had a little son.

"I'm not the kind of woman who likes to run around. In fact, I'm fairly traditional. When I was married, even though I couldn't stand it sometimes, I never thought about anyone else. Pitiful, wasn't I? Thirty-five years old, married without love and yet afraid to look for it. It's ironic how nobody called me immoral all those years, but now that I'm truly in love, they call me immoral, unethical. This is a problem worth thinking about.

"Divorce gave me freedom and a desire to find real love. I knew what I was looking for, what I needed. My thinking on sexual morals had developed way beyond what I knew before marriage. Married men weren't outside my range of possibilities. I knew what went on between a husband and wife — a loveless marriage wasn't going to keep me from loving another woman's husband.

"When I met him, he and his wife had been living apart for more than three years. The tremendous energy I felt deep inside told me it was a love to throw myself into, a love I could die for. I was convinced he shouldn't go on holding his marriage together.

"People tell me what I'm doing is terrible, breaking up a family and ruining their child's life....

"It seems normal to blame me like that. Quite honestly, I think those who get the most excited are the ones who are having problems at home. Probably a good number of them have spouses who want to leave them. Like a vine around a tree, they'd rather strangle it to death than let go. That kind of person doesn't love anybody but Number One.

"Of course, I've thought a lot about their child. I'm a teacher; I understand young people. When they heard I'd been given a disciplinary warning, some of my girls came to see me. They asked if I loved him—I said yes. They asked if he loved me—I said yes again. Then they said: 'If that's how it is, then you should keep on loving each other.'

"I was moved by our conversation. I realized that the first to understand me were these kids of the younger generation! They're far more open-minded than their parents. They understand the world in a much deeper way. They value themselves and place high expectations on independence of thought. We ought to ask ourselves, how should we understand this new generation? What is their standard for happiness? Is it possible their parents' style of happiness isn't right for them?

"Our case hasn't been settled yet, but more and more people are coming to my side. Last year was a critical time. He was laid up in the hospital, misdiagnosed as having stomach cancer, and his wife, with whom he'd been separated for years, was busy settling his property and financial affairs. She even went down to the bank and falsely claimed his savings account as her own. I stayed with him in the hospital for twenty-one days. My entire bonus was deducted, and the principal called me in for a talk. But suddenly it seemed people began to understand — they began to be nice to me again.

"You know, I didn't cry once with all that pressure, but when I saw those apologetic smiles on the faces that used to give me such hard, cold looks, I broke down. Maybe there is such a thing as progress; maybe public opinion is fair after all."

Thirty-eight years old, E is from a worker's family. She spent four years in the army in Inner Mongolia, entered the Beijing Foreign Languages Institute in 1973 and is presently a middle school teacher.)

*   *   *

F. *A woman set on conquering men.*

She insisted on seeing me, having heard I was compiling interviews for this article. I knew about her— how she'd quit her job and started her own business and how people called her the "Saint Mother." But I wasn't prepared for what I saw when she stepped into my office.

"You don't have to hide it. I know I startled you. I'm probably the ugliest woman you've ever seen. Nobody's ever liked me, so don't worry, you can't hurt my feelings."

She was extremely calm, caustic almost; I could feel her deep-seated hostility.

"They hated me as a child. My father liked to whip me for no reason at all. My mother often just threw me out of the house. My little brother and his friends would chase me around, calling me names and spitting on me ... somehow I managed to grow up. I knew I had to fight. I had to be stubborn. They wanted me to fail, so I had to succeed! They wanted me to die, so by God, I was going to live! I know how much they despised me, not only for how I look, but for my pigheadedness — but it was them who made me that way!

"After high school I went into the countryside for three years during the Cultural Revolution. In those days, the city and country were so different; a city person was something to stare at in the villages. When the farmers first set eyes on the city girls, they could only think of one thing. They talked about us like horses for sale at an auction.

"One time they were sitting around in the shade smoking, discussing their favorite topic. One girl, they said, with creased eyelids and big almond eyes, was worth 1.50

141

yuan a *jin*;[6] another with round eyes and snub nose could go for 0.80 *yuan* a *jin*. Then they said, even if someone gave them 1.50 *yuan* a *jin* for me, nobody would want anything that ugly! They knew I could hear every word — they were just trying to hurt me for their own entertainment.

"I got so upset I shook all over. I was used to insults like that, but I'd just turned seventeen and was beginning to understand what went on between men and women. I had no idea I'd have to face that kind of treatment in the countryside! I thought about dying; I thought about killing the people I hated most. In the end, I decided how I'd get my revenge: I'd make them respect and admire me. I'd make the most handsome, arrogant men bow down at my feet!

"I went back to the city and worked five years in a factory doing menial labor. My health began to deteriorate; the worst part was the antagonism between me and the others, especially the good-looking men. To tell the truth, I wanted one so much — all my life I'd lacked beauty — even then, that's all I wanted. I yearned for the one who would finally notice the single decent part of my body — my hands. I always kept my nails neat and clean in hopes that one day a handsome young man would tenderly take my hands in his own. I'd have given all my love for that; I'd have given my life. What young woman wouldn't bloom when offered a little tender affection? All I wanted was a measly touch on the hand.... Every time I thought about it, I'd get so worked up, I'd start shaking. But nothing, not even a look from a man, let alone a handsome one....

"In 1981, when the economic reforms got going, I decided my time had come. I'd finally get the revenge I'd been waiting for! I couldn't go on like that, not really living, feeling suffocated by it all. I had to do something unexpected, create a stir, surprise everyone ... I had to do something to get their respect. I wanted to see their flattering smiles, see those men humble themselves before me.

"I quit my job and began work setting up the first nongovernmental charity organization. I didn't have any money, so I had to go to factories and mines to collect donations. It was then I discovered how good deeds made people forget my face. Describing the miserable fate of those cast aside by society, I'd watch them look long and hard into my eyes. I could see how they were moved by my words. I was completely worn out after six months, but I'd moved from my tiny room to a two-room office with a couple desks and chairs. My plan was becoming reality.

"The most important thing was that people began to notice me, talk about me, admire me. Newspaper reporters came to take their pictures; TV reporters came to film. It wasn't long before organizations abroad came to contribute money and equipment. I built a dormitory for my new staff. I had a base, prestige, money; people began to show some respect.

"With all that, I wanted a man more than ever!

"I'm a woman. I knew how much I needed a man, especially when I had everything else. And he had to be someone with looks — beauty was all I lacked.

"A crew from the regional TV station came to interview me about my work. The MC was a handsome young man, charming and very funny, the idol of many young women. I was thrilled to have him there. I poured out my heart into the microphone. I talked about kindness, morality and benevolence; I talked about compassion and love. I pulled out all the feelings I'd hidden at the bottom of my heart for thirty years. I cried, talking about the unfortunates of this world, and in that moment of passion, fainted dead away. He was standing in front of me holding the microphone, and when he saw what was happening, quickly reached out to grab me.

"He brought me home. When I came to, I was lying on the bed with his arm around me; he was wiping the sweat off my forehead with his handkerchief. That was my first time to be so close to a man — a man so beautiful I'd never dared imagine. I was close enough to hear his breathing, breathe in the air he exhaled, feel his heartbeat, feel his warmth.

"He could obviously feel my excitement, and growing excited himself, he said over and over again: 'You are so good, so holy and pure, like the Saint Mother herself ... you are so beautiful....'

"He stayed with me that night.

"He may have been unmarried, but I quickly found out how much he knew about women. When he loosened my bra, I realized what an old hand he was. He must have fooled around with hundreds of women! Suddenly I felt a great desire for revenge; I hate people like that who can rely on their face to get anything — they take it all so easily. Haven't they had to learn anything from life? Haven't they ever had hard times? Well fine, I thought, I'll give him a taste of what it's like ... I'll make up for what he's been missing.

"My desire for revenge subsumed any sexual feeling I had for that beautiful young man. I pulled the quilt around me, and though he tried to win me over, I wouldn't give in.

"After a while he fell asleep. I turned on the light and stared into his face. There he was, that untouchable TV personality — the first man to ever call me beautiful. Catching such a man wasn't so difficult after all; revenge had come easy. I realized then how much I despised men. I knew the joy of victory — I'd proven my power over men. I'd gotten my revenge. I'd won!

"He kept after me for more than a year. The more I held out, the harder he tried, until finally he got to be a nuisance. 'The circus is over,' I told him. 'I've seen enough.'

"Not too long after that a striking reporter from a large newspaper came to interview me. I strung him along for a while, then got rid of him like the first.

"I'm not a virgin by any means. I've been going out with someone for a while, even back when I was playing around with those handsome men. He's just a plain-looking guy who walks with a limp. We're a good match; he'll never say I'm beautiful, and he'll never say I'm not.

"I plan to keep up my work. I may not always be kind, but I still advocate benevolence. I've had enough of revenge, but I'll never get married... though I do want a man in my life.

(Thirty-four years old, F is from a poor urban family. She went into the countryside after junior middle school, worked in a factory for five years and now runs a charity organization.)

Widows

G. *Love and sex are two different things.*

Dalian, Fujiazhuang Beach; thirty thousand sunbathers, one woman in a bikini. The blazing summer sun enhanced her sensual good looks. A dark muscular young man joined her where she lay; it was obvious I had interrupted them, but that didn't seem to bother her.

"I can't figure out what I'm supposed to be," she said in a soft, floating voice. "Every time I have to fill out a form, there's always the question: 'married or unmarried'.

"How am I supposed to answer that one? I have been married, but I'm not now. Is that 'married' or 'unmarried'? There's no place for me on the form. It's obvious there's a reluctance to admit the huge numbers of people in China who are divorced.

"I looked up *guafu* (widow) in all the dictionaries and found the same definition in each: a woman whose husband has died. That can't be me— my ex is as healthy as ever. So what am I? A man can be called *guanfu* (wifeless man) whether he's lost his wife through death or divorce, but all I get is *guafu*. I've even been elected chair of the widow's association affiliated with our studio."

Her head tilted back to the sun, she went on in a loud voice as if no one else were around. Heads turned from all directions to listen.

"I had a fight with the head of our film studio a couple years ago. What was their excuse for not giving me an apartment? My films were big hits; I was earning a lot of money for them! Divorced eight years, and I was still living cramped in a nine-square-meter room with my mother and daughter. When it rained, the roof and a hole in the wall leaked. Everything we owned — the furniture from Romania, the refrigerator, color TV, stereo, piano, carpet — everything was piled up around us. We had no room to move. I wasn't going to stand for it any longer! Why shouldn't they give me a place when everybody who sits around in the office, drinking tea and cracking sunflower seeds, had all been allocated their own apartments?

"I finally took the matter into my own hands and picked the lock on an empty apartment. I knew it was ridiculous to wait for those old bureaucrats to acknowledge that a troublesome, uppity widow has any rights. I know what I'm worth— our two-room apartment still isn't enough.

"The head of the studio called me into his office, but before he had the chance to begin, I laid it all out on the table. He wasn't interested. 'Keep it short, alright?' he said. 'It's too much for you, is it? My family has been living in a nine-square-meter room for eight years, and you can't take a couple minutes to listen?!' I walked out and slammed the door!

"My mother's the anxious type; she lives in fear of having her life support cut off. She told me to write a report and make it up with my boss. I said to her: 'Go ahead and leave. You can kneel down all you want, but I'm going to keep standing.'"

I asked about her personal life.

"Personal life? Of course I have no secrets! I don't care if you use my real name; I'm long past that. I can tell you all you want to know about my thinking on love and sex.

"I believe in staying single. Don't get me wrong— single doesn't mean I go without sex. I'm a woman, and women need men. I just do it differently, that's all. Life without sex would be like slow suicide.

"I'm the assertive one when it comes to men. I take the initiative and usually get what I want.

"I haven't always been like this. In fact, I used to be very conservative. My first love was the most popular boy in high school. I was so naive back then; I loved him with all my heart. When he wanted to have sex, I agreed, because I thought we'd be together forever.

"But two years later that playboy took off with another girl. I was left completely heartbroken and didn't really recover until someone introduced me to a technician in the factory where I was working.

"My ideas back then were extremely traditional; I thought losing my virginity was such a big deal, so before we

146

got married, I told my fiance everything. When he said he could forgive me, I threw myself crying into his arms and vowed to serve him the rest of my life. I thought then losing my virginity meant losing myself, that I'd become the lowest, most despicable person possible.

"We got married, and I began to work like crazy. I did everything for him. I did everything to satisfy him sexually, whether or not I was in the mood, even if it was a bad time of the month. I had four abortions in three years! But whenever it occurred to him I wasn't a virgin when we got married, even if we were making love, he'd swear at me and slap me around—I was always covered with bruises. It got worse when he started graduate school, as if he'd gone up in the world, and my debt to him had compounded.

"I finally had a baby—a girl. It almost killed me. Did he come to the hospital once to see me? Of course not! It was the lowest time of my life.... But I knew I had to keep on, if only for the child's sake. My thinking then was: 'Marry a chicken, follow the chicken; marry a dog, follow the dog.'

"Not too long after that, some film studios began to recruit new talent, and I was hired as an actress. Life began to look up; my world was growing. I wasn't going to take any more abuse at home, so for half a year I didn't go back, sleeping nights on a wooden bench in the office. I was starting to build a new character: my ideas were changing. I began to understand then that women and men are equal.

"After the divorce I was like a race horse set free; I moved quickly from actress to director. It's strange, you know—when my career took off like that, I also changed. People began to call me a 'strong woman.' They said I was fast and efficient, that I moved with force. My complexion improved; men began to look at me. My ideal then was to find a good husband and settle down peacefully for the rest of my life.

"I found another man to love, a recent college graduate five years my junior. We were together for half a year, but when I brought up marriage, he hemmed and hawed. I was no longer the old me. I had confidence and a strong sense of myself. He couldn't make up his mind, so I threw

147

him out!

"I thought over each relationship. The more I gave, the more serious I was, the more I got hurt.... So I tried to forget about it all and threw myself into work. I began to make a name for myself in film and TV. An American film producer asked me to co-direct a movie. I made several trips abroad. I was too busy to think about anything—and essentially shelved the relationship problem.

"That particular period determined how I'd live the rest of my life. It was a time of re-evaluation and repudiation. Having worked through my sadness, I was ready to look objectively at the psychology of interaction between the sexes. One day it came to me—why make marriage the goal of my entire life?! You give so much, and all you get in return are shackles to tie you down. Are you crazy? Your world is so big, how can you fit a man in?

"But I wasn't about to give up sex. Sexual restraint inhibits creativity. Stay single but enjoy a healthy sex life—that's the best plan I've come up with for the second half of my life.

"A lot of women say they can't feel sexual desire without love. But as far as I'm concerned, sex and love are two different things. If you can't find a man worth loving, are you going to give up the chance to enjoy sex?

"Some men are pretty pitiful as well. One time I met an attractive editor in a publishing house. He couldn't take his eyes off me. I knew what he was thinking, so the next day I arranged for us to meet and sent a taxi to pick him up. But he didn't have it in him; he couldn't deal with it. What good is that? You want to play around, but you don't have the guts! And you call yourself a man?!

"My mother always goes on: 'How can you keep this up? Find a good man and settle down!' I don't listen to her. She was widowed as a young woman, her life sacrificed to feudal morals. My daughter's just the opposite: she's afraid I'll get married and leave her. She once crawled into my bed crying because she dreamed I'd left with some man. Pressure from one, fear from another—I know it's hard on them too, but I've got my own ideas, and I can't listen to anyone but myself.

148

"There's nothing good about marriage. All the men interested in me have a wife at home. A man doesn't love his wife; he loves his mistress. Besides that, men are too selfish. I'll never forget what one said to me, leaning against the head board with a cigarette in his hand. 'My wife was a virgin when we got married — a true blue virgin.' He seemed so proud, I had to ask: 'And were you?' 'No,' he answered. I asked if it was alright if his wife slept with other men. 'Absolutely not!' he cried. So I asked him: 'What would you do if I were your wife?' 'Beat you! Beat you till you knew your place!' he said viciously.

"Just look at that. Men are so selfish it makes me sick! I'll never get married again."

(*Thirty-eight years old, G is the daughter of a revolutionary soldier. She spent two years in the mountains during the Cultural Revolution, five years working in a yarn factory and is presently a film director.*)

*　　　*　　　*

H. *Without love, she had to turn him down.*

She didn't look like a woman over forty. In a striped dress and necklace of precious stones, she carried herself with grace and composure.

"Something happened two years ago to make me start thinking about this. My husband had been dead five years. He was killed in a bus that fell off the side of a mountain. It was a terrible accident.

"We had a good relationship. I often think about him — little things bring back memories, bring back the old feeling.

"I have nothing against remarrying. Even before, I believed that every woman has the right to do what she wants. In some villages, even to this day, widows aren't allowed to remarry, but here in Beijing, those old-fashioned morals mean nothing.

"Also, if a woman remarries, it doesn't mean she's negated her first marriage. Some people think if a woman takes a second man she's committed blasphemy — that her body belongs to someone else and is his for eternity. We can excuse that kind of thinking among uneducated people, but how can scholars and Marxists get away with it?

"Everybody has the right and the need to seek a normal life — who doesn't hope to grow old with one's spouse? But accidents happen. After you get through the pain, you think: Will I live off the old memories or plunge back into life?

"I've never forgotten my husband, but I know he's in my past now. I will get married again — I just have to find the right man. My only condition is that I can love him. I wasn't always so clear about this, but something happened two years ago....

"I'd just started to pull myself together after my husband's death when he came into my life. Actually, we'd known each other several years. He'd helped with the funeral arrangements when my husband died and was very good to me. He and his wife had been on bad terms; she'd gone abroad a couple years before, leaving him with only his writing to keep him going.

"One time we were out walking when it began to pour. We ran to his house, but by the time we got inside, we were soaked through. My dress was clinging to me, water dripping all over. He was staring at me like an idiot. Embarrassed by his look, I turned around to the books on his shelf, but before I knew it, he had his arm around my waist. I was so flustered I couldn't speak properly. 'Stop it,' I said. 'Our relationship before was fine. I've always respected you, but I don't want this....'

"He let me go. He said he respected me and would never force me to do anything against my will. He then walked to the other side of the room — a dignified, solemn gentleman.

"We sat down on opposite sides of the room. I wanted to understand him better, so I asked how he'd been getting on since his wife left. 'You want to know?' he said. 'I've been repressed! Every day I write five to six thousand characters, enough to make me feel like I've done something. In the evening, I start to get restless. I've never been able to write at night ... it's then I feel really lonely. I walk to places where I can be around people. Last night I went down to Tian'anmen to watch the old men fly kites... but I can't watch kites every night! I don't know what I was doing just now. Seeing you there like that did something to me. But you're proud—I know you. I can't force you to do anything... just forget it.'

"He sank back into his leather chair, exhausted, his eyes dark. I'd never seen him so weak and helpless. My heart warmed to him. We were so much alike! Both of us just needed a little companionship.

"We women rely on our intuition when it comes to men; we can get a general feeling with one glance. Men are probably the same—they probably have some intuitive sense too. He seemed to know what I was thinking and rushed over, kissing me gently on the hair. Perhaps, I thought, there was some way it could work.

"But we couldn't do it. I just didn't have that feeling for him. I respected and understood him, but there was no love and no sexual need. Without that, for me it was impossible.

"That got me thinking: he likes me, and I don't dislike him. Why can't we become lovers? Why can't we make love? Why can't we break through that wall?

"It's not a question of morals. My husband's been dead for some time now; I am free. Though he and his wife aren't officially divorced, they may as well be. We can both do what we want—we have our own apartments; we have birth control; we've both had experience. In other words, practically speaking, we're completely prepared. We also know what we could be for each other—we could fill that empty space. But it never works... it doesn't feel right.

"Even if he did get a divorce, I wouldn't marry him. A married couple has to enjoy being together; the basis for that is love. Since that happened I've known what I must do—find a man I can really love. I can't have sex without love."

(Forty-three years old, from a poor but educated background, H is a teacher of Chinese at her Alma Mater.)

"Old Maids"

I. *She wants a child but doesn't want to get married.*

Her beautiful face was set rigidly along the brow. She gestured as she spoke, her hands moving in hard, fast lines.

"I've never been excited about getting married. I think I'd probably go frigid. I'm just not interested in men.

"Men these days are quite inferior. They work their way up to department head or section chief, but when you get right down to it, they don't know what they're doing. They don't have any experience. None of the boyfriends I've had were very interesting.

"But I do want a child. I don't think it's anybody else's business but my own who the father is. I went at lunchtime to have a talk about this with the Party secretary.[7]

" 'I plan to have a child,' I announced to him. He looked happy to hear the news. 'Well then,' he smiled, 'when are you getting married?'

"I'd been thinking over the problem for some time — when he said that, I broke out angrily: 'What makes you think I should get married to have a child?!' Food from his chopsticks splattered all over his lap. He probably couldn't believe someone like me, the 'backbone of the office'[8] and a grassroots cadre,[9] would think about a child without getting married. He stared at me for the longest time, then asked, 'Why are you bringing this up? Is it morally right?'

"I got even more excited: 'Why bring it up? Because it's my right! I'm a woman, and it's in my nature to have children. Restricting my right as a woman to give birth is inhumane! Nature has given me not only the ability to procreate but also the inclination to do so. Giving birth is my right!'

"The secretary finally managed to get down a bite of food. He said: 'What you're suggesting is a question of policy. How can you have a child if you don't get married first?'

"I told him: 'According to the law, all citizens enjoy the same civil rights. I'm no different from any other woman in my right to give birth. The marriage law also stipulates that the children of both married and unmarried mothers have the same rights of succession and inheritance. In other words, the law acknowledges children born out of wedlock and grants them equal rights. My application to give birth is no joke. I like children and will be a very responsible mother. I want my own child.'

"The secretary thought for a while before giving me the usual answer: 'We'll have to bring this up before the Party committee to discuss it more thoroughly.' I said, 'Fine, and while you're at it, why don't you thoroughly discuss my housing situation. I'm thirty-four and have never once had my own place. I share a ten-square-meter room with my nieces. We all want to study at night, but I'm not about to take the only desk. They're young and have their whole lives ahead of them. So what do I do? I use the storage room at the office.'

"They call me the 'backbone of the office,' and it's true I don't do much else but work. I don't smoke. I don't drink. I don't buy cosmetics. I only buy a few books once in a while. But I haven't even got a place to put them! They're all stacked under the desk and bed. I have to pull out the flashlight to find what I want; I always come up with my hair covered in dust and cobwebs.... But when I go to apply for housing, everyone looks at me like I'm crazy! At work, our leader says things like: 'You don't have any responsibilities at home — go take over for so-and-so.' When it's time to donate blood, he says: 'So-and-so's husband isn't in good health; she shouldn't have to give....'

"I don't get it.... Why not judge us based on what we've done for society rather than on our marital status? I don't want to get married, but I do want my own child. My purpose in life is to work for society, and I've never shirked my responsibilities in that regard. Why can't I be accorded my proper rights?"

*   *   *

J. *A woman preoccupied with proving her virginity.*

The lines on her face pronounced a coldness; thick polaroid glasses blocked the expression in her eyes. She pursed her lips and peered at me from behind those lenses for so long I began to worry she was going to refuse my interview. She then opened her mouth and began to talk:

"I loathe that question." She wrinkled her brow.

"You're right. I am an old maid, but I loathe those words! I hate them all — spinster ... virgin ... all of them!

"Ever since I can remember, at least since I've been aware of my own sex, I've been worried about preserving my virginity.

"No one's told me why, or for whom, but I know I must save myself for one man. I don't know whether he's alive or where he is; I only know I must save myself for him!

"I spent several years during the Cultural Revolution in the mountains of Shaanxi.[10] The mountain folk are bold, uninhibited, rough and very poor. I was only seventeen. Those people taught me a lot; they taught me what it means to be a woman.

"I'll never forget that young bride holding high a blood-stained cloth the morning after her wedding. She was showing everybody outside guarding the door — her new parents and grandparents and all the neighbors — that she had been a chaste virgin. The in-laws sighed and grinned proudly. But when I saw that blood, my heart turned cold.

"When I was in junior high, I rode a bike all the time, even when I had my period. I wasn't very tall but still managed a big men's bike. We used strips of rough strawboard for sanitary napkins back then. Once, riding the bike, I rubbed my crotch raw, and it got infected.

"My mother took me to the hospital and talked for a long time to the doctor. I remember only one thing from their conversation: The doctor said, 'Her hymen was thin and has already been broken.' My mother stood stock still

154

in disbelief, then fell back in her chair.

"Something began to bother me. I could sense this hymen thing was a big deal. Later on I heard people say things like 'virgin's treasure,' and I began to worry I was missing something without one. What I saw that day in the mountain village made me realize: I could never show off my blood on a white cloth — regardless of the fact that I was virgin.

"It's not that I've never known love. I've had plenty of men interested in me... I've even loved a few. But I wouldn't have sex with them. It was hard to know what to do.... They're grown men — their desire is normal. I used to think: I'm not a kid anymore. I've got that desire too. But I wouldn't do it. I was afraid they'd think I'm not a virgin and wonder about my unclean past."

She lowered her voice, betraying a trace of regret.

"How could I prove my virginity? I'm a virgin without a 'virgin's treasure.' I've seen a lot of marriages break up because the woman wasn't a virgin when she got married. What could I do?

"I learned to put my feelings aside. I wasn't about to admit I haven't got that thing men value so much. I used to really want a man, but I knew I had to protect myself. They finally gave up trying... all of them.

"I'm not going to get into any more relationships. It's not because I'm afraid of men. I just feel like I've already lost so much, I couldn't stand to lose any more.

"I can't stand anything that has to do with men, sex or relationships. If they start kissing on TV, I turn it off. I've walked out of theaters in the middle of love scenes. When my colleagues begin to discuss the men in their lives, they see how upset I get and stop talking.... They say I'm too serious. I don't want to be like this, but I can't help it. I don't know how to change.

"Physically, I've got the desire, but psychologically, I'm afraid. The only way I could manage was to learn how to ... to masturbate."

Her voice trembling, she spat out this painful confession.

"I can't find any way out. I've asked myself over and over again: Why have you given up the right to love?

All you're missing is that 'virgin's treasure.' Do men have to prove their chastity to women? What makes them think they can demand this?

"Sometimes I think: I should liberate myself. To hell with this 'virgin's treasure.' But then I think about that wedding night when my bed will remain spotlessly clean....

"So I've decided against relationships. I'm not going to get married. I'm a virgin, and I'll stay a damned virgin for the rest of my life! As long as I never let a man touch me, I can prove it's true."

(Thirty-seven years old, J is presently working as a company section chief.)

Final Words

When I'd finished with these interviews, I felt, both as a writer and as a woman, a complex tangle of emotions. It was difficult to pull the loose pieces into a cohesive whole. What is implied by connecting their stories into one long piece? Is there a deeper social meaning?

Ten years ago I would have never thought of writing on such a topic. Successfully tape-recording these conversations seems even more far-fetched. Although sex has been a part of our lives since Day One, nobody would have answered my questions. Making it a secret, something dirty, a phenomenon occurring only within the realm of capitalism, is an emotional deformity. That these women were willing to speak out is progress, a step forward.

I want to thank them. They discussed openly with me their secrets about love and sex and what it means for them; they held up their own lives as examples. In revealing themselves, they've allowed others to understand and evaluate. The facts speak clearly about a great many undisclosed truths.

Notes

1. The article on which this translation is based covers twelve of the original twenty-four interviews of both women and men published in 1988.
2. During the Great Proletarian Cultural Revolution, Mao Zedong called on urban youth to go "up to the mountains and down to the countryside." The said purpose was to "learn from the peasants." Most of the women interviewed for this article were teen-agers at the time and spent three to five years in rural army units, living and working with the peasants as "educated youth." (See Note 5 of the Introduction for more on the Cultural Revolution.)
3. In China, the term "intellectual" generally refers to those who have completed a university education and hold a white-collar job.
4. To "eat vinegar" is to be jealous. For a man to "wear a green hat" means his wife is running around with another man.
5. Refers to their return to the city after some period of time in the countryside as "educated youth" during the Cultural Revolution.
6. One *jin* equals half a kilogram.
7. In an effort to curb population growth, the government adopted a family planning program in the late 1970s epitomized in the "one couple, one child" policy of 1980. Tactics to enforce the policy include persuasion, peer pressure and propaganda—speeches, banners, broadcasts, stories in the press and posters. Family planning representatives in the neighborhood committees counsel, pressure and provide contraceptives. In the city, couples must "apply for a child" through the woman's work unit or neighborhood committee, which is allotted a portion of the births planned for one year in that locality. The woman (*I*) went to speak to the Communist Party secretary in her office to make such an application.
8. This term refers to the hard-worker in the office, the one everyone turns to in a pinch to get something done.
9. There are two broad occupational categories in the state sector: workers and cadres. *Workers* ("blue-collar") are line personnel in industrial and commercial enterprises. *Cadres* ("white-collar") are executives, managers and officials, as well as staff members of government enterprises, offices and organizations. A "grassroots cadre," at the lowest managerial level, works directly with the workers.
10. Shaanxi Province, located in northern central China, borders on Inner Mongolia.

Brothers

Wang Anyi

They called each other Lao Da, Lao Er, and Lao San, like three brothers,[1] when they were in school together. They called their husbands "family,"[2] as if they were three men talking about their wives. The only women in their college class, they showed up the men on every count. Their dorm room was the messiest — dirty dishes were washed before the next meal, dirty clothes before the next shower. The plaster bust Lao Da stole from the drawing studio, embellished with a mustache by Lao Er and glasses by Lao San, was crowded onto the desk with the rest of their clutter. They were the latest risers on campus — Sundays and holidays, they slept through from one night to the next. The morning sun would beam in upon their motionless quilts, and sinking into the west, would be followed by the rising moon. And they were the earliest risers — they'd sometimes slip into their sneakers before dawn and creep across the dark campus to climb Phoenix Hill. Disregarding the well-trod, generations-old path, they'd pick their own way through the brambles, until, reaching the summit, the sun fresh from the heart of the river, the wind whipping their hair out behind, they'd stand alone, silent, forgetting time. Mornings like those, they'd be the last into the classroom. Everybody would be leaving by the time they arrived, the lunch line already forming at the dining hall. But there they'd sit, oblivious to all, just the empty classroom and a bird outside the window singing its afternoon song. By the time they'd decide to eat, the dining hall would be closing. They'd just laugh and laugh, as if they'd pulled off some great trick. First in line at the dining hall for dinner, they'd pile their bowls with food and go out to buy fruit wine for a drinking party back in their room. Just like three brothers.

Sleep would be forgotten; they'd open up their hearts to each other in the deep, dark void and share their most secret thoughts. Times like that are so few in this life. Most people never meet one such opportunity to explore and expound upon the inner recesses of the heart; they find no distinction between inner world and outer face. They have no secret place. They pass the nights as if in the busy, crowded world of daylight, sleeping earnestly alone, without a thought as to what makes up their existence. Sweet sleep engulfs them, but what a pity! The three brothers, on the other hand, were among the very few who knew how to create the opportunity for self discovery, and as luck would have it, they'd been brought together from all the people on this earth to share a room together. Cut off from the others, any one of them would have gradually sunk into loneliness and melancholy for lack of stimulation. Isolation often destroys the chance for self-awareness. But they'd met. And every time they came together, they found unexpected inspiration; a shocking jolt of motivation would catch them by surprise and power them with excitement. They never failed to seize the moment. If one of them faltered or struggled to unearth some inner part of the Self, the other two were always there to lovingly encourage and push her along, to help her over the crisis and dig in deeper. They talked to extraordinary depths. Turning off the light, they shared their secrets in the pitch black. By the early pale of dawn, they'd all begin to sense a creeping embarrassment, and feeling ashamed to look each other in the eye, they would do so deliberately, but the moment their eyes met, they'd turn away again, more embarrassed than ever. Then there were the times, a regular event in fact, when the conversation ran so deep, they'd lose all sense of direction or find themselves on the wrong track. They'd struggle to regain their bearings and pull themselves out of the mire, but they'd flounder only deeper, thrashing the water into a muddy mess. All talking at once, fighting to get a word in, they'd forget their original topic, till finally at a complete loss, they'd clamp their mouths shut as one. Then would come disappointment and frustration. They'd put out so much. They'd emptied their hearts and minds but found in the end they were even more confused than before. Long, perfectly flat, normal days would follow, in which they'd sleep, eat, go to class, do their homework and write to their husbands.

The three brothers came from Shanghai, Nanjing and Tongshan County in northern Jiangsu Province. Lao Da's husband worked in a Shanghai factory, Lao Er's was stationed as a battalion commander in the Northeast and Lao San's was a secretary in the county Cultural Center — he often came to Nanjing on business. Whenever Lao San received his telegram, she went immediately to reserve a room in the college guesthouse. She'd bring him first to the dorm to wash up and then to the dining hall to eat. He always treated the three of them to their first meal together — using Lao San's meal tickets. He'd talk on and on while they ate, the three bent over their food in silence. Her face hot with embarrassment, Lao San wouldn't dare look at the other two, sensing a quiet condemnation in their grim expressions. She felt she'd done them wrong. When their meal was finished, she'd grab up the dishes, but no one fought with her over the washing. They'd just sit there, angry at the way she was scrubbing the bowls, and share a chilling smile. She'd duck her head low, well aware of their resentment, and scour every speck away. Back in the dorm, the three would line up on one bed while he sat alone on the far side, trying his best to humor them across the messy desk. They'd frown at his vulgar names "Big Sister" and "Second Sister" until Lao Da would finally stand up and say: "It's getting late. We should go to bed." Lao San and her husband would scurry from the room as if they'd received a royal pardon and rush to the guesthouse. The two left behind would twist their lips into a ridiculing smile, a look of tacit understanding between them. They'd slowly rise and lay the bedding, putting out the light as soon as they'd climbed into bed. Staring blankly into the darkness, they were saddened by the empty bed at their side, hurt, as if a member of their ranks had abandoned ship. Their heart-to-heart talks of nights gone by suddenly seemed empty and meaningless. How easily they'd been destroyed and wiped away! Lao San was a traitor to have left them.

Lao San's first thoughts would be of her "brothers" as she stretched out on the hard guesthouse bed with her husband. Their silence oppressed her, made her angry at him. If he hadn't come, things would have gone on perfectly fine as before. But he'd ruined everything. Gradually she'd forget them, forget herself and relax into a deep slumber. Waking in the middle of the night, she'd think about the curious situation they'd created. They called themselves "brothers" and their husbands "family," but there was no getting around it, women were still women, and men were still men. They could never change that fact. She'd then fall peacefully asleep and not wake until the sun had cleared the tree line and the dining hall had closed. Walking into the classroom, she'd spot them in the front row, eyes fixed seriously ahead like two conscientious, diligent students. Shame would burn at her cheeks. She hated herself, but knowing she could fall no further, she'd boldly approach with a winsome smile and sit down at their side.

The rift between them would squelch all good long talks for a time, but when they did eventually find that connection, the rift would close, if only superficially. Surges of excitement at their reunion would bring tears to their eyes. They told their love stories, from first meeting to marriage, describing the journey as destruction of the Self and the struggle for a new life. What they discovered shocked them: If they didn't keep working at it, if they didn't put up a fight, they'd lose the Self completely. What a precarious position they'd found themselves in! On the very edge. Luckily the three had met and were there for each other — you hold me up, I'll hold you, and none of us will sink back down. But the opposite shore stretched so far away; they couldn't for a moment relax their grip. They wondered about the pairing up of men and women, where two obviously different people synthesize into a single unit and still want to do their own thing. People look for someone like themselves in their desire for a peaceful, harmonious home, but don't they know how easy it is for two like beings to subsume and merge with each other? Preserving the Self, on the other hand, free from that merged union, means paying the price of loneliness, and only the most exceptional can endure such a fearful thing. Didn't the fact that God provided the world with equal numbers of each sex prove that people weren't meant to put up with loneliness? But fear of being alone, pursuit of a common factor and the subsequent merged life ensure untold misfortune and unhappiness.... One question after another welled up and encircled them, trapping them in a tight ring. One answer led to the next question; their final conclusion pointed back to where they'd begun. They sensed the hopelessness of the human condition and grew excited that they'd arrived at the very core of life, at a universal black hole. So long as there was no escape but death, they decided, and for that they lacked the courage, they might as well do something to bring a little happiness, no matter how concocted or transient, to this unfortunate world and themselves. They'd begin right at home. They'd start small. They'd follow Lei Feng's[3] example.

The semester would finally draw to a close and winter or summer vacation begin. They were always reluctant to part and return home. How weak we humans are, they thought, our strength insignificant when matched with the natural forces around us. We're no more than ants trying to shake a tree! But off they'd stride, laughing and talking in loud voices to hide their depression. Lao Er lived in Nanjing; she always saw the other two off before going back to close the windows and lock the door. Gazing about one last time at the deserted room, those bright, sunny days and dark, bottomless nights would swim before her eyes. When she couldn't stand it any longer, she'd quickly bolt the door and rush from the silent dorm. There were a couple vacations when that husband of hers stationed in the Northeast was dispatched to areas so remote he couldn't make it home. She'd spend her holiday alone, returning to school a week or two before the semester began. Staring at the two empty beds, she'd think: Those two are enjoying themselves now! The days dragged on, but, knowing she could make it through, she felt proud of herself. At least there's one person in this world who can hold out through the loneliness, she thought. She'd sit alone in the drawing studio amidst the pale, lifeless plaster busts, sketching one after the next; gradually a deep inner peace would settle into her heart. She'd begin to talk to herself: You lonely devil! Who in the whole wide world is thinking of you now! Everyone has somewhere to go, something to do.... And when she remembered that battalion commander on who-knows-what peak in what mountain range, she'd suddenly feel very wronged. Well, I'm busy too! In fact, I have too many things to do! She'd plunge into a frenzy of activity; she'd climb Phoenix Hill alone before daylight, charge through the brambles to do her sketching and descend to campus exhausted. How painful was that long wait for the first day of school when she'd welcome Lao Da and Lao San back with a peaceful, magnanimous smile. She'd imagined that smile a thousand times. They'd see how busy she'd been. Busy doing what? She never got around to answering that question, but she'd be busy and they'd come, calling "Lao Er, Lao Er." When the time finally came, however, she'd go home and wait until the first day of class to show up at the classroom door. She'd waited for them so long, they should now wait for her, she reasoned. Their delighted smiles would warm her, and looking down at the pile of snacks and special treats they'd brought for her from home, she'd feel the tears well up in her eyes. Happy days are back, she'd chortle to herself, and in her happiness, she felt a certain revenge toward that commander in the mountains.

That night the early autumn breeze wafted in the open window, rippling the mosquito netting around their beds. A lone cricket chirped in the courtyard. They chatted drowsily about whatever came to mind, careful to avoid one subject — their vacation —though it meant sacrificing all the thoughts they'd had in connection with it. "Lao Da, Lao Da!" someone yelled up through the window, but they ignored him, disgusted that an outsider would use one of their nicknames. When he changed his tune and called her by name, she got up to see what he wanted. He'd come to return the laundry soap she'd forgotten by the side of the sink after washing her clothes that evening. By the time she'd crawled back into her mosquito netting, they'd lost all interest in sleep and were laughing uproariously at the boy who'd remembered such a ridiculously minute detail as whose soap was whose. This led to a discussion about the deterioration of men; those heroes of days gone by were already too few and far between. A real man, they said, as if they had come straight out of the classic era, was broad of chest and shoulder, strong enough to take on all the difficulties of the world. A real man would never concern himself with soap. How unfortunate to have been born into this crumbling age! Then came the wisecracks about the funny things their husbands had done over vacation. They rolled on their beds in laughter. Stifling their giggles, they thought how men had been assimilated by women and had already lost their inner Selves. What was there to worry about? What did they have to fear? The union between a man and a woman was a contest of strength in which men had been reduced to prisoners of triviality. Women had come out on top. But what a letdown if men really had lost their masculinity! They laughed and laughed, then sensing something was terribly wrong, stopped laughing altogether. One of them suddenly came up with the question — what would the world be like if there were only women? Another black hole gaped before them. Quiet descended in the late night as they crawled back into bed.

Refreshed and relaxed the next morning at dawn, they recalled their discussion of the night before and discovered they'd climbed a step higher. We must make a difference in this degenerating world, they valiantly resolved, and filed off like martyrs to the dining hall with their dirty bowls and chopsticks.

The last semester was finally upon them. Saddened by their eventual permanent separation, they knew even if they met again, they wouldn't be the same. They'd reached a pinnacle; they were the most liberated and aware they'd ever been. Never really conscious of themselves before, they'd just followed along like everybody else, but in knowing each other, they'd discovered their true Selves. Discarding all obligation, all worry, they'd freed what lay at the core. Bundled in their quilts, they talked from one night straight through to the next, putting off food till the follow-

ing day. Would parting mean a return to that old addled ignorance and dissolution of their recently discovered and solidi-
fied Selves in the domestic world of two? It scared them to
think how without free expression, their inner Selves would
gradually be extinguished. They'd spend the whole day at
Xuanwu Lake, gazing raptly at the pristine waters and
wishing the moment could last forever.

Lao San's husband, however, showed up more than
ever that last semester. He came every two or three weeks,
his look of hostility toward Lao Da and Lao Er deepening
with each visit. He clearly resented the name "Lao
San." Every time they called her that, he'd pull a long,
surly face. He looked for chances to order her about in front
of them. He waited for her to empty the basin after he'd
washed his face. He stopped calling Lao Da and Lao Er
"Big Sister" and "Second Sister" and called them by
their last names instead.

Two paths stretched before Lao San. The first was to
return to Tongshan County, where her husband had arranged a job for her in the Cultural Center; the second was
to stay at the school as a teacher. When they'd heard that
one of them was to be chosen for that coveted teaching position, Lao Da and Lao Er had agreed to give the chance to
Lao San. They both already held city registration permits,[4]
but Lao San's only alternative was to return to her little
county town. Taking the job would mean a new life for her.
She couldn't make up her mind. Her husband's repeated
trips to Nanjing were for the express purpose of taking her
right back home. Whenever he came, she agreed to the first
path, and as soon as he left, she'd change her mind. Lao
Da and Lao Er prevailed upon her, arguing that this was the
only way she could change her life. She said she knew that.
They said life in Nanjing would be completely different than
in Tongshan County. She said she knew that too. They said
as soon as she was settled, she could arrange for her husband to join her. That, she lamented, was out of the question. He felt he'd lose his self-respect if he were to follow a
woman. They laughed sarcastically: *If that's the case, he*
needs a woman behind so he can hold up his head, but the
woman can only trail silently behind. No, no, that's not what

I mean, Lao San replied anxiously. *What else could it mean?* they sneered. *Wouldn't we be disappointed if men weren't there to help us out?* Lao San blurted desperately. They gaped at her, shocked at such a statement. Then, very slowly, Lao Da replied: *Lao San, you're all mixed up. You mean to tell me he's trying to help you? He obviously hasn't got anything going for him but wants you to give up your future for the sake of his pride. A real man would encourage you at a time like this,* Lao Er added. *In fact, that would be a great gesture on his part,* Lao Da smiled. *I don't want any gestures. I just want to get along with my husband!* Lao San cried. Her expression of this perfectly ordinary female aspiration left the other two speechless. Lao San whimpered on: she'd never forget the night he'd walked twenty-five kilometers from town to her commune by lantern light through the snow to ask her to marry him. After a while she calmed down and, embarrassed about the way she'd carried on, said with a laugh: *The most important thing is whether or not a man and a woman love each other. If they do, assimilation of one by the other is worth it. What good is that inner Self we keep searching for if it can't bring happiness? If it only has the power to destroy?* She said that was all she'd been thinking about the last couple days. They'd made everything too complicated, too extreme, and as a result talked themselves every time into those dead ends they called black holes. They'd be better off to back up a bit, to regain their sense of purpose. Heaving a sigh of relief, she said she already knew her purpose in life, and with that, walked off to wash her bowl and chopsticks. She went to bed early that night and fell right asleep. A deadly hush hung over the room where Lao Da and Lao Er stared into the darkness. They knew Lao San was already far away.

When it finally came time to say goodbye, they held a small going-away party for themselves in their room. Gathered awkwardly around the desk, they had to search about for conversation like three strangers. They opened the fruit wine and gulped down big mouthfuls from their tea cups until gaiety overtook them and hysterical laughter filled the room. They recalled their first meeting: Lao Da had been the first to arrive, then Lao Er and finally Lao San. Not a word passed between them that first night, the next morning it was to ask what time the dining hall opened for breakfast. This memory struck them as unbearably funny, and doubling over, they hooted with glee. Then Lao San lifted her head and asked: *Can you guess what I was thinking about today walking down the street?* They stared at her excitedly, and smiling, she answered her own question: *I was thinking how easy it would be if I got run over by a car.* They shrieked with laughter and laughed until the tears came. Clutching her tea cup as if to warm her hands, Lao San stoically went on: *You're really going to make something of your lives. You've got everything ahead of you. For me there's nothing. Everybody knows each other in a small town. You can spot a newcomer a mile away, then before you know it, they're just one of the rest. There's only one market, so everybody knows what everybody else is cooking for dinner. There's nothing new to get excited about, no secrets to uncover….* She said her family had lived there for generations. Originally from Henan,[5] it was probably her grandmother's grandmother's grandmother who'd been pushed to Tongshan County by the Yellow River. Her family had been forced to move every several hundred years by the river's wanderings, but now that it had been dammed up and strict residency regulations imposed, there was no chance of ever leaving again.

Lao San laughed at her own words. Lao Da and Lao Er sobbed. Gazing at them tenderly, Lao San said that although they may not realize it, she was really very fond of them. She felt so free and uninhibited in their company, free like never before, free like she could never be again. At home with her family there was no such thing as doing what she wanted. Take mealtimes for example. It wasn't until she met them she realized she could eat when she was hungry and didn't have to wait for the clock to tell her it was time. In the future, as wife and mother, she wouldn't be able to let things slide. She might not feel like eating, but there would be her husband to consider. A family has to plan its mealtimes together. In fact, it's impossible to realize this inner Self, she said. It just makes a good conversation topic. And it's not men who swallow us up, so we shouldn't go

167

around blaming them. They've got a tough time too. We should try to help each other, not fight. Lao Da and Lao Er bawled all the harder.

Singing resonated through the halls that night; all were so busy with their own farewell parties, no one noticed how the three brothers carried on. The next morning they woke up with terrible headaches, said their goodbyes and went on to the train station. Lao Er left with Lao Da to avoid the lonely chill of the empty room, and the two parted quietly in the deserted street outside the campus gate.

II

Lao Er settled into a teaching job at a high school not far from her home in Nanjing, thus embarking on a more or less normal lifestyle. Her schedule consisted of two art classes and an extra-curricular art group that she organized herself. When one of the paintings from this group was selected for the National Youth Art Exhibition, parents came to her in droves, entreating her to let their children join. Her battalion commander was demobilized the following year and returned to an administrative job in some government office. He was allocated a two-room apartment and, other than an occasional business trip, the two of them fell into a regular, peaceful routine. She was close to a couple of colleagues at school; the beauty parlor and shopping were their standard activities.

The three of them once planned a Sunday outing to the Sun Yat-sen Memorial with their husbands and children. She and her husband had gone to the same school; he was a freshman the year she began junior high. He sent her a love letter in the heat of the Cultural Revolution, proposing they join for life, but after an initial surge of emotion, she put it in an envelope and sent it back. He never asked her about it again, but they stopped talking and began to avoid each other. That was the beginning. If a day went by without seeing each other, they'd feel empty, as if missing something. When it came time to be sent to the countryside[6] and they realized they might not see each other for years, they couldn't stand it any longer. They met one day on the street, and with paling faces and wildly beating hearts, asked where the other was being sent. One said Danyang, the other, Huaiyin. Who are you going with? they asked. Neither wanted the conversation to end. You ask one question, I ask the next. A full two hours passed before they exchanged addresses and said goodbye. Years later they met at Mochou Lake before he went off to join the army. Neither knew how to kiss — the best they could do was press their lips together for a while — but they always remembered that first time as the most exhilarating, a kiss to never forget. She worked for a couple years as a metal forger and went to college; they got married, and so the story goes. Bringing him along that Sunday, she emphasized the word "bring." He was her dependent, her "family."

Her colleagues brought their children — one had a boy, the other a girl — and their husbands. The children took center stage; a full morning of maternal boasting was concluded with an afternoon impromptu show. Six adults sat watching the two children sing and dance. One was required to smile cordially and clap enthusiastically at the end of each act. Her face aching with the endless smile, she swore she'd never have a child. Then making an oath against all future Sunday outings, she turned to her colleagues and exclaimed: "Today was so much fun! We'll have to do it again soon." They parted at long last near the memorial entrance and went their own ways to catch the bus home. A wave of relaxation surged through her, unhinging the tension in her face, restoring its usual animation. On the bus home that day, she thought of her brothers Lao Da and Lao San, and her throat tightened at the sudden pleasant memory of their happy times together. Poised on the summit of Phoenix Hill, they'd vowed to the Yangtze River to never have children. Being married, they said, left only half their freedom. How quickly that half would be eaten up by a child! Precious freedom! There were already too many responsibilities and things to do in life, too many roles to take — they must not add one more. Lao San was unreliable. She was the kind of duty-bound woman who'd sacrifice herself for her husband, and once the temporary liberation she'd found through her brothers wore off, she'd pick up her responsibilities and go on sacrificing herself as before. She thought back to what Lao San had said their last night together, the words she'd spoken from her heart, the way she'd expressed her Self. She and Lao Da, on the other hand, had never really articulated their true Selves. All those long talks into the deep of the night about who the Self belonged to seemed to fade into a confusing haze. What was it they were trying to get at? That evening at home she wrote a letter to Lao Da, a how-are-you-I'm-fine-remember-the-good-old-days letter. Only a page and a half. She addressed the envelope to the teacher training college in Shanghai where Lao Da had been assigned a job as an art teacher. But who was to say she was still there? So many people had been going abroad or to Shenzhen[7] in the last few years. At first she looked every day for a return letter but after two weeks began to give up hope and eventually stopped thinking about it altogether. Their school days were over, she reasoned. She might as well let them pass.

Time went on. Her husband was promoted to section chief and then to deputy division chief. The boss at work, he let himself be ordered about at home, seeming to enjoy the change in roles. Her bossy commands never bothered him; if she softened, he'd begin to worry she wasn't feeling well. Sometimes when he was trying to cheer her up he'd call her by her old nickname, "Lao Er," but she'd turn a stern eye and warn him to stop fooling around: Can't you see I'm busy? He'd clamp his mouth shut, and, embarrassed, wonder what was wrong with her. Nothing was wrong; she just didn't like him to call her by that name. "Lao Er" represented a particular time in her life, and even though she couldn't quite remember what it had been about, she didn't want him to bring it up again. Her mind had grown lazy since graduation. She'd probably squandered all her thoughts during those school years, and now there was nothing left. Ever since they'd bought a color TV, she spent her evenings from eight to the last "Thank you and Good night!" leaning against a stack of pillows in bed. A deep, dreamless sleep always followed. She gained weight; clothes that used to fit were impossible, and those once too baggy, she began to wear with style. In an effort to cut back, she forced herself to get up at six every morning to write several pages of big characters[8] before the breakfast of *youtiao* and *doujiang*[9] that her husband bought at the corner shop. But instead of losing weight, the regularity made her gain that much more. Determined to avoid pregnancy, they had calculated precisely the days of the month, thus regulating their lovemaking into a strict monotony.

One of the students in her art group was accepted into the art department of her Alma Mater. She felt gratified — her work had not been in vain, and excited — a student to follow in her footsteps. She invited the boy for dinner, cooked by her husband. He came, awkward and embarrassed, but her husband joked around, and after a while, he began to loosen up. They toasted with beer, and soon his soft white cheeks flushed rose, his eyes gleamed as if he were about to cry. Stumbling over his own words, he told them how he'd loved to draw as a child, how he'd filled the courtyard with chalk horses and old men. His parents had pinched their pennies to buy him paper and brushes, but being semi-literate factory workers, they only knew quantity, not quality. It wasn't until he'd joined her art group that he'd learned what it meant to paint. He promised he'd do his best so she could be proud of him and not lose face. Tears nearly fell as she listened to his little speech. Standing up, she suddenly opened the bookcase and pulled out a large art book, which she deposited in his lap. Stunned, he tried to refuse the expensive gift, but she proved the more obstinate, and the book went home in his hands. She took him to campus the first day of school to show him around and introduce him to her old teachers. They greeted her warmly: "Just think, you're a teacher now! You cut class more than any of them. You and those two you called 'brothers' slept all day long and didn't know what to do with yourselves at night. What a delinquent lot!" A labyrinth of feeling pressed down on her. I was once like that, wasn't I? she thought dejectedly, and leaving the student at school, went home alone.

Another year went by, and another student from her group was accepted into the fine arts department of the

171

Shanghai Theatrical Institute. She didn't get as excited as the first time; in fact, she didn't think much of it at all. She was just doing her job. The thought of Shanghai did bring to mind Lao Da. Where could she be right now? No letter had come, her whereabouts still unknown. It was about this time she began to take an interest in knitting. She bought new wool and ripped apart old sweaters; knitting came to occupy all her free time. Peaceful calm enveloped her when she sat, needles in hand, fingers working through the motions — up, down, through, back around — motions that lent a soothing rhythm to her thoughts. It made her happy. Just the thought of picking up her needles made her happy. In a few short months she became an expert knitter, and putting her creative ability to work, she designed her own unusual patterns. Her husband brightened up the office with his colorful, exotic sweaters. When one of his colleagues asked her to knit him one as well, she happily agreed, and he rushed off excitedly to buy the yarn. She had her husband help wind the balls that very night. Eager to get started, she counted out the first row of stitches, but the moment the real work was to begin, a wave of irritation filled her. A big sweater like this will take forever, she thought. One boring stitch after the next. Knitting had been so pleasant before, a leisurely walk, a carefree stroll, but it had become an oppressive task, each step burdened by the goal ahead. Thinking then about life as a whole, she sunk into dismal despair. With no ultimate purpose, there was nothing new to get excited about from one long, insipid day to the next. Knitting lost the power of peace and happiness; all she could think was to finish that sweater so she could put her needles down forever. Every day she found some excuse to put the work off. The man who'd bought the wool couldn't very well hurry her along. He came once in a while to see how she was progressing but found the sweater much the same, not a stitch further than before. Some six months later, the sweater season long past, he showed up to collect his yarn. Knitting, from its happy beginning to its wearisome demise, thus became a permanently closed chapter in her life. Her long-suppressed depression rose to the surface and with it the question: What was she living for anyway? That mind of hers, gone soft from disuse, awakened and leapt into action, throwing her daily routine into disarray. She lay awake deep into the night listening to her husband's peaceful snore. How that snore irritated her! It was the snore of the entire sleeping human race, the symbol of its ignorance and apathy. She'd doze off just before daybreak, when the alarm clock would jerk her back awake, and, exhausted, crawl out of bed and sit there fidgeting until it was time to go to work. Her swollen eyes pierced by the morning sun, she'd somehow make it to school. As she watched the students arrive in twos and threes, her melancholy would turn to compassion. How sad for these children to be born into this world! she thought.

Her husband kept an eye on her shifting moods, from her exhilarating highs to those bottomless lows. He knew her better than she knew herself. He knew she had too much energy and nowhere to put it. He knew she lacked the reasoning to positively direct this force, causing it to rage like turbulent water against a dike. He wasn't worried though, that the surging mass would burst through its embankment —not that he held any illusions about her power of intellect— but because he knew the dike was built up from the intellect of others, including his own. He did not, nonetheless, let down his guard, carefully tracking her mood shifts and trends so he could take appropriate measures when necessary. He loved her because, like an unfortified city, everything was etched clearly across her face. She could hide nothing. He knew what she needed and wanted, and at the same time he did everything in his power to give it to her, he purposely held it away. She shouldn't be satisfied at every turn, he thought. She has to learn to curb her desires; the world wasn't made for her alone. Everybody has to learn to restrain themselves, or we'll all have a hard time getting by. A man of intellect, Lao Er's husband understood about survival of the fittest. He felt the true essence of a man was not necessarily to be upright and outspoken, but to be capable of coping with a quickly changing world. Well aware of how different she was from him in this respect, he gave her space and made it look like he was letting her have her own way. He knew perfectly well her image of a "real man" was purely aesthetic; what she needed was a firm, steadfast man like himself. Without that, the smallest step would prove difficult, hopelessness would come again and again. He kept their arguments to a minimum, though every time these questions came up, she grew terribly excited, as if she alone were awake in a slumbering world. Mornings when she sat fidgeting, when she refused breakfast and wouldn't make the bed, he didn't force her, but neither did he go along, carefully folding the quilts before he went out to buy the *doujiang* and *youtiao*. She didn't have to eat — she could do whatever she liked — but life around her would go on as usual. She'd gradually start to come around, but rather than relax, he'd tighten his regime, coming home exactly on time, leaving on schedule every morning, airing the quilts, washing the windows, keeping the house fastidiously neat and clean, until, feeling completely ridiculous and ashamed, she'd pull herself back to a normal routine. Home and career for this man factored as two equal parts of life — one the means, the other the purpose. It lay before him like that, so simple and clear, in brilliant contrast to her chaos and impulsive change. But it was just this upheaval, her capricious chaos, that gave his life fluidity, that sharpened the dull edges and spiked the flat water. It defined for him a sense of aesthetic he valued so highly he was willing to give up a number of other things, his dream, for example, of becoming a father. She gave him a rich sense of beauty that allowed him the humanity stifled by pressures at work, and for this he was grateful. But in no way did this confuse his vision of life's true path; it only gave him energy to work harder. He considered the two of them a pretty good match as husband and wife.

There was a limit to her depression. When she could fall no further, she'd pick herself up, and perceiving some hope and purpose in life, find she could put up with the monotony of her passing days. She discovered a new talent in her art group, a bulky, broad-shouldered young man who, though he stood a full head above her, was still a little boy at heart. Determined that he possessed exceptional artistic potential, she put all her time and energy into helping him develop, and with absolutely no discretion, told him that so long as he put his mind to it, there was a chance he could get into the Central Art Academy. He listened to her advice, and from that day on, devoted himself entirely to art, laying aside his other schoolwork to paint. She began to ignore the other students and concentrated solely on him, until in the end, her extra-curricular art group was reduced to one teacher and one student. They painted together every afternoon until the sun set, but as time went by, she realized that his talent was actually very generalized. If you told him to study dance or music, he'd perform just that much better than the rest, but would never stand out in any one field — the perfect candidate for a four-year university, she realized with irritation. Her enthusiasm cooled; she spoke less and less to the boy. He was fortunately an easy-going sort and didn't take her rejection to heart. Putting down his brushes, he crammed for several weeks and tested into university with a decent exam score. Her art group never picked up again, and without that, her workload was lighter than ever. Art wasn't a core class and didn't even rate the importance of P.E., which at least had some objective standards for performance. She did whatever she felt like in class. She often just put a vase of plastic flowers on the podium for her students to draw, and sitting to one side, read a novel or do some quick sketches, which she'd rip up on completion. A full semester passed like that.

Then came the morning, brushing her hair, when she noticed wrinkles around her eyes and a soft sag to her skin. She suddenly felt sick at heart and thought: Youth has nearly passed me by. Aren't these few remaining years about to go as well? Urgency pressed upon her. She had no time to lose; she had to enjoy what remained of her fleeting youth. She began to practice with make-up, and borrowing fashion magazines, added a fresh look to her wardrobe. Her artistic touch was transformed to new wonders on her face — with the right eye shadow, rouge and lipstick for each lighting situation and each outfit. She knew how to blend and vary color for subtle changes, to create a new look. Everybody thought something wonderful must have happened to her, she shone with such vibrancy and life. In fact, it was nothing of the sort. Changing her image and walking down the street with an attractive flair gave her hope and confidence, that was all.

She developed a taste for going out, and every time, whether it was to go shopping or to the movies, or even to a friend's house, she had to reapply her make-up. It was about that time she joined another Sunday outing organized by her colleagues. The children, elementary school students already, were learning to play musical instruments — the electronic organ and violin were cheerfully toted along for a little concert on the grass. She almost didn't make it through the day, nearly getting up and walking out on their party. Back home, she thought about how shallow she'd been, and fed up with it all, decided to give up trying to retrieve her youth. She never stopped with the make-up though. Women love beauty, and though she'd once been called "Lao Er" like a man, she was still a woman at heart. Where was the one who'd called her "Lao Er" now? Depression hit again.

That night, waking from a deep sleep, she roused her husband and said: *I want to have a baby*. He thought it was a dream but, reaching out to touch her, found she'd tunneled through to his quilt and was lying at his side. *Aren't you acting on a whim?* he asked worriedly. *So if it's a whim, let it be a whim,* she answered. *What if you regret it later?* he asked. She laughed: *Regret won't work. Once a baby's born, you can hardly push it back.* Her voice resonated clearly in the thick of the night, then echoed strangely, as if it wasn't her own. He wondered: What's gotten into her now? But his body had already begun to move, and soon their joined heat had reached melting point. She wanted more than anything to have the baby right then and there, to fill up her empty, meaningless life. She'd heard about a mother's love, how women were willing to sacrifice everything for their children. So long as I can't realize my inner Self, she thought, I might as well have a kid and sacrifice myself in a big way. Better that than this dull, empty life. She fell peacefully asleep, awoke calmly at daybreak, brushed her hair, washed her face, straightened up the room and sat calmly waiting for her husband to return with breakfast. They ate together, walked their bikes to the street and went their separate ways to work. Aware of the solemn sacrifice forming in her belly, she moved with slow prudence; slowly she pedaled, carefully she dismounted, cautiously she walked to her

176

office. There was someone with a timid smile standing carefully behind her desk. Her heart skipped forward several beats. Who was it? In that split second, all she could think was: Something's about to change.

Stepping forward, she suddenly shouted: *IT'S YOU! LAO DA!* That name hadn't passed her lips in ages, but the way it fell out, it was like she'd been using it every day. Lao Da smiled apologetically, like a child who's misbehaved, and finally, after a long time, answered softly: *Lao Er ... Lao Er, look at me. I look terrible. I'm so pregnant.* Lao Da's protruding stomach brought back last night's scene with uncanny clarity. She reached out and touched her belly with tears in her eyes: *It doesn't matter. How many years has it been? Can you remember?* Lao Da said: *Too long, too many years. Look how far along I am. It doesn't matter,* Lao Er said; *it doesn't matter. Aren't we back together again? Isn't that what's important?* They stood facing each other, wanting to hug, yet too embarrassed, afraid a handshake wouldn't be enough. So they just stood there. They recalled the times they'd slept all day in the dorm room; the times they'd let the dirty dishes pile up on the desk, the times they'd crossed campus before daybreak to climb Phoenix Hill and share sunrise over the Yangtze River. Their tears streamed down. How long ago that was! Did anyone climb Phoenix Hill to watch the sunrise now? Did the sun look the same floating on the river before it leapt free and soared into the sky? They'd always thought those beautiful days would never pass. They'd come through rough times [10] and assumed once they'd pulled in some happiness, they could hold onto it forever. *Lao Da, Lao Da, why didn't you write to me? I wrote once but didn't get anything back. Did you get my letter?* The other teachers had gone off to class, but she wasn't scheduled to teach until the third period; the two of them were left alone in the office. The sun shone brightly outside, birds chirped in the trees. *Lao Er, it's not that I didn't want to write. I just didn't know what to say. I didn't have anything new to tell you! You would have been bored to tears by anything I wrote. But when I didn't get a letter back,* Lao Er said, *I thought you'd left the country or gone to Shenzhen. Isn't everybody leaving these*

177

days? She began to sob. *But I didn't go anywhere. I've been in Shanghai all along. I can't imagine going to a strange place like Shenzhen, much less abroad,* Lao Da explained. *If you had gone, I'd be the only one left; I'm sure Lao San's forgotten all about us,* Lao Er said, still crying. The mention of Lao San reminded them again of how happy they'd been, and they continued to stand there talking, forgetting the time. When the bell suddenly rang, they jumped in surprise, thinking they were students once again late for class.

III

Lao Da stayed at Lao Er's house that night. They stopped using their old nicknames to avoid thinking about Lao San, calling each other instead by their last names.[11] They took the double bed in the bedroom, and Lao Wang's husband made do on an army cot in the outer room. But they didn't sleep. Slipping between sleep and semi-consciousness, Lao Wang's husband wondered vaguely what it was the two women had so much to talk about. At around four or five in the morning, he listened to the silence inside and assumed they'd finally drifted off. "It's light outside," a voice broke through his thoughts. The living room curtain beside his makeshift bed slowly bloomed into color with the coming light. They seemed to be getting out of bed, talking and laughing softly, moving about the room. Then they were at the doorway and creeping past his cot. *Where are you going?* he asked. The two women leapt in surprise then fell over each other laughing. *What are you trying to do, scare us to death?!* his wife cried. *I was just asking where you're going this early in the morning.* He sensed she was near that madcap, reckless edge again. She said: *We're going to the market to buy some vegetables. We'll pick up breakfast while we're out, so you can stay in bed and sleep.* The sun must be rising from the west today, he thought, lying back down on the cot. He listened to them close the door and clatter down the stairs. A moment of quiet passed before their melodious "pit pat" came to him through the window and gradually faded away. Curiously touched picturing the two

178

women walking together in the day's first light, he lay thinking for a while before getting up and pulling on his clothes.

They walked down the street. The sun hadn't lifted above the horizon yet, but its rays washed the sky with the fluctuating shades of morning. Feeling light and refreshed, even after their sleepless night, they promised each other they'd keep in close touch; they'd write regularly — no more repeats of the past. We have to help each other through this dull world so we don't sink further into depression, they said. They hadn't imagined there was anything more to get excited about, but for their reunion, they rejoiced. It had been so many years, and though they'd been ground down by daily life, rubbed into respectability and boxed in by convention, they still held the spark to light their friendship anew. They'd paid the price to preserve that bit of warmth; they'd held out alone through long, lonely days. Lao San had deserted them and, fearing they'd lost each other as well, they'd put off making contact, put off even writing a simple letter. What good would that last remaining spark be if they'd lost each other? they wondered. If they idled away their years, waiting for something to happen, wouldn't it eventually burn itself out? Responsibility oppresses with irresistible force. You've got a whole long list of things to do even before you get up in the morning. You can't sever one link of the chain — break one off, and the next comes loose; the next comes loose and then the next, until the whole thing falls apart. It doesn't matter if you come undone, but what if other people get messed up along with you? What right do you have to destroy the order in their lives? They've done nothing to destroy yours; in fact, they've helped you maintain it. One clamps to the next in this long connecting chain, and to preserve themselves, none of the individual links can permit a destructive thought among the rest. Caught in the clutches of these binding shackles, any warmth, any spark of enthusiasm, is just one more burden to bear. They'd managed, however, to save that spark, and now, coming together, they could bear the burden and destroy the chain as one. Like two restless wild horses, they saw their meeting as a mileage post marking a new phase in life. They burned with a freshly kindled fire.

Their market plans forgotten, they walked all the way to Xinjiekou and feasted on a big breakfast of wonton and steamed rolls in a small street-side shop. They then turned and headed home, neglecting to buy the portion they'd promised Lao Wang's husband. The sun hung, a bright orb over the roofline; bicycles flowed, a noisy river of morning traffic. Lao Wang had also forgotten about work, but she did remember to call the school from a public phone to reschedule her classes for later that afternoon. They browsed through small shops on their way, buying five-spice pumpkin seeds and other snacks to nibble on as they walked. Lao Wang's husband was gone by the time they got back, but he'd left a note on the table: He hoped nothing had happened, that they'd just forgotten the time. He thoughtfully added that he'd call her school to ask the day off for her so they could enjoy their time together, and he reminded them about Lao Li's train at two. *Now that's a real man!* the two women exclaimed. They settled down to talk, the prospect of lunch erased from their minds. What is a man anyway? they wondered. He is the natural complement and companion to a woman. There are some things women can't do together. Like sex. Like have children to carry on the family line, to ensure continuity of the species. A woman needs a man to get through the various stages of life, to complete the tasks set out for her as a member of the human race. Inseparable as they are, man acts as woman's heaviest, most burdensome link. Man and woman collude into a mutual prison: He imprisons her; she imprisons him. Men, in fact, are nothing more than a high cell wall. They felt they'd made great headway in putting these pieces together, but then, with a confused rush of emotion, they realized they were just one more step down a dead end road. Crouching on stools over a basket of spinach to be cleaned, they reflected on their own imprisonment and on the small convict in his mother's womb. Lao Wang, in her high-strung way, felt like she was going to be sick. She pressed back the uneasy feeling in her throat and thought about the terrible crime they were committing. Lunch was out of the question.

Neither was hungry; the idea of three meals a day repulsed them. And it was time to go to the train station.

Slowly rising from their wooden stools, they picked up Lao Li's bags and trudged out into the blinding midday sun. The bus was nearly empty; they both got a sun-baked seat and bounced lazily along to the station without a word. Across the vast square and into the waiting room, they parted by the ticket checker, purposely not buying a platform ticket, both to avoid a long, emotional farewell and to assuage their fear of parting. With calm goodbyes, one turned and walked inside, the other retraced her steps out of the station. Daring not focus her mind, Lao Wang hazily followed the chute of benches to the exit. The square outside gleamed with sunlight like a huge, horizontal mirror. Almost summer, she mused; summers in Nanjing are terrible! Descending the flight of concrete steps, she felt light-headed, dizzy. Could it be she was pregnant? The solemn fervor of that night had trickled from her mind and seemed a remote fantasy. Was it real? Crossing the square, she was suddenly subsumed by hopelessness: she was a lone sailboat navigating a boundless sea. She sailed aimlessly, the opposite shore nowhere in sight, until at last she found the bus stop. Back home, she collapsed on the bed and fell fast asleep.

It was about that time Lao Li's train began to pull out of the station. She sat by the window watching small groups wave from the platform, and her mind wandered back to Lao Wang. What could she be doing now? Fatigue slowly crowded out consciousness; her eyelids drooped. "Clank!" The sound of the train changing tracks jerked her awake in time to see the last sign for Nanjing Station sweep by. What had seemed hours of sleep was but a few short moments. She watched the trees dart by like the thoughts flitting through her mind. One thought, more persistent than the rest, pressed forward — in two months, two short months, her child would be born. She'd wanted this child for so long, dreamed of it though she knew she shouldn't. They'd promised each other in school to add no more restrictions to their overburdened lives. She was a woman of sensibility, of emotion so rich, she could not help but feel the constant pressure. A child would add to her burden; all hope of preserving her freedom would be destroyed. She wanted the child anyway, dreamed of a child to fill up her emptiness. She'd given up hope, thought it was too late, when suddenly, when they stopped trying so hard, she'd gotten pregnant. Joy and the rich moment-by-moment awareness of a life growing within her had transfused her soul, and with her awareness had re-emerged the Self they'd talked so much about in school, the Self which until then had lain dormant and out of reach.

She had to get up every morning at dawn to cram into a city bus. Shanghai's buses are crowded like that, the streets so noisy. Leaping from the crush into the din, she'd arrive at school, from which, once the dismissal bell rang, she'd join the wildly impatient crowd in the fight to get home. She never stopped running; feet back on the pavement, she'd hurry to the market to haggle over prices, then straight to the kitchen to cook their supper. Her husband ran a small factory and never got home until after dark, always too worn out to talk. Lao Li figured they'd been too tired all those years to get pregnant; physically, there was nothing wrong with either one. Bound by her hectic, exhausting run-around life, Lao Li had not the leisure of Lao Wang to strip away everything and soar above the mundane to explore her Inner Self. Her most critical problem was managing to get through the day. Just to stretch out on the bed and catch the closing of the last TV show at night was enough. Time and energy to contemplate her Inner Self had become an extravagance, an amusement she could not afford. If not for her deep reservoir of feeling, her Self would have long ago vanished, never to surface again. But she had merely hidden it away within her enormous heart: hearts of such capacity can conceal things at astonishing depths. Unlike Lao Wang, who liked to flaunt her Self about in public, Lao Li always appeared calm and at peace. But the fact of the matter was, inside, she was all astir. The moment she'd discovered a seed of life had been planted within her, her Self rose from where it lay hidden and sparkled forth like light on water. From that day on, she could feel a part of herself growing in her womb, growing day by day. Separation from herself allowed room to explore. What am I all about? she wondered.

What of myself will be embodied in the new life in my womb? Though her reflections brought no answers, she still enjoyed turning the questions over in her mind. Thinking about the Self gave her great pleasure — nothing like those vague, cumbersome late-night discussions in their dorm room and certainly nothing like Lao Wang's gloomy deliberations. She felt happy, and it was this happiness that had inspired her to visit Lao Wang. There'd been some business to take care of for her school in Nanjing; she'd jumped at the chance to make the trip, imagining the two of them reminiscing about the old days together. What she hadn't guessed was that their meeting would spark such a fire of excitement. Something new had started. New life pumped through her veins. She was shocked to realize how she'd trudged through all that time in such a blind stupor! Was bringing a baby into this world such a good thing after all? Was she really meant to let her child follow her into this rat race? What's the point of one more rat anyway? Was there no hope for change? The image of her child caught up in such a life called up the endless toil and utter ignorance of her own. Her heart sank at the thought.

Lao Li was a kindhearted woman of great empathy. Her tears were invariably shed for others, but when it came to herself, she was tough. Women of this sort are thought to have forfeited the Self for their offspring. They're thought to live in a dark, unenlightened world, their best intentions often misconstrued. But don't they, in fact, stand the most squarely inside themselves? Don't they know better than most their inner Self? So sure of where they stand, they can let go and focus their attention on others around them. Not like those who go on all day about the "Self" — that's only fear, fear that if they drop it for a moment, they'll never find it again. Then there are some who wear chatter about the "Self" like a fashionable new outfit while their old discarded life lies crumpled nearby. Even the word "Self" for a woman like Lao Li felt awkward and un-wieldy; she wasn't any good at throwing it about casually like Lao Wang. To her it was a natural part of existence, nothing to get excited about, certainly nothing worth special mention. You can be sure, however, that when a woman like

Lao Li does turn her attention to the "Self" and begins to ask questions like "What am I?", that exploration will be of no ordinary intensity or significance.

Fields swept by. The sun balanced, a shimmering ball on the edge of the earth; speed seemed to hold it there in place. Staring out into the moving picture, Lao Li suddenly felt a wave of distress. I wonder what Lao Wang's doing now? Lao Wang was still asleep, her room fading into darkness. The sun then dropped, a flat coin into a slot along the horizon. It's so crowded in Shanghai right now! Lao Li thought. Her husband rode a bike to work. He had to circle every night round all those streets closed to bike traffic, so that by the time he made it home, he was exhausted and set on a querulous edge. It grieved her to see him like that. She knew the extra work she'd taken on for his sake, unnecessary work that made her life that much harder. Like cooking three dishes and a soup every night for supper. Like heating up a couple ounces of rice wine for him when he got home. She'd neglected to point out to Lao Wang earlier that day that the prison they'd talked about was actually a prison of love. Lao Wang's weariness grew from responsibility, Lao Li's from love. Love is an exhausting thing! It requires a higher level of awareness than responsibility. You can have responsibility without love, but never is there love without responsibility. Every once in a while she wished she'd grown up an orphan — to be free from that web of love for her family. She'd wander then like a young shepherd boy in those childhood tales, wander all day on lush green mountainsides with her flock of sheep. Oh, to be a shepherd boy! She couldn't understand why there had to be so many people on this earth, people who were forever connected to each another. Lao Wang, she knew, saw responsibility in those connections; she saw love. To make matters worse, she had to live in the most congested city in the world. Smashed together, they all had to fight their way through Shanghai's narrow streets, delicate sensibilities pulverized by the constant friction. How easy to lose patience, lose control, and how difficult to pick one's self-confidence off the asphalt after yet another quarrel and round of curses! How pitiful we are! She closed her eyes with that thought,

184

and rocking gently with the train, tried to drop off. But sleep would not come. Looking up again, she saw the lights had been turned on. The dull yellow glow inside pushed out the last rays of sunset to the fields below where a shepherd boy was herding his flock back to the fold. She asked the child in her womb: Is it really right to bring you into this world? They would become a triangle, interlocked. They'd been two, but then with one more, everything suddenly became so complicated, so time-consuming. Ah, to be a wandering hobo! She'd shoulder her dusty old bag and follow the wind all over the world. No one to wait for her and no one to wait for. Again a shock of incomprehension. Why, in this world of so many people, why must two, and only two, join as one? They seal their fate eternally through physical union and bear a child as proof of their devotion; they form a blood-linked circle of three. But joined thus, none can enjoy freedom of movement, every step felt by the other two. Lao Li's heart ached thinking of these things. My loved ones! she cried out inside, I will never leave you! Yet even so, another part of her yearned for freedom, dreamed of shouldering that tattered bag and wandering like a vagrant over the world. The oppression of love fanned her desire for freedom with incredible force. She couldn't take it lightly, no more than Lao Wang could take responsibility lightly. Love was serious, painful, the cause of all grief and misery in the world.

The train pulled up to the station, and she wondered again: What's Lao Wang doing now? Following the shuffling crowd toward the open door, she stepped out onto the platform. A half-orb of milky white dangled above, illuminating the black rails and olive green cars at her side. All around, the great swaying army surged, the thunder of footsteps and hum of voices crowding out her train of thought. Borne like a small boat in a rushing torrent, she was pushed past the exit and straight to the bus stop where she climbed aboard the waiting bus. The driver finally arrived to coax the grumbling vehicle into gear; drowsiness fell over her. Closing her eyes, she could vaguely hear an argument in the back, anger rising to a critical pitch then tumbling down and breaking into laughter. Noise pressed round, drowning out reflection. She could only articulate one thought: Is he home yet? She got off on a secluded side street and walked home in the dark, the dim street light glow and city clamor rising like steam somewhere off in the distance. Craning her neck, she peered anxiously ahead, looking for that second-story light to tell her she was almost there, when suddenly, spotting the warm beam behind their flowered curtain, she felt her throat tighten, her eyes mist over. She was willing, she realized at that moment, to hand over all the freedom in the world for that spot of warm light. She'd taken out her key long ago, but the back door hung open, the neighbors outside saying goodbye to some guests. Without even a hello, she squeaked up the stairs and pushed open their door. It was an evening to warm her heart. Her husband told her how he'd bowed out of dinner with the manager of a joint operation so he could go to the market and cook for her. Too bad the food was already cold. She poured boiling water over the rice to heat it up and listened to him go on about what he'd done over the last two days, her heart filling with tender affection at his childlike chatter. Suddenly her mood changed. She put away the rest of her meal, washed up and climbed wearily into bed. "Don't you feel well?" her husband asked. She said she was tired, and closing her eyes, fell fast asleep. Lao Wang at that moment, well rested from her afternoon nap, was sitting bolt upright in bed watching TV.

Lao Li's husband watched her sleep and thought: It's not easy to be a woman. He reflected on all the difficulties women must face, all the hardships women have to deal with that are beyond a man's capability. He thought how his wife had never enjoyed a day of happiness with him, how hard their life had been and how she took it all in stride without a word of complaint. His family didn't have any room for the young couple when they first got married. They'd borrowed the corner of a friend's garage as a temporary little nest, but when the agreed upon month was up, it was back to their respective homes and meetings under the trees at night. She'd always been the one to console him. Kindhearted and intelligent, not like many kind women who are just plain stupid, she knew how to make other people happy. She could

186

describe some small incident with so much animation you'd think it had all happened to her, when in fact, it was only something she had heard about. Her imagination and creative power were that great, and her classes so interesting, even the other teachers at her school liked to sit in and listen. Knowing how she had it in her to be a completely different kind of women, he sometimes wondered if she wasn't to be pitied. Times when work was going well and he could turn his attention to other things, he found she was not exactly as she appeared. He could detect an agitated undercurrent flowing deep under her peaceful, composed surface; it was with fear and humiliation he sensed its terrible destructive power. He tried not to think about it too much, and fortunately, she was always calm and steady, their home lulled by her gentle, peaceful air. He was grateful for this, and it was for this he vowed to always love and cherish her. He knew how well she understood love — but on the other hand, he considered it a dangerous thing for a woman to possess such understanding. He sometimes had the unsettling feeling he was going to be caught off guard, that he'd come home one day and she wouldn't be there or he'd be waiting for her and she wouldn't show up. Where could she have gone? He'd rush home madly on his bike, narrowly miss the fender of a car — a slew of curses in his wake — bound up the stairs in threes and throw open the door to find her by the window, painting a small water-color of the shadowy, sunset rooftops below. Why had he come home so early? she wanted to know. Was something wrong? His throat caught with burrs, he mumbled something about forgetting a package, but when she tried to help him look, he pushed her roughly aside and grabbed a bag from the cabinet. It wasn't until he was on his way back to the factory that he discovered he'd come away with a ball of leftover red yarn, and his eyes filled with tears. In times of more coherent thought, he determined to let that dangerous undercurrent loose, knowing how pressure can build without some form of release. He'd bring the roughest, wildest factory workers home to drink and let them carry on until the neighbors came round, banging on the door for quiet. She'd remain her dignified, sedate self through it all, and those workers, who knew no respect for anyone, couldn't help but show some restraint, making him feel ridiculous and completely unjustified. Climbing gingerly into bed, he lay down quietly at her side. He hadn't slept well the night before, but now she was back, and curling up beside her like a little boy, he fell asleep.

IV

Her reunion with Lao Wang brought everything back for Lao Li. She wasn't like Lao Wang, who could pick things up and just as easily put them down again.· Once something started, she couldn't let it rest. They began to write regularly, exchanging three or four pages crowded with tiny characters each week; their correspondence developed into one of life's daily pleasures. They hoarded time alone to devote to their letters — in one week, there were three days for reading, three days for writing and one day to rest. How is it we have so much to say? they asked each other. We both have husbands, and a husband ought to be closer than a friend, although there is a limit to what one can talk about. By the next letter, they'd both come up with an answer: they were too close to their husbands. Together every day, morning to night, they'd gotten so they could communicate without even opening their mouths. As time went on, they'd grown lazy, passive; they'd come to assume there wasn't anything new to think about. One of them might want to suggest more open communication, but afraid the idea would be laughed down, would keep the thought suppressed inside. New ideas had thus been diluted into water by their daily life, by the trivial details that fill the space between husband and wife and render abstract conversation absurd and meaningless. Husband and wife are bound in flesh, by material objects; it is for this material foundation they give up the spiritual world. Abstract dialogue, they realized, can only be carried out between those who maintain a certain physical distance. For two of the opposite sex, the body takes over the mind, material concerns outweigh spiritual convergence, the flesh ultimately cuts off the spirit. It took them dozens of pages to solve this dilemma. In the end, when they had it all straightened out, they breathed a deep sigh of relief and relaxed. Writing to each other, they happily noted, brought them back to their girlhood — to that age of best friends when every girl has a buddy with whom to share the secrets of growing up, to promise eternal friendship. The promises get broken later, however, when boys step into the picture. Girls learn to betray and tell lies; they sneak away to meet their boyfriends and keep the secret locked inside, until eventually a huge gulf separates one from another. They'd gone back a couple of decades, these two. They were learning anew what it means to enjoy a pure, innocent friendship unfettered by sexual desire. Girls again, but not really, because as mature women, they brought that much more to the relationship. They made themselves out to be free, autonomous beings in their letters, and in fact, when they immersed themselves in their correspondence, they forgot everything around them and did achieve, on a fictitious level anyway, their ideal of freedom.

Lao Li's time came. As for Lao Wang, well, nothing had come from that night — it had all been the work of her imagination. Three o'clock one morning Lao Li gave birth to a son. His cry filled her with a joy as she had never known. Lao Wang couldn't sleep that night; she tossed and turned, inexplicably upset. When word finally came from Lao Li, she remembered that night and realized it had been her sixth sense at work. How mysterious the human ties, she thought, and wrote back to say she wanted to be the child's godmother. She'd never read the Bible but did know from translated novels that the job of godmother was not unlike that of a *gan-ma*.[12] She searched everywhere for a present, finally hitting upon a long life talisman cut from a precious stone. We have a child, she thought, her eyes filling with tears as she gazed at the stone. In her mind, the father was already out of the picture; their child had only two parents   a mother and a godmother. We must teach him and raise him well, she thought; he is the fruit of our soul. I must go to Shanghai, she thought, tightly clutching the talisman; Lao Li needs me now. It was the middle of summer vacation, a typical broiling hot summer in Nanjing. Lao

189

Wang's husband agreed she should go to Shanghai and cool off for a couple days. He bought a ticket for her, packed her bags and saw her to the station.

She went without announcing her plans. Lao Li was so surprised by her abrupt arrival, she bolted upright in bed, stretching her arms out to her friend. Lao Wang rushed over and pressed her back into the pillows, thus commencing her month of postnatal duty.[13] Her first job was to get rid of the housekeeper Lao Li's husband had hired. She claimed the woman was no good, devious, scheming, and obviously had it in for mother and baby. Announcing she could take care of everything, she told the husband to relax and let her do all the work. Truth of the matter was, she didn't know the first thing about her newly adopted profession; all she had were a bunch of old wives tales to go by. Closing the doors and windows against drafts, she wrapped Lao Li's head with a cloth in the 34 degree[14] heat and fed her poached eggs in boiling water. She wiped her down three times a day with a hot washcloth but wouldn't let her move her own arms and legs, declaring exertion of energy would lead to leg and back problems. Lao Wang had never been able to stand the heat. It fanned her irritable nature; her sweat flowed like rain. She determined, though it was absolutely unnecessary, to stay awake every night and keep watch over Lao Li. Seated on the bamboo couch to one side, however, she'd soon be slumped over and fast asleep. With a startled jump, she'd jerk awake. *What's wrong?* she'd ask. *Nothing, absolutely nothing,* Lao Li would reply. *Then why aren't you asleep?* she'd ask. *I slept all day long. How am I supposed to sleep at night?* Lao Li would answer. She'd then say: *You go ahead and get some rest. I'll stay awake.* But her eyelids would droop and off she'd go again. Early mornings, she went first thing to pick up the milk and then straight to market for vegetables. She learned to haggle over prices so viciously everybody in the neighborhood began to wonder who had hired the tough new housekeeper. She cut her finger open learning to clean fish. She crept quietly around the baby, gently changing his diaper while warning Lao Li's husband about the careless father who had yanked his son's little thing off with the cloth. To hear her talk, it was obviously something she'd made up. Having no experience with housework, everything was a big project. Dirty diapers she washed immediately. Warming up the baby's milk required a half hour of preparation. Never before had she been so diligent, so patient, but in her frenzy, she left behind a trail of destruction. Countless bowls were shattered, and spilled water rained more than once on the neighbors downstairs. Touched by this woman from Nanjing, the neighbors didn't complain; they tried rather to help with advice and guidance. By the end of the month, she'd developed a quick and dexterous hand.

Lao Li's husband was extremely grateful, and surprised moreover, to discover women could have such loyal friends. A good or bad job was all the same — sincerity was another thing entirely. He didn't know how to pay her back, but for her part, all she wanted was for him to keep out of the way. He finagled a ticket to a restricted movie for her, but she wouldn't go, unwilling to leave his wife for a moment. It was the hottest time of year, and there was only one room in their apartment. Nights, he left the room to the women and baby and slept outside by the street on a canvas cot. Stretched out alone under a tree, he fixed his eyes on the dim light above, sensing as he lay there a creeping contradiction. On the one hand, he felt grateful to this woman, somewhat anxiously apologetic, but on the other, a vague dissatisfaction told him she'd broken up their home, separated him from his wife. He felt sorry for himself, sleeping like a castaway beneath the trees. What really surprised him was the way that woman called his wife "Lao Li." The first time he'd heard it, he assumed she was referring to him. "Sorry. My name's not Li," he'd replied. "I wasn't talking to you," came her unexpected response. That name grated on his ear. It made his wife into someone else, a man perhaps — not his wife. Every time she used it, he pretended not to hear. But he felt like he shouldn't react to her like that, as if it were an act against his own conscience, and forced himself to be calm.

Lao Wang had already drifted off that night when she suddenly jumped back awake to see Lao Li staring up at her.

What's wrong? she asked. *Everything's fine,* Lao Li smiled.
*Then why aren't you asleep? You go to sleep; I'll stay
awake,* Lao Wang commanded. *I don't want to sleep. Let
me stay awake for just a little while!* Lao Li implored.
Alright, for just a little while, Lao Wang softened, *but it's
the middle of the night. What do you want to do?* Lao Li said:
*Let's talk for a while; you've been here so long, but you're
always running around doing everything while I lie here doing
nothing. We haven't even had a chance to talk!* Alright, let's
talk then, Lao Wang agreed. They sat very still for several
minutes listening to the clock. *Life's really a strange thing,*
Lao Li began. *How so?* Lao Wang asked, though she knew
perfectly well what she was getting at. *Just think how a
human being is reproduced,* Lao Li continued. *Like on a printing press?* Lao Wang asked sarcastically, then added, as if
pained by the thought: *But it's actually the reproduction of*
two *human beings; you can't say it's only one. Then it follows,* Lao Li said, *that we're talking about the reproduction of
six. The mother and father are already reproductions of their
parents — No!* Lao Wang interrupted, speaking quickly; *there
are so many more than that! We've got the blood of millions
of relatives we've never met flowing through our veins!* She
hunched over, pinching her shoulders together as if she were
cold. They got up to look at the sleeping baby and stared at
him as if he were some kind of freak. *What are we really?*
they gazed at each other in speechless despair. *There are
some things we shouldn't question too deeply,* Lao Li said in a
quivering voice. *It's like facing a deep pool,* Lao Wang
added; *one slip and it's all over.* But they'd already begun
to creep down that dangerous path and, curious to explore
further, had no intention of turning back. Wasn't the first
human a pure being? they asked each other. And if so,
where did we come from? Their course became more perilous
yet. They saw that humans were reproduced not only from
other humans but from animals themselves —monkeys and
fish. They had the blood of creatures from the primeval for-
ests flowing through their veins. The human "Self" they
realized, wasn't so spotless after all. It had been tainted
from birth; they couldn't be responsible for it. They groped
in fearful despair, searching for a way out, until they thought

of the advancement of life, of how far humans had come from that animal state. Life, it turned out, was a process of cleaning and filtering, a means to elevate and purify the human condition. A pale wash of light the color of a fish's belly rose evenly along one edge of the sky. They let out a deep sigh — they'd made it through the long black night. Daybreak had come at last and with it joy and new hope. They took turns kissing the baby and agreed he was the most perfect, the highest form of life yet to be born. A superior being, they said, draws both naturally and knowingly from the finest of many lives. That being the case, they thought, it was possible for them to perfect their own worn-out existence. They recalled the night and their trek up that perilous mountain. Gratefully they acknowledged that without each other's support, they would have never had the courage to attempt that dangerous path, much less to pull through to the end. If they hadn't fallen in the darkness, they would have turned around long before the path really began, leaving a terrible impression to haunt them like a nightmare. The memory of how their souls had passed through this danger was to remain for them, in times of need, a source of comfort and support.

At the baby's first month,[15] Lao Li's husband arranged a small party to celebrate and thank Lao Wang for her help. School was about to begin, and it was time for her to go home. Lao Li didn't invite any other friends; their party consisted of three adults and one baby. They drank fruit wine and beer until, taken by a light giddiness, the two women returned to that night years ago when three of them laughed and cried around a table of such wine. Forgetting all about Lao Li's husband, they rattled on with increasing fervor about things only they knew about. Remembering how they ditched class together and slept right through the day, they doubled over with laughter, tears gleaming in their eyes. Back then, they said, life was so good, so carefree. They had no responsibilities to speak of. On and on they went, then, rediscovering Lao Li's husband at their side, they began to fight for his attention, interrupting and being interrupted, yanking his arms back and forth to make him listen. The water was boiling. He wanted to get up and make some tea, but they wouldn't let him go. They suddenly remembered something terribly funny—both knew without even saying it—and burst out laughing so hard they couldn't talk straight, leaving him completely in the dark. On and on they went, releasing him to his tea, but he came back to find them facing each other, tears glistening in their eyes. A carefree time like that, they said, would be a blessing if but a single day, not to mention the three full years they'd had together. Now they had to pay it back with this dull, ponderous life, they sobbed. He thought they'd really gone off the deep end. It was the first time he'd seen his wife in such a state, and he wasn't enjoying it. She'd changed into something ridiculous, ugly, somebody he couldn't recognize. He backed off from the table, lowered himself into the couch and lit a cigarette to watch their performance. He felt like he was watching some crazy comedy with all the punch lines taken out. But they weren't actresses and there was nothing to laugh at, nothing remotely amusing, only a disgust that left a bad taste in his mouth. They finished off the wine and picked at the food left on the table, a weary silence enfolding them. Nobody said a word. The baby slept. *I'll never forget this summer*, Lao Wang said with tears in her eyes. *Neither will I*, Lao Li agreed, her eyes as wet. *Let's spend next summer together too!* Lao Wang suggested. *Okay*, Lao Li agreed; *let's go to Qingdao or Beidaihe or Dalian.*[16] *Yes*, Lao Wang went on; *with nobody else, just the two of us!* Excitement built as they dreamed about their summer together. Lao Li's husband was horrified at the thought of the two women running wild on the beach and determined then and there to destroy their plan. But they'd already dropped that idea, summer being so far away, and moved on to their winter vacation plans. One wanted to see the flower show in Guangzhou,[17] the other, the ice festival in Harbin.[18] They debated back and forth until, spotting him on the couch, they told him to decide whose idea was better. Guangzhou, said one with a tug to the left; Harbin, said the other with a yank to the right. He looked at this one and at that— a gaudy flush from the wine hung on their cheeks, their eyes gleamed with unnatural light. These crazy women! he shuddered. *TO HELL WITH BOTH OF YOU!* he bellowed, pretending to be drunk, and pushed them away. They staggered back, laughing as they went; he joined in to cover up his anger. The next morning when he left for work, they were still asleep, one curled up on the bed, the other slouched on the bamboo couch, the remains of their meal scattered over the table. His temper flared, his head pounded. He walked out the door without any breakfast. That night, however, he came home to a clean room: the freshly mopped floor shone, the table was set with small plates of chilled vegetables, the baby, washed and powdered, lay on the bed mat. His wife, fresh from the bath and in a clean change of clothes, was reading a book under the desk lamp, waiting for him to come home. That Nanjing woman was nowhere in sight. The room felt so large all of a sudden, his heart so light. What an insane month! he thought, washing his face and hands and seating himself at the table. His wife scooped out a bowl of rice for him. The early autumn breeze drifted in the open window. Looking at her, he felt a rush of emotion. My woman's back, he thought. Yesterday she was taken by the devil, but now she's back. Curiously, neither of them brought up Lao Wang. He didn't ask if she'd gone, and she didn't say she had.

Lao Li resumed her normal schedule after Lao Wang's departure. She found someone to take care of the baby while she was at work and went mornings to drop him off, evenings to pick him up. The summer had emptied them of conversation; they didn't correspond for a long time, and when they did, it was only an occasional greeting. The baby occupied every minute of Lao Li's time. She watched him grow day by day, marveling all the while at his expanding repertoire of tricks. Today he can make noises, tomorrow he can wave his hands in the air, the day after he's learned to throw a tantrum and roll around in anger. Feeling like her pain and heartache had been worth it, Lao Li was consoled. And he learned how to get sick. First diarrhea, then a fever, then diarrhea and a fever; two out of three days she'd be rushing to the hospital, child in arms, heart on fire, thinking: My sweet little darling, if anything happens to you, it'll be the end of me. Her entire world seemed to be hinged upon his tiny, fragile body; and she sensed her own weakness, not knowing what might happen from one day to the next. She couldn't sleep when the baby was sick, fearfully imagining death and the horrible pain and terror he'd face if he died alone at night — when, in fact, all he'd have was a common cold. Her anxiety struck Lao Li's husband, who saw her cool composure slipping away and being consumed by a quick testiness, as a bit neurotic. She'd sometimes snap at him for coming home late, even if he was just a few minutes past the usual time. Thinking that she must be tired, he tried to lighten her load, and in no time had learned to change a diaper like an experienced nanny. Two weeks would go by without a problem, and she'd start to relax, but whether by coincidence or the workings of an adverse force, just as she was feeling a little happy, his temperature would soar, and they'd have to race again to the emergency room, another night of sleep destroyed. She came to the conclusion that she must never ease up; the moment she let her guard down, the baby would get sick. On the days he was well, she'd fret and pace anxiously, but as soon as he came down with something, she'd sigh in relief. It was that absurd. Her husband would try to cheer her up by saying: *The baby's looking really good these days!* But she'd pale unexpectedly and in a quaking voice tell him to never speak like that again__ once said, he was sure to get sick. He'd try a different tactic and say: *He's not looking a hundred percent today, is he?* She'd panic and run for the thermometer, leaving him speechless. One night in bed he tried to talk her around. They'd tried for so long to get pregnant, he said, and finally when they'd given up, the baby had come, as if by the will of Heaven. His life, therefore, his very existence, waited upon his own destiny. They could do nothing to force it along. She burst into tears: *What do you mean by that? Parents aren't supposed to take care of their children when they get sick? We're supposed to just close our eyes and let him suffer? Let him die?* He struggled to defend himself, but she cried all the harder, falling so deeply into depression she thought everything was going to come crashing in around her. He realized arguments were of no use and turned to consolation, finally easing her from her outburst. Later, when she was more coherent, she could see how in her exhaustion she'd become like a bowstring drawn tight, ready to snap at any moment. She decided she'd have to relax. The baby had been pampered to such a fragile state, however, one afternoon outside without his hat and he began to cough. She thought she'd wait to go to the hospital and try some cough syrup at home, but when it developed into whooping cough, she vowed to never be careless again. Ever since this baby's come into my life, she thought, feeling the fatigue creep along her spine, it's like I've been walking on thin ice. Every day there's a new danger to look out for. How wonderful to be free from it all! Ah, to be a wandering hobo! The thought exploded like a shooting star, then fell and disintegrated as she gazed bitterly over at the baby. If I were to leave, she thought, what would become of you?

The wandering hobo image stirred her up at times of utter exhaustion, when she couldn't trudge another step. If there ever comes a day, she thought, that I can't take it anymore, I'll just leave. Believing there was a way out helped, but that day would never come—her ability to endure was endless. When the baby was a little older, she took him to the day-care center near her school, squeezing every morning onto the bus with her fat little bundle. Even if someone had wanted to offer their seat, it was impossible to break through the wall of bodies; so she'd stand, clutching her child and feeling a hand move where it shouldn't. She'd want to scream at the top of her lungs, but she'd hold her silence, reasoning it was perfectly normal under those circumstances to bump up against one another. Her school was a good distance away, and she had to leave home early. She'd come close to tears to pull the sleeping child from his warm nest in the quilt on those bitter winter mornings. I'll just quit my job, she thought, knowing that would be impossible. She couldn't let him support the family alone —besides, he didn't make enough money. Squeezed and pushed on the bus, the baby would sometimes cry out; she in her frustration would join in, giving the spectators around a good show on their way to work. There'd be a few sarcastic comments, but when it came time to get off, they'd do what they could, usually with a helpful shove to push her out the door.

It wasn't much, but that small gesture consoled her to know there was some warmth in the world. Lao Li was the kind of person who could pick out the goodness in anything and blow it up into a balloon of patience and restraint. She didn't have much time to write letters and often just sent a postcard with the baby's footprint pressed on back in colored ink. Over time, Lao Wang's stack of increasingly larger footprints grew, and with it, food for her imagination.

These two women worked out a thousand and one intricate ways to pass messages. Creative, perceptive — they knew how to capture and convey the most intimate feelings. If their paths had not crossed a second time, they would have lost the touch, for to live in this crude world, they'd been forced to steel themselves with courage and cunning. Sensitivity had no place. Their men had knuckled under in the process, becoming somewhat like women, and if not for their mutual inspiration, they themselves would have folded into complete boorishness. Together they cultivated a small plot of tender, tenuous flowers — flowers that over time grew tall and hardy. They sent each other beautiful hand-made birthday cards inscribed with hidden meanings, and when they didn't have time to write, they simply directed each other to a particular line in a book. When Lao Wang found "Finally, that which I have been anxiously anticipating has occurred," she knew Lao Li's baby was sick again. And when Lao Li read "A girl's worry; her husband leaves home to make his fortune," [19] she knew Lao Wang's husband had gone away again on business. Their husbands, had they known about this little game, would have teased them to no end. But they didn't give them the chance. They wrote to each other at school and never mentioned a word of it at home.

V

Feeling responsible for her godson, Lao Wang went back to Shanghai during winter vacation. She'd picked up her needles again and knitted several little winter outfits, which she tried on the baby first thing through the door, working him up into a fit of agitation. Having come this time as the "godmother," she reclined comfortably on the sofa and chattered idly all the day, without so much as lifting a finger to help around the house. She didn't sleep at night and spent her mornings in bed buried under a quilt while Lao Li's husband ate his breakfast and got ready to go to work. Sleep being contagious, Lao Li soon picked up the habit as well. The two women huddled every night on the bed with the baby between them and whispered to all hours. Lao Li's husband, on the sofa now due to the cold weather, had the feeling, listening to them talk through the night and watching them sleep through the morning, that they weren't quite normal. It didn't matter generally — he could get his breakfast and leave. Out of sight, out of mind. But Sunday, when the sun shone high in the sky, he felt a clutching irritation looking down at the two sleeping women and clutter all over the place. He couldn't get a thing done in that mess. Lao Wang was their guest; it would be wrong to show his anger, but when he couldn't stand it a minute longer, he finally said: *Rise and shine, ladies. It's almost noon.* The two bodies shifted slightly in their nest. *IT'S ALMOST NOON!* he yelled. The clear, light explosion of mirth beneath the covers told him they hadn't been sleeping after all, merely lying there in quiet repose. That irritated him all the more.

Lao Li fussed less over her son with Lao Wang around. They took him along to the art museum on a windy day, but he was perfectly fine, didn't even get sick, as if he knew they weren't worried about him anyway. That made Lao Li's husband all the angrier. He thought he could see witchcraft in Lao Wang; a light brush up against her and his woman had gone mad. Nothing came out right anymore — whenever she went in the kitchen, every dish his wife tried to cook was burned. Unfortunately, there was no chance of her leaving soon. The school holiday had just begun, and she showed no sign of going home early. He came up with the idea of inviting Lao Wang's husband, thinking that after so many years of married life, he of all people ought to know how to deal with her. My life was so peaceful before, he thought, but it's fallen apart since she's been around. He could see the power this woman exerted over his wife and knew, that without his wife's own deep undercurrent, she'd be incapable of stirring up so much trouble — they wouldn't even be friends. How strange, he thought, in this whole wide world these two would have to meet. Their luck was just too good. Though his suggestion surprised them at first, it wasn't long before their excitement caught on. *What a great idea!* they said. The only problem is where to sleep. *Don't worry about that,* Lao Li's husband said; *I'll take the bamboo couch and Lao Wang's husband can have the sofa. It'll be a little crowded, but that'll make it all the more fun. What's New Year's without a big crowd!* Lao Wang wanted to go that very night to send a telegram; Lao Li wanted to go along. *Go ahead,* said her husband; *I'll stay home and watch the baby.* The two women rushed excitedly out the door and straight for the telegraph office. When Lao Wang's husband got the express telegram at three the next morning, he thought at first something must be wrong, but taking a second look, he realized it was only an invitation. The morning of New Year's Eve he squeaked up the stairs to Lao Li's apartment, his arms loaded with Nanjing pressed duck, roast chicken and other Spring Festival[20] treats.

Lao Li's husband felt a certain closeness to Lao Wang's husband from the start. He asked, and found out they'd gone to the same high school — that gave them something to talk about. He didn't know whether it was having her husband around or just the psychological effect, but he felt somehow that Lao Wang was more under control. She went to the market that afternoon to buy celery for the squid and asked not Lao Li, but her husband, to go with her. She even helped with preparations for their New Year's Eve meal and made a few egg dumplings, twisting the skins into crazy shapes. He listened with satisfaction as her husband sternly reminded her she was a guest in someone else's home, and realized then everything he disliked about her had to do with the way she'd moved in and treated their home as if it were her own. Seeing what a polite, sensible man her husband was helped him forgive Lao Wang; and sitting around the New Year's table later that evening, he agreed to join her in a drinking game. Lao Wang's husband watched his wife's flailing arms and threatening gestures with secret amazement. Why was she so happy? All the gloomy restlessness that plagued her in Nanjing had drained away; she looked like she'd come home to a place she belonged. He scrutinized Lao Li and her husband, thinking first there must be something with the husband, but he saw the polite way he treated her and realized the cold distance there. Turning his attention then to Lao Li, he saw the indulgence and warm, encouraging looks, even when his wife was at her wildest. He remembered the night the two women talked until dawn and thought: Yes, these two really have something good! But what is it? He sat to one side thinking while Lao Wang, her face flushed bright pink from the wine, bent over with laughter, shouting: *Enough! Enough!* Lao Li tried to get her to play one more time. *Now you're both out to get me!* she cried. They fell over each other in hysterics. When the ruckus died down, they took several deep breaths and got on to the serious business of talking. The two women talked about themselves; the men talked about the two women. Now that Lao Wang's husband is here, Lao Li's husband reflected, at least I have someone to talk to. I don't have to sit and watch them perform. The women said: *Another year has flown by, just like that.* The men said: *Another year is about to begin.* The women said: *Last year we didn't get much done. What should we do next year?* The men said: *What a hectic year, and another's already upon us.* The women said: *The New Year's TV show is getting worse every year.* The men said: *It's never as good as it was before.* The women turned and laughed: *Why are you talking about the same things we are?* The men laughed back: *You're the ones copying us!* They all broke into laughter and turned again to their conversations. Lao Wang and Lao Li began to make plans for an art show. They'd call it "Brothers" and hold it in Nanjing or Shanghai. Thinking about the money they'd need to rent a hall and print tickets and brochures, they sunk into a discouraged silence. They drank some more wine, picked at the food on the table and listened to the men talk about politics. Then they got going again. They'd found a solution to the money problem: they'd teach art classes to finance their show, charging fifty *yuan* a student for one semester. The only problem was, once they got the tuition money, they'd have to teach for six months. They'd be ready financially but have nothing to hang on the walls. Besides, at fifty *yuan* a student, they'd be getting only five hundred for ten, five thousand for a hundred. Could the two of them take on a hundred students? What about their jobs? Their eyes gleamed at the thought of quitting — work was such a nuisance, day after day, month after month, year after year. Thrilled by the thought of leaving it forever, they wondered why they'd put up with so many years of torment before coming to this solution. Quitting would mean freedom to do whatever they liked — freedom, for example, to hold an art show. But that brought them back to the problem of money. Quitting would also mean one less salary around the house, and that would mean difficulty just getting by. A short depression hit before they came up with a new idea: they'd go into the countryside to paint and photograph the peasants. They'd go to Guangxi, Sichuan, Yunnan,[21] or to the west — Shaanxi, Qinghai, Tibet![22] They argued briefly over which route to take, but then put it aside to continue with their plan: they'd have something to show when they returned, they'd have money, they'd even have pictures for a photo exhibit. Intoxicated by their dream and having found hope and purpose on the eve of the New Year, they drank glass after glass of celebratory beer. At midnight, when the bang of firecrackers exploded through the sky, they tied their string to a bamboo pole and held it through the window to join the roaring symphony outside. Coughing back the smoke, they laughed and laughed, thinking: What a lucky New Year's this is!

Lao Wang's husband had to leave on the fourth day of Spring Festival; he had to get back to work. Lao Wang said classes wouldn't start for another week so she'd stay a couple more days. Lao Li's husband looked expectantly at Lao Wang's husband, waiting for him to say something, but to his surprise and disappointment, he didn't force the issue. It was a long, depressing day, as if they'd celebrated too hard for too long. No one talked much or felt like cooking. They heated up some leftovers, ate a little and went to bed early. The two women whispered on the bed for a while before dropping off, and though the TV next door blared on into the night, his house was perfectly still. Depression hung over Lao Li and Lao Wang that evening for some reason. They sensed something was wrong—somehow they'd made a mistake, missed some opportunity, but didn't quite know what. They sensed some small regret but couldn't lay their finger on it.

Up bright and early the next morning, the two women bustled about making breakfast and cleaning the room. Lao Li's husband went to work in a good mood. It was a beautiful day outside. *Let's take the baby for a walk in the park,* Lao Wang suggested. Lao Li thought it was a fine suggestion, so the two set off with the baby in the stroller. The park was quiet—only a few old folks practicing *taijiquan* [23] and some young parents playing with their children. They sat down on a bench facing the sun, stroller at their side. Threads of white cloud floated above in the deep blue; early winter jasmine dotted the branches with tiny yellow blossoms; the ground around the tree roots had already begun to thaw; birds filled the air with their morning songs. Happiness gradually opened their hearts, and as they relaxed, they began to talk. *If only we could go on like this forever,* they said. *Why can't time just stop altogether? New Year's was great, a lot of fun really, but too noisy, too many people. How seldom we get the chance to sit down quietly, just the two of us! Good thing I didn't go back to Nanjing,* Lao Wang said. *That's right,* Lao Li agreed, *it's a good thing.* Their earlier unease seemed unreal, a figment of their imagination—everything was in fact perfectly normal, perfectly fine. Suddenly they grew excited and said, as they'd repeated so oft before, how lucky they were to have met and found each other again. How dismal life would be without each other! Their friendship, they realized, had helped them preserve something poetic, something which had almost been eroded away by their dull, uninspiring days, something which had been ignored in the material world they shared with their husbands. Coming together, they'd recovered the poetry, without which, their dismal days would have grown even more depressing. Men were such monsters! Pragmatists all, they knew only goals, end results; they had no appreciation for process, the path to those goals. Shocked at what they'd always taken for a granted, they thought about how men led women racing along that path, the scenery slipping by before they could get a good look. Men, they admitted, were far more realistic — a short rest to smell the flowers or a jaunt through a green meadow would mean straggling behind the pack. Beautiful fantasies can't exist without a solid material base. The men are out there struggling for something real, if only to protect the dreams and poetic illusions of women, they mused tenderly; that in itself is a great sacrifice. It's the women's job to hold ground and keep those dreams intact — men have already done their share. They lingered thoughtfully for a moment over this idea, then with a start, realized they were wrong: Men hadn't taken on the whole struggle at all. They'd borne up only half and left the rest to women. It was by joining the fight that women's spirituality had been lost. They felt resentment but knew they couldn't blame men entirely, thinking: It really is a social problem. In any case, they could keep each other on track and help each other from withering away further. That's why our friendship is so important. That's why we must cherish it forever. So pure and noble, free from sexual motivation, it relied solely upon their rational minds; it lay in the higher realm of human existence. Lao Wang suddenly came up with a crazy idea. *What would we do,* she asked Lao Li, *if we both fell in love with the same man?* Lao Li thought for a while before answering: *I'd let you have him.* Lao Wang persisted: *I'm talking about a love so strong you could never let go.* Lao Li replied: *Then we'd have to kill him.* Tears sprang to Lao Wang's eyes. They didn't know it, but they'd already pushed the conversation, like their relationship, to a precarious point of no return.

Neither was paying attention to the baby. Excited by the blue sky and bright sunshine, he'd pulled himself upright, and bouncing gaily, was rocking the stroller back and forth. It tilted with each bounce, as if to spill its contents to the ground, but righted itself every time. He loved the terror of the moment, the adventure, and tried again to create that precipitous point where danger fell back to safety. Gradually he worked out a law of balance and return, but

204

he wanted more, and bouncing harder, he increased the angle of tilt, pushing himself closer to the edge. He was lucky; that point never came. His game eventually began to bore him, but though he wanted to stop, he'd gotten so used to the motion, he couldn't control himself. Rocking carelessly, he poised on the verge of tipping, then let the vehicle settle upright again. The sun shone like a big warm wheel overhead; drowsiness filled him, his body moving mechanically as before. The stroller finally tipped and deposited him on the soft, muddy ground. There was very little danger of injury—as he fell, he knew only a sudden intense moment of happiness. But the soft flesh near his eye was cut by an exposed tree root, and the flow of blood blocked out his vision. It didn't hurt, but the blinding red terrified him, and realizing that something critical had happened, he let loose a great cry.

The two women turned to find him sprawled on the ground in a pool of blood. *MY BABY!* Lao Li screamed, sending a tremor through Lao Wang. She stared at her friend—the ashen-faced woman with clenched teeth and arched eyebrows at her side wasn't anyone she knew. Lao Li rushed to pick him up, but when the unwieldy bundle of heavy winter clothes got caught in the stroller, she panicked. Her loose hair swept across her face and brushed through the child's blood, painting her face like a demon. Lao Wang moved over to help, but Lao Li turned on her. *DON'T TOUCH MY BABY!* she screamed angrily. Lao Wang gasped, her heart torn to shreds, but ignoring the pain, did what she could by righting the fallen stroller. Lao Li sat down with the bleeding baby in her lap. Peaceful in the safe world of his mother, he gazed quietly at the blue sky. She pressed along his brow to find the wound, her own face sketched in blood. When her hand came up dripping, she broke into a long hoarse wail. The gathering crowd tried to calm her and helped her find the spot, but when she saw the fragile white bone exposed through the pink flesh, she cried again, stamping her feet in frenzy. Somebody gave her a handkerchief to press against his head and told her there was a hospital behind the park. Somebody else offered to show the way, and, grabbing the baby, sprinted with him toward the back gate. Lao Li staggered behind, wailing like a peasant woman. Lao Wang kept up the rear, pulling the stroller in her wake. She wanted to give Lao Li a shoulder to lean on — but didn't dare, sensing the terrible force of her hate. Lao Li obviously blamed her for the accident. She'd accepted the help of strangers, let someone she'd never seen before run off with her child, and yet had screamed at Lao Wang: *DON'T TOUCH MY BABY!* Those angry words reverberated again and again. If only there was something she could do, something to make up for her nameless crime, but Lao Li wouldn't give her the chance. She tried to pull Lao Li out of the way of an approaching truck, but Lao Li waved her arms and shoved her back with such force she almost fell. Regaining her balance, she saw Lao Li miraculously cross to the other side, the rushing stream of cars closing behind. She waited until the traffic eased, then crossed and followed her at a distance, knowing with bitter chagrin that a hugely important part of her life was slipping away.

The baby was stitched up and sleeping quietly at home before Lao Li fully regained her senses. She paced the room, her cheeks flushed bright red like a tuberculosis patient, reaching out the window periodically to check the clothes, then lifting the thermos to check the water, then back to the window again. Lao Wang huddled in the corner; she wished she'd relax and stop wasting her energy, but didn't dare say so. Lao Li seemed to have forgotten about her anyway — she never glanced in her direction. The baby slept all the while, a finger in his mouth, white gauze wrapped round his head like a little hero. The squeak of footsteps on the stair sent panic through the room; their eyes met, and in that moment, they saw the tremendous gulf already separating them. They watched the door with pounding hearts, an ominous foreboding filling the silence. He came in and glanced around at the peaceful scene — food on the table, baby asleep, clean, quiet — a welcome sight he'd missed for weeks. *Let's eat!* he called to them cheerily, sitting down to taste the vegetables. He was waiting for his wife to tell him to go wash his hands, but when she didn't react, he had to get up and do it himself. That minor disappointment didn't spoil his mood. He walked happily back to the table and called to them again. *Just think,* he said to Lao Wang, *your husband's eating all alone right now. What's wrong? Aren't either of you hungry? Here, I'll put rice in your bowls ... but you're not going to get me to feed you! Ha, ha, ha!* He laughed heartily at his own joke. They finally stood up, and walking slowly toward the table, glanced again at each other. In that look they saw the fear. Hate filled them, but it was a nameless hate, something they couldn't lay their finger on. Lao Wang straightened up and said in a loud voice: *We had an accident today. The baby....* Spinning around, Lao Li's husband saw the gauze bandage. *What exactly happened?* he asked, slowly putting down his chopsticks. Lao Wang told the whole story, beginning to end, then stood there before him, head held high like a martyr facing execution.

Lao Li's husband felt his blood run hot, then cold. He thought: They tricked me into this good mood. I walked right into their trap. He thought: They ruin everything. Tonight, just like every other night, has been destroyed because of them. CRASH! He hurled his rice bowl to the floor. Lao Wang jumped in surprise. She turned around to look at Lao Li, who by this time had backed up to the edge of the bed and was sitting there as if in shock. *What's that supposed to mean?* she said evenly, holding back her anger; *It was an accident! What little kid hasn't grown up without a few knocks and scrapes?* Lao Li's husband laughed sarcastically: *Well then, you mean to say it's perfectly fine that he fell? I even ought to* thank *you for it!* Lao Wang responded in a chilling voice: *You certainly don't need to thank me, but you shouldn't blame me either. I didn't make your child fall.* A pang of grief shot through her as she uttered those words, "your child." She knew that Lao Li, watching apathetically as they exchanged verbal blows, wasn't about to help her out — hat hurt as well. Lao Li's husband snapped out of control. Ever since this woman's come into our life, he thought, I haven't had a day of peace. *Yes, I'll blame YOU!* he yelled, pointing his finger at Lao Wang's nose. *This isn't fair —* Lao Wang started to say, but her voice caught in her throat. She couldn't cry now. She had to defend herself. But no words came out. Her lips shook with the strain of holding back the tears. Her face contorted into a mask of restraint. This woman is repulsive, thought Lao Li's husband. Why does she always hang around here? This isn't her home! Why doesn't she just leave? His last thought he yelled straight in her face: *GET OUT!* When she heard that, her tears dried and she forced a laugh. *I will not,* she said in a trembling voice; *This room isn't only yours.* She then turned and seated herself on the sofa, shooting a glance at Lao Li for support, but Lao Li, deaf to all around her, sat silently on the bed patting the baby with one hand. He was awake now, quietly sucking his hand. Lao Wang curled into a ball and stared at Lao Li's back. *It's over, Lao Li, finished,* she cried out in her heart. Tears fell and rinsed over her face. She didn't move from the sofa that night. Lao Li's husband took the bamboo couch. Lao Li and the baby had the bed alone. No one slept, all busy with their own thoughts. Lao Li's husband began to regret the way he'd acted. A little excessive, he thought. He'd lost control in the fury of the moment, but there was no way he was going to apologize. Lao Li, it seemed, had transformed that day into a perfectly mediocre housewife — not a thought in her head but for the baby. Each time she got up in the night to give him water, take his temperature, give him his medicine, she could see Lao Wang's eyes glittering at her from across the dark room like a cat.

The next morning Lao Li's husband ate his breakfast and left. Lao Wang didn't move from the sofa; when Lao Li called her over to eat, she just gave her a strange look. Lao Li sighed and put the breakfast things away, then sat on the bed to crochet a cashmere jacket for the baby, who, having long forgotten his adventures of the day before, was playing happily on the bed with a thick wooden knife. Sunshine filled the room. Lao Wang sat, ashen-faced. Could she be sick? Lao Li thought anxiously. She tried to strike up a conversation, but Lao Wang said nothing in return, giving only a slight nod or shake of the head in response. Lao Li gradually remembered what she'd screamed at the time of the accident and the fight with her husband. She felt awful. She wanted to explain herself but didn't know where to begin. She felt like she'd been through something terrible, but didn't know what it was. All she knew was that it had happened, and there might be no going back. She tried to approach Lao Wang, wanting to smooth her short boyish hair like she'd done in the past, but those fierce bright eyes forced her back every time. At noon she fixed some noodles. Lao Wang didn't touch hers, and after taking a few uninterested bites, she cleaned up and put everything away. Later that afternoon, when the baby was asleep, she said to Lao Wang: *Will you watch the baby for me? I have to go buy some things.* She then rushed out the door before Lao Wang had a chance to reply and raced downstairs to the street, where she frantically wondered what she should buy. She decided on a roll of toilet paper, but then realized she'd come away without any money. That was her way of apologizing to Lao Wang for yesterday's *DON'T TOUCH MY BABY!* She walked once around the block, bright with sunshine, and went home to find the baby sound asleep where she'd left him and Lao Wang motionless on the couch. Approaching uneasily, she asked in a gentle voice: *Don't you want a little something to eat?* Lao Wang shook her head, eyes glittering. At dusk she finally rose to brush her hair and wash her face. She set the table for dinner, and as soon as Lao Li's husband walked through the door, she sat down without a greeting and began to eat. Their sleeping arrangement that night was as before, Lao Li's husband happily taking the hard, bumpy bamboo couch by way of apology to Lao Wang. Three days passed. Lao Wang spoke not a word to Lao Li but did say a few things to her husband. He answered every time quickly and respectfully, as if receiving a great unexpected favor.

Lao Wang prepared to leave, as according to her original plan, on the tenth day of the New Year. Lao Li said she'd see her off to the station. She didn't get a reply, but when she reached out for her bag, Lao Wang let go. They then walked single file out the door to the bus stop. On the bus and off again, neither spoke. Silently they crossed the square, blown cold by a raw spring wind, remembering the day in Nanjing when Lao Wang had taken Lao Li to the station. They looked away to avoid each other's eyes. Lao Li walked with her to the platform entrance, and seeing that she was about to go in, suddenly grabbed her arm and yanked her out of line. *LET GO OF ME!* Lao Wang yelled, struggling to get free. The crowd looked on, but Lao Li paid no attention to their curious, derisive eyes. She held firm with two hands and said: *I love you. You've got to believe me, I do love you!* They'd never used that word before, that word fouled and corrupted by sexual liaison. Tears sprang to Lao Wang's eyes. *It's too late. Do you hear me, IT'S TOO LATE!* she shouted. *No, it's not. It's not too late, it's not....* Lao Li was also crying. *Yes it is,* Lao Wang's tears streamed like two rivers. *Some things,* she said, *some beautiful things are very fragile. Once they've been destroyed, that's it, forever—we can never get them back.* Shaking her arm free, she pushed through the booth and disappeared into the crowd.

They never saw each other after that. Several years later, when the trauma had passed, Lao Wang took a boat trip alone through the Yangtze River Three Gorges.[24] She remembered how on that New Year's Eve they'd promised to make the trip together and how they'd made plans for an art show called "Brothers." Smiling to herself, she shook her head, as if to make the past go away. She changed jobs several times in the past couple years but has never really been satisfied. To this day, she doesn't know what it is she's looking for. Her boat worked its way through the narrow gorge, the rock walls plunging skyward to a narrow strip of blue.

Notes

1. Literally, "Eldest," "Second" and "Third," these nicknames are commonly applied to the boys in one family to distinguish birth order. In so naming themselves, the three women take ownership of this conventional male model and proclaim their bond to be as tight as "brothers."
2. Women are sometimes referred to as so-and-so's "family."
3. Lei Feng was a People's Liberation Army (PLA) soldier in the late 1950s who gained a reputation of performing selfless works for others. Mao Zedong's famous phrase "Learn from Lei Feng," uttered at Lei's death in 1963, has since been resurrected as a slogan to encourage

sacrifice for the benefit of the country.

4. In China, the right to live in cities is controlled by the Household Registration Bureau. All urban residents must hold a city registration permit, which is arranged through the work unit, school or neighborhood committee.

5. Henan Province is located in the heart of the country, south of the Yellow River.

6. During the Cultural Revolution (1966-1976), Mao Zedong called on urban youth to go "up to the mountains and down to the countryside" to learn from the peasants and bring revolution into the rural areas. (See Note 5 of the Introduction for more on the Cultural Revolution.)

7. The Shenzhen Special Economic Zone, a former village on the border with Hong Kong, has in the past decade of economic reforms burgeoned into a modern high-rise city of joint-ventures and job opportunities for aspiring youth.

8. Calligraphy practice of large characters requiring a certain amount of physical exertion.

9. *Youtiao* are strips of dough, deep-fried until golden; *doujiang* is soy milk. The two are often eaten together for breakfast.

10. In reference to their years during the chaotic Cultural Revolution. (See Note 4 of the Introduction for more on the Cultural Revolution.)

11. Friends often call each other by last names, using the customary "Lao," meaning "old" or "Xiao," meaning "little" or "young," to denote familiarity.

12. *Garrma* refers to a close friend of the mother, who, though has no legal responsibility, treats the child as her own.

13. Chinese traditionally believe that when a woman gives birth she has used up "half her life." Strict measures are required to bring her back to strength in a period of postnatal confinement. She and the new baby must stay indoors for the first month; windows and doors are shut against drafts; she is not allowed to take a bath, wash her hair or eat anything cold for fear of catching a chill.

14. 34 degrees centigrade is equal to about 95 degrees Fahrenheit.

15. Chinese customarily invite family and friends for a celebratory meal at the baby's first month to mark the end of postnatal confinement.

16. Three seaside resort towns along the east coast of China.

17. Formerly known to Westerners as Canton, Guangzhou lies just north of Hong Kong in Guangdong Province.

18. Harbin is a major industrial city in the northeastern province of Heilongjiang.

19. Taken from *The Dream of Red Mansions*. Bao Yu, the central character in this mid-eighteenth century novel, composes a poem in which he borrows lines from the Tang Dynasty poet Wang Changling.

20. Chinese New Year, marking the onset of spring on the lunar calendar, is also known as Spring Festival.

21. Guangxi Zhuang Autonomous Region, Sichuan Province and Yunnan

P rovince are located in southwestern China.

22. Shaanxi Province, Qinghai and Tibet are located in the far west.

23. A Chinese martial art employing slow, graceful movements and regular breathing. Also known as "shadow boxing," *taijiquan* is a favorite form of exercise among older people.

24. The stretch along the Yangtze River between Yichang (Hubei Province) and Fengjie (Sichuan Province) is known for its spectacular scenery, distinguished by sheer rock walls lining the narrow ravine.

You Can't Make Me Change

Liu Xihong

A friend told me about Lingkai, saying, "She's a strange one."

And said, "She wants to meet you. She always points you out and tells me I have to introduce her to you."

I smiled. My friend's an unimaginative type who can't handle anything out of the ordinary. "Why?" I asked. "Why is she set on meeting me?" Nothing but trouble comes from trying to be someone's teacher. That's not for me. And I'm not the kind who likes to play older sister or confidant. I haven't got it in me to show a young girl how to live.

But I said, "We can get together if she likes. Set a time."

Lingkai showed up a whole hour early, way off the mark. I rolled out of bed, and folding up my blanket, went to open the door.

There stood a sixteen-year-old girl — typical Cantonese face, features etched clearly within the rounded contour of jaw and brow. Her delicate mouth could excite passion.

I let her in. She walked over to my best chair and sat down, crossing her legs at the knee. I looked at her closely. She wasn't exactly a crane among chickens, but she was attractive. That skin made me think of the young girls in Renoir's paintings.

But her hair had been cropped so short you could see the sideburn. I frowned.

"Have you had breakfast?" I asked in Cantonese.

"A glass of milk."

"Have another."

"No thanks."

I left her with a pile of magazines and went into the kitchen to get something to eat.

By the time I got back, she'd messed up my stack of newspaper clippings, pulled open my desk drawer and was examining my six-color lipstick set. Nothing had prepared me for this.

"Hey!" she yelled. "You like natural tones too."

I forced a smile and sat down.

"You smoke?" she picked up a pack of cigarettes.

I shook my head. "A friend left them behind."

"Boyfriend?"

"Yes, my boyfriend."

"Oh...." Lingkai pondered this for awhile then asked, "What's his name?"

"Yidong. You know him?"

She shook her head. "What's his last name?"

I'd had about enough of this. "Who are you? The Household Registration Bureau?"[1]

She wouldn't let it drop. "What is it?"

"Liu. His name is Liu Yidong,[2] for Christ's sake!"

"Ah...." Lingkai peered at me strangely. "You have the same last name. The same last name! Don't you know close relatives can't get married?"

I didn't know whether to laugh or cry. "What makes you think we're related?"

"How d'ya know you're not?"

"I don't have a big family. I know every single one of my relatives by their first name."

"How d'ya know he's not your long-lost brother?"

"Listen, little sister, I was born in 1953. A new life had just begun. Families got along. The new government was pushing for everyone to have lots of kids, and women were all trying to outdo each other as mother-heroes. We didn't have problems of infanticide and child abandonment back then."

I reached over and patted her cheek. "Besides, we're just friends. It doesn't mean we're getting married. Alright? Can we let it drop now?"

She said nothing. For a long time. Then with amazing

214

speed, she pulled a cigarette from the pack, lit it and exhaled an experienced breath of white smoke.

"You smoke?" I stared at her in panic. "How can you?"

"Do you believe in love?" she asked, solemn as a Taoist priest.

"Lingkai," I pulled my face back to normal, "I'm happy to have you come visit me, and I'm glad you can make yourself at home, but the least you can do is ask whether or not you can smoke in my room."

Snuffing out the cigarette, she repeated her question, "You have a boyfriend. Do you really believe there's something called love?"

"Yes," I answered without a moment's hesitation.

"That's weird. Older people never believe in love. My mom doesn't."

So she was equating me with her mother. "Your mom?" I muttered indignantly, "Do you really think someone as old as your mother would still believe in love? Love is for the young. It's especially sweet at your age," I smiled.

"But I don't believe in it."

"Love is like soap bubbles. When you blow them out and fill the sky, it's really there, a whole sky full of color. But when they pop and there's nothing left, you stop believing. People like your mother make the mistake of not believing in something they had before just because they haven't got it now. They don't understand the soap bubble theory.

"I'm blowing now and have been for a long time. I do believe in love," I added.

"A whole sky full?"

"A whole sky full." I chuckled. "If they ever disappear, I won't have anybody but myself to blame for not blowing. Why do you want to know? You shouldn't be worrying about these things."

She smiled good-naturedly at me, eyes narrowed intently as if turning something over in her mind.

"When I was your age, I studied hard like I was supposed to. If I went to a classmate's house in the evening, I

215

told my parents. If they said to be in at nine, I didn't dare get back at a quarter after. Not like kids now," I said. "You've all got bikes to ride to school, watches, even lipstick, permed hair."

"What about it? It's not like we're doing anything wrong," Lingkai retorted. "You're too uptight."

Our conversation had taken an outrageous turn. "Uptight? You want to know what uptight is? Uptight is saying people with the same last name can't get married!"

We threw back our heads and laughed out loud together.

"You're different than most people. I like you," Lingkai announced when it was quiet again.

I managed a tight little smirk. This *was* outrageous. I was letting a sixteen-year-old evaluate my character.

"You even know how to smile without showing your teeth. That's really great!"

Laughter burst from my throat, teeth all out in the open.

"I ask too many questions, don't I? Are you mad at me?" she grinned guilelessly.

"No, I'm not mad at you. I know you grew up reading *A Hundred Thousand Answers to Why*. Passion for learning when young is normal. How could I be mad at you?"

When it came time for her to leave, I walked her to the door. "Aren't you going to see me off downstairs?" she wanted to know.

"I never walk my guests downstairs. Come and see me anytime, Lingkai."

"You see what I mean...." She looked dejected. "You're too uptight."

"You can't call this uptight. Look what I've got on. I can't go running around outside in my pajamas. I'm a civilized person, you know."

She flung her head back and with a you-are-absolutely-impossible tone, stated emphatically, "You still don't get it. That's just what I mean by uptight!"

I pressed her small hand in mine. Warm and soft, it felt nice. "I like you too. Come and see me often."

"You should tell me if there's anything special you want me to do."

I thought for awhile before replying: "I want you to do well in school. If you're smart, you'll study hard. And let your hair grow out. I can't tell if you're a boy or girl with it like that. Girls your age look good with long hair."

She nodded, eyes wide.

"One more thing — don't smoke." I suddenly felt I had the right to tell her what to do. I liked her and could almost imagine myself being responsible for her, taking care of her like a legal guardian. "I won't allow you to smoke."

"It's not like it's a habit or anything," she interrupted in a soft voice. "Just once in awhile. It helps calm my nerves."

"I don't care. I won't allow it," I persisted. "It looks terrible. Besides, advertisements all over the world say that smoking is bad for you!"

Lingkai called me at the hospital just before quitting time on Saturday. I was adding the last ingredients to a complicated prescription of Chinese herbs when the phone rang. I ignored it to go over the list again and carefully wrap the small bundle in paper. Finished, I walked over to the phone.

"Are you busy?" She obviously wasn't pleased to have been kept waiting. "Let's go out for *dim sum*[3] tomorrow morning."

I thought about it. "No, tomorrow's a bad day. I have something to do. But let's go another time. I'll treat."

"You don't have to pay for me. We can go dutch to the revolving restaurant."

"Go dutch? Absolutely not. You're a student. You don't have any money. Let me take you out. It's just tomorrow I'm busy."

"I do too have money! Why can't you go tomorrow? Why?"

"Lingkai, if there's something you want to talk about, come over to my room. You're a student, for goodness sake! What do you know about revolving restaurants? Put your time into your studies; if you've got extra money, buy some of those self-study magazines...."

"So is it yes or no?"

217

"No. I already told you I'm busy."

"You're getting together with Liu Yidong, aren't you?"

"No."

"I'm sure! If you don't want to go, just forget it. You're so boring."

"Shut your smart little mouth, Lingkai. You're too big for your britches. I have an exam coming up next month and a huge pile of books to get through. I don't intend to be a third-rate pharmacist for the rest of my life."

Silence.

"Hey," I said, "Where are you calling from? Are classes out? Don't call me from school. Teachers think students who are always on the phone don't really care about...."

"Click." The line went dead.

There was nothing I could do.

Lingkai didn't show on Sunday. I waited for her all day. Nor on Monday.

I took my exam. She still didn't come.

I began to get anxious, wondering where she could be. I didn't know where she lived and thought better of looking for her at school. What could she be up to? That little rascal. When I had nothing better to do, I'd write her name over and over again on a scrap of paper... Lingkai, Lingkai, Lingkai....

I had to leave town for a six-month study course. Yidong came in the afternoon to help with my luggage.

"Don't write unless there's something important," he was saying, squatting down to lock my trunk. "I'm too busy to think. My work's piled up all the way through the end of the year...."

Lingkai appeared at the door.

"Lingkai!" I called out in happy surprise.

A disheveled circle of hair hung around her face like the fringe on a stray puppy. I put my arm around her neck and pulled her over. Why the disappearing act? What have you been doing? You waited so long to come around, and I'm just about to go away....

"I've been busy," she answered, looking at Yidong.

Busy, busy, busy. Everyone says they're busy. Too busy to do anything. I'm the only one with nothing to do.

Yidong straightened up and clapped his hands free of dust. "Kong Lingkai," he said.

Lingkai, you're famous. Everybody knows you.

Yidong turned to me, "You don't know? Your friend is a model in the third art studio at the Youth Palace."

A model?! That was news to me.

"I know who you are too!" Lingkai shouted. "You work in the advertising agency on the sixth floor of the Youth Palace. I've seen you carry billboards up to the roof like any old worker. I never would have guessed *you* were Liu Yidong." She gave me a look to say: this is the best you can do? He does *that* kind of work?

"Very tough," Yidong laughed. "No wonder your boss goes around complaining about you. Do you argue with them about everything?"

I couldn't join their laughter. Lingkai, a model in an art studio?

"Do you still smoke? I've got a pack around here somewhere," Yidong offered.

I was furious. "Lingkai! You still smoke? What did I tell you!"

Without so much as a glance in my direction, she replied indifferently, "When I sit for a long time and can't move, all my muscles turn to stone. I wouldn't be able to walk home if I didn't have a cigarette. Besides, I always go down to the restroom."

Still angry. "Are you going to listen to me or not? Who told you to go and be a model anyway? Are you going to buckle down and study like you should? Are you going to ever grow up and be somebody?"

"But I *am* doing well in school. My grades are fine. I even got to the third round of finals in the physics competition last June. Why can't I model if I've got the time? It's not getting in the way of anything else."

"So you've got all the time and money in the world to go to some revolving restaurant, is that it? Do you have any idea what I think of modeling? Why don't you go find a job pulling a hand cart? Why don't you set up a booth and sell carmabola [4] by the side of the road?"

Yidong tapped the table with his middle finger. "Alright, alright. Enough. I have to go now." He shouldered the trunk to be shipped and walked out.

Lingkai and I went out on the balcony. He called up from the street: "I'll send someone over with the receipt for your trunk. I don't have time to come back with it."

"Whatever," I shrugged.

Lingkai stood behind me, hands on her hips, eyes cast down, like a music star surveying the crowd.

"I noticed him a long time ago, but I thought he was at *least* forty." Lingkai followed me into the room.

"Don't be mean. He's only a couple years older."

"But you look a lot younger." Lingkai peered carefully into my face.

How depressing. "That's because all I do is sit around and eat."

"He works like a coolie. I once saw him on the tower putting up those decorative lights for the Cypress Clock. He was hanging there on the roof eight stories up like a kite.... God, it was dangerous."

That moved me. Yidong always took on the most difficult, most tiring, most dangerous work. Something about him touched me very deeply.

"Lingkai, tell me how you're doing. How've you been lately?"

She ignored my question. "Do you know why I like you? Because you don't treat me like a kid. You treat me like a friend, someone your own age. You know how to respect people."

Flattery. She was trying to seduce me. I answered tersely: "Friendship is of course based on mutual respect. I can respect almost anyone. That I can do."

We walked out into the street. The late sky was full of watery stars and a faint, milky moon. When I was little, the moon always shone big and bright. It would follow me as I walked along the lane by my house, from one end to the next.

My arm rested on Lingkai's shoulder. She was wearing a pink scoop-neck blouse and flat summer sandals. Everything about her reminded me of when I was young. Can anyone get back the past?

"There's a story in the Bible, in Luke, about a time when Jesus was out healing the sick," I began. "People were crowding around him, pressing in from all sides. A woman who'd used up her savings trying to cure the disease she'd suffered from for twelve years squeezed through the crowd and touched his belt. She was cured instantly. Jesus turned and asked, 'Who touched me?' but no one stepped forward. Peter said, 'There are so many people around you....' but Jesus insisted, 'No, someone touched me. I felt healing power leave my body.' The woman saw it was impossible to hide and kneeled down to tell Jesus her story. Jesus said to her, 'Daughter, your faith has healed you. Go in peace....'"

"It's important to have faith," Lingkai said. "Daughter, your faith has healed you," she repeated, looping her arm through mine.

"That's right."

We faced each other over yogurt in front of a small shop. I pointed out the Wangji Roast Goose Restaurant across the street, where the shopkeeper's family sat eating their dinner in the doorway under a street lamp. The grandmother, a baby slung across her lap, slurped soup from a bowl held high before her face. The young wife chattered about something between gulps of food; the shopkeeper picked at his teeth. Fat dripping from the roasted birds hanging in their cabinet glistened in the light of a high-watt bulb.

"I see that family eating dinner every night when I take my walk. They put out at least twenty *yuan* a meal," I told Lingkai.

She looked over at the cabinet of birds, her mouth watering. "It'd be great to sell roast goose. You could eat it everyday."

"Don't be a fool," I retorted. "Look at what they've got on the table. Their favorite dish is mouse-speckled carp. It's not cheap, that's for sure."

221

There was a time when Yidong and I were so poor we ate beef noodles and fish-head soup for dinner every night. That gets old fast.

"Come on, let's go. There's nothing to see here." We turned and walked away.

I could tell she had something on her mind. "Lingkai," I stopped walking to face her, "I know there's something you want to tell me."

"No there isn't." She couldn't hold my gaze; her eyes bounced off whatever moved.

"Yes there is."

"......"

"I'm treating you like a friend, someone my own age. Come on, talk," I urged.

"......"

"I'll respect what it is you have to say," I smiled at her.

"......"

"It's important to have faith. Daughter...."

"I want to be a model," she blurted out before I could finish my sentence.

"You...." Pause. I had to force the rest out. "You—already are a model, aren't you?"

"I want to quit school and become a fashion model at the Weimei Company."

I pulled her up short. "Become a model? How'd you come up with that idea? And what do you plan to do when you hit thirty? Don't you know models are a bunch of brainless ninnies? You're good at physics. You could study astronomy at Fudan University.[5] Astronomy! You've got a career ahead of you...."

Lingkai looked at me. And with an impatient edge to her voice, said: "I've already decided, so don't try to change my mind. I told you because I respect you. You can't make me change."

Shaking with agitation, she leaned against a telephone pole.

"Lingkai, I'll make a deal with you. If you promise to get your mind back on your studies and concentrate on getting into college, I'll give you a carton of Marlboros every month...." No sense of principle, I was practically begging her.

"I quit smoking a long time ago. It's not in anymore." She pushed off from the telephone pole with both hands and kicked a popsicle carton a few steps down the street. I followed.

"That's just great. You're young, you have everything ahead of you. Now's the time to study...."

She stopped and turned to face me. "My mom says it's okay. I don't see why anyone else should worry about it," she sneered.

The beauty school had put out an advertisement for ten new models. More than a thousand applicants, accompanied by mothers and husbands, had shown up for the try-outs. Things had taken a new turn — Lingkai didn't give a damn about what I thought. That made me mad.

"You're so out of it, it makes me sick," she said, turning her back on me, the corners of her mouth pulled tight.

I couldn't take it any longer. "Get out of here! You brainless fool, get out of my sight!"

But it was me who turned and walked away. Rounding the corner, I was hit with a wave of remorse. I was supposed to be the adult. And I'd promised to treat her with respect. Why was I being so unreasonable? Simply atrocious.

I looked back over my shoulder. The telephone pole stood alone.

But she really shouldn't go into modeling. It just wasn't right for her. Those wandering eyes drunk with laughter, that face, rich and full, like a good book waiting to be read. She was too expressive — a model hardly needed so much life in her eyes. Why a fashion model? I'd rather see her go into acting and become a movie star than waste her time like that.

I didn't go out that evening. I shut myself in early, turned off the light and fell asleep.

Lingkai was like a string of pearls in the palm of my hand. I'd held her carefully, I'd protected her, but now she was slipping through my fingers. It was very depressing.

I studied for a semester, a long, stifling semester.

Thoughts of Lingkai filled my free time.

Not a single letter from Yidong, just as he'd promised. A man of his own mind, he was not to be pushed around or wheedled, but no matter how long he ignored me, I'd never leave him for that. We understood each other. When my birthday came around, I knew he'd be there knocking at my door.

But Lingkai.

Lingkai was also a big part of my life.

Watermelon and lichee filled the markets by the time my training course was over. The sun held strong twelve hours a day; the air at three o'clock shone gold. I pulled a crate of books off the train, and waiting for the crowd to pass, rested a minute beside the luggage car. Yidong wouldn't be coming to meet me. He didn't even know I was back. But he *was* my boyfriend — meeting me at the station should have been his duty. Fanning myself with a handkerchief, I glared at the heavy box. In my anger, I almost missed the robust middle-aged couple walking up ahead: M'am, could I ask your husband to help me out a bit?

My room was the mess I'd left it six months ago. I'd given Yidong a key, but he naturally hadn't come around to straighten anything up. Naturally.

A layer of dust coated the chairs. I couldn't even sit down.

With a sweep of my arm, I brushed the clay dolls Yidong had given me from the desk. Those damn little toys were as stubborn as rocks; they clattered about crazily on the floor, then were silent, unscathed by their fall.

Crestfallen, I plumped down on the floor and kicked my feet up on the bed frame to let the blood flow. I popped open an icy cold beer, and tilting my head back, drank deeply. A soothing chill ran from my throat to lungs.

There was Lingkai at the door.

How did she know I was back? But she always did.

I flashed hot then cold, dazed and disoriented. She had on a bright red blouse and three-tiered pleated skirt. Her long hair hung loosely about her shining, rosy face.

I beckoned to her with a sloppy, pretend-drunk wave of

my hand. We huddled together like old long-lost friends.

"I saw your windows wide open, so I came up." Her mouth and eyes flashed in a brilliant smile.

I grinned back, stroking her silky strands.

She began to move quickly about straightening up the room. Boil some water. Plug in the fan. Let me do that; I jumped to my feet. We rushed around together. When we were finished, I filled a bowl with pumpkin seeds for us to snack on.

"Liu Yidong doesn't know you're back?"

"He was too lazy to even write."

"You guys have it tough. No home together, no room you can share. I bet Liu Yidong eats instant noodles everyday. You don't have anything."

For a moment I couldn't figure out what she was talking about. My smile faded as it sunk in. "We've got trust," I said.

"You're dreaming," she replied, "but you don't have to make up anything for my sake."

The little smart aleck. You certainly couldn't pass her off as a kid.

Yidong himself probably didn't think we had much in the way of trust. I know for a fact he didn't have a whole lot of faith in me. He sometimes looked at me like I was one of those women in the market who'll fight over a skirt on sale. He held himself at the center; he'd submit to no will but his own. It was useless to think of changing him. And for that, I loved him. But then again, I'm just a simple fool.

Lingkai had already cracked her way through most of the seeds. A mountain of shells piled high before her.

I covered the bowl with my hand. "Save a few for me. There isn't much. I don't have much as it is. No, not much at all!"[6]

I glanced up at the ceiling. Lingkai was right, but she shouldn't be saying these things to me. I was almost old enough to be her mother. I felt a rising bitterness in my throat, against Yidong, against Lingkai.

"I'm right, aren't I?" Lingkai smiled playfully.

"Right about what? No, you're not!" I spit out a seed.

I had to save face. I really was another Kong Yiji.[7]

"There's only one good thing about men," Lingkai grinned cunningly, "and only one bad thing about you."

"What's wrong with me?"

She deliberately twisted the subject in another direction: "You've got energy. It shows in your face. I bet you never have nightmares."

"You're wrong there. I dream all the time, day and night. I've got energy because I force myself to be happy."

"You do have nightmares? What about?"

"Nothing like what you're thinking of."

Wild animal dreams haven't scared me since I was a kid. All I have to do is yell: Get away from me! Then fly up into the sky. They don't frighten me at all.

But I have had one terrible nightmare: Yidong comes into my room in the middle of the night, and drawing back the mosquito netting, says to me: "You can't make me change. A-yuan, there's a limit to what you can do, and you can't make me change." He then laughs gently and disappears. What?! My name isn't A-yuan! He called me by another woman's name to tell me I can't make him change!

Waking with a start, I looked in the bathroom, on the balcony, everywhere, but no Yidong. I turned on all the lights, my face covered in tears.

The next time I saw him, I was afraid to ask about that name. He'd look down on me even more. And I'm not about to tell Lingkai either.

Swinging my legs, I said listlessly, "The one bad thing about me is you think I want to change you, right?"

And I said, "Everybody always thinks they're right and everybody else is wrong."

Lingkai's a smart girl. I didn't have to treat her like a child. "That's how it is with friends," I continued. "So long as both are willing, we adapt ourselves. We shouldn't be afraid to acknowledge the influence we exert on each other. It's an inherent, integral part of the relationship. Why shouldn't we acknowledge it? I feel good when I make other people happy. It's a kind of instant happiness."

I stroked the back of Lingkai's hand. "Would you like an instant happiness? A surprise present? Chocolate?"

226

Bubbling up with laughter, she bounced her head back and forth like a little chick. "Yes! But I don't like those liqueur-filled chocolates. They taste like cough syrup."

I went downstairs to buy tomatoes, carrots, celery, mushrooms, jelly fish and water chestnuts. Stir-fried together, they made a beautiful plate of red-orange-green-blue-and-purple that was complimented by the sparkling rose wine in our glasses.

Lingkai rolled up her sleeves and sat down. "Yidong's going to be mad you didn't invite him over for this great dinner."

"Yidong? No way. It takes a lot to make him mad."

I thought about him.

Yidong's got a lot going against him, but I still like him the best. I'm not too sure what he thinks of me, and I'm not about to ask. Whenever we fight, I walk out the door to the park where I can find a quiet green hill to stretch out on. Back in my room, I throw around all the stuff he's given me. I've never broken anything when he's around, but he gives me only unbreakable wood and metal toys, as if he's known all along. Sometimes I think: If he ever wants to leave me, I'll let go with a smile. A heart can't be tied — that I do know. He's so strong; provided he doesn't die an unnatural death, he's sure to outlast me a good twenty years. I want him to curl up at sixty in some corner of a theater and fondly reminisce about that independent, gentle, tolerant, unassuming girlfriend of his youth. I want him to acknowledge deep down that I, of all his friends, men or women, understood and believed in him like no one else. I want him to be wearing shabby, tattered old clothes and thinking about me miserably, so miserably.

When I told him this, he just laughed, "You're really something!" and walked over to tap my forehead with his index finger: "You shouldn't think so highly of yourself."

He didn't even care. Doesn't care right now anyway. I made a fool of myself over the whole thing.

With Lingkai came a different state of mind, the feeling I was facing a clear little creek, a gurgling stream flowing out to sea.

Is it ever possible to recapture the past? To escape the future?

227

Lingkai invited me to watch her fashion show, "Silk for '87," at the Grand Palace. I carried the dishes into the kitchen, came back, and told her I wouldn't go.

She stared at me unhappily.

"I don't like to go to parties or dances. I don't have the right clothes," I explained.

"Who cares? Besides, I've seen your three-hundred-*yuan* fur jacket."

"That was a display item. My mother bought it for my birthday, but I've never even worn it. I need a car to match before I can wear a coat like that. Just wait till I get my Benz, and I'll drive you around with a fur coat draped over my shoulders."

"You'll never own a Benz," she said sharply.

I thought about it. She was probably right. Yidong was practically a manual laborer, and even though he could afford milk and beer over plain water, he'd never fatten up. Better not put too much faith in him. Besides, I'd made up my mind long ago to support myself, to rely on my own two hands to make a living. I was a pharmacist with a future. I wanted to learn everything possible about the profession and was ready to spend my life dedicated to it. You couldn't take away my work and give me a Benz, or even a Rolls Royce. I'd dry up and die. That was a fact.

I held my hand upright. "How do you know? If you stand life up like this, it appears very long. Not knowing life, how can you know death? Perhaps someday I'll have it all."

In the end, she talked me into it.

Yidong sat beside me. He was the stage designer for the show. A few minutes before eight he went to speak with the lighting man then came back and sat down.

I couldn't believe that was Lingkai up there. Number five or six in line, she blew in like a whirlwind from the right, the music a cha-cha, Lingkai a beautiful raven.

Somebody from Weimei Fashion Company had complained to Yidong that Lingkai was planning to quit. She wanted to get into photographic modeling at the modeling center.

228

"Popular, isn't she?" I asked.

"Very. A big name," Yidong answered. "She's got the most potential of anyone in the troupe, and Weimei can't give her what she wants. They'll have to let her go, see what she can do elsewhere."

"Give her what she wants? She's such a hot-shot?" Lingkai hadn't mentioned any of this to me. I had no idea. But she shouldn't be too presumptuous.

"You don't understand. Weimei can only do so much, but Lingkai can really go places. She's not out of line at all."

The music changed, and Lingkai appeared again, this time in a double-breasted gown. The curled ends of her silky hair floated in soft waves behind her ears. I stared up at her, lost in the hazy beauty of some other world.

So lovely, so healthy, so young.

I've said before that Lingkai's face is a moving laby-rinth of expression, a face you can never get enough of. Only a fool would care about her clothes. The other flowers were pressed back into a pale, indistinct bouquet by her bright loveliness.

There was a stir in the crowd as photographers pressed forward, camera flashes piercing the dark. I saw my chance and held up two fingers in a victory sign.

She saw me. She looked around, turned and smiled, turned again, then held her pose. Another turn, two quick spins in my direction and an "okay" sign back to me.

Yidong leaned over, "You messed up her pattern. Don't fool around like that."

Lingkai was such a star. A few hand signals could hard-ly matter.

"So now you're satisfied? Proud, huh? Now it's okay with you she's not in school," Yidong said.

"Don't be so sarcastic. I'm not that dumb. Ten, twen-ty years from now, masters and doctorates are going to be a dime a dozen, but a good model is born into the job. Not everyone can do it, you know. They ought to be given professional status for more job security."

Yidong laughed.

Lingkai came rushing over after the show. I pointed at a

229

chair, but she said the manager would make a fuss if he saw her sitting in her hand-painted silk dress.

"Can you tell I've got false eyelashes on?" She asked. I said no, nobody would notice just that.

"What'd you think?" she asked. "You saw sixty sets. How'd you like it?"

She had on a sleeveless evening gown with a low scoop neckline. I ran my hand down her smooth glowing neck, shoulder, arm. I saw the layer of make-up. Make-up that thick in this weather should have melted and smudged into a big messy puddle, but Lingkai sparkled, clear and cool as jade.

She'd won me over completely.

"I feel cool. Nice and cool."

She bent before me laughing, eyes and teeth like bright pearls, so fetchingly bashful.

Even if she did stay in school, passing the university entrance exam, not to mention getting a degree, would have been difficult. She just didn't care. She'd already found her profession, her career, and she was doing a very impressive job at it.

Everybody should make the most of what they've got. With Lingkai, it was beauty.

I saw her next at the modeling center. Yidong and I were sitting in the shade of an umbrella eating ices when a big noisy group crowded round an umbrella nearby. Yidong went over to say hello. I spotted Lingkai in the pack. She'd recently joined the center and was meeting with the manager to discuss work.

She flew over to my umbrella. "I've grown up a lot," she informed me. "I've got my own ideas now, so I won't be going over to bother you all the time like I used to. You won't think I'm ungrateful, will you?"

"Why would I think that? What new ideas have you come up with?" I asked.

"They want me to have a stage name. I've decided on 'Mimi'," she announced with a twist of her head.

"Mimi!" I cried. "Why don't you just call yourself 'Wildcat'? Come on, Lingkai, how could you pick such a horrible name?'' I virtually shuddered with repulsion.

"But they want to use our stage names for advertisements. What am I supposed to pick? We might be going to Japan in October,'' she said in a hurt little voice.

"Horse shit,'' I spat in their direction. "Is that all they care about? Tell them you've got a perfectly good name, and it's Kong Lingkai.''

I fell silent, too sluggish to go on. Lingkai retreated, then returned. "They say I have to have one.''

She looked at me. "They all have English stage names. You've studied Japanese. Pick a Japanese name for me.''

Studied Japanese? Ages ago. I glanced over at Yidong, but he was concentrating on slicing an orange.

I lost all sense of dignity. "Lingkai,'' I lashed out, "haven't you got a brain at all?''

I watched Yidong eat his orange, hands sticky with the sweet juice. "He's got a Japanese name. It's Shiye Tailang.''[8] I pointed to myself, "I'm Zhongyi Yinzhi.''[9]

Lingkai puckered her lips, highly displeased.

Yidong wiped his hands with a paper napkin and lit a cigarette. Shielding his face with one hand, he avoided eye contact. I knew that expression. I was acting like one of those vulgar women in the market who fight over a skirt on sale.

I shut my mouth in humiliation and said no more.

I felt terrible.

What's really terrible is that Lingkai never comes over anymore. If I want to see her, I have to watch TV or go out on location when they shoot commercials.

Last time was on the beach, noon straight up. The waves washed in, washed out. Lingkai's group took up a huge area over near the water. When he saw who it was, Yidong said he wanted to go over to look at the proof sheets they'd sent that morning. Lingkai spotted me and tilted her head with a half wave, then turning, kept fussing with her face.

They were shooting a Sunshine brand milk commercial. A group of teen-agers jumped into an open jeep, small cartons of milk in hand, and made a great show of enjoying

231

themselves. The jeep careened wildly over the yellow sand, Lingkai's long hair flying — what a sight!

Someone was chanting the words to the commercial in Cantonese: "Sunshine people look better, sunshine songs sound better, Sunshine Milk tastes better...." But nobody was listening; all eyes were glued to the young people in the jeep racing along the line of surf.

I pulled Yidong over. "Yidong, is it true the sky's higher for these kids? Is the land wider, the wind stronger? Are they any happier?"

We sat down to have lemon tea with them at the break. Lingkai came over and leaned against my chair. "You're not like us," she said. "We've only got our youth, nothing else."

As so often in the past, I couldn't figure out what she was trying to get at. But this time she didn't seem to care.

"What're you talking about? You're young and that's everything." I suddenly felt helpless, resentful.

I stood up and waved to Yidong to leave.

Somebody called out, "Yidong, you haven't seen the proof sheets yet!" But Lingkai turned and whispered to him, "Let them go. Mr. Liu's friend is too far behind the times."

I walked over and twisted her ear, "Smart aleck. You should learn when to keep your mouth shut."

We rode away on our bikes, rode and rode.

Yidong knows me. He knows I'm old-fashioned. He knows I won't wear sun dresses or backless tops. He knows I'm from a small, simple family. He knows, he knows, he knows....

We rode until the sky dropped black around us.

"Yidong, is it true when you're young, you've got everything, and when you get old, there's nothing left?"

"Of course."

He didn't look at me.

"Really?" I felt pale.

We stopped under a street light. I could see the warm, gentle pool of his eyes. "Oh, sure!" I said.

"Wisdom," he said. "With wisdom comes everything.

'God waits for man to become childlike through wisdom.' Tagore said that.'' He patted me on the back. "You're both afraid to gain and afraid to lose. I don't want to get involved in this.''

He said I was afraid to gain and afraid to lose. That's a good joke. Brother, if I had everything, if I were Ali Baba's cave, I could certainly care less about a little loss or gain.

But all I've got are two empty hands.

If someone were to ask me: What is it you really want? I wouldn't know how to answer. But Yidong's a genius. Yidong knows me. He'd never ask me that.

He asked if I wanted to get something to eat. I shook my head. I wanted to go home and study my herbal medicine texts. I wanted something real to hold onto, something I could grasp. Everybody else, when they reach fifty or sixty, can stand around grandson-in-arm and gossip. They can steam a different shape taro cake for every day of the week. But I'll be useless at that age if I don't do something now. All I'll be good for is lying in bed and reading Eileen Chang [10] novels.

I said I wanted to go home.

"Well then,'' he good-humoredly comforted me, "Go home and get a good dreamless sleep. Don't think too much. When you get up tomorrow morning, you'll see the sun's still there.''

I nodded and smiled at him, then turned and left on my own.

Notes

1. In China, urban population is strictly controlled by means of residence permits. The Household Registration Bureau is in charge of issuing permits and keeping tabs on population movement.
2. In Chinese the given name is preceded by the surname.
3. Also known as *yum cha, dim sum* are Cantonese-style pastries served with tea in the morning.
4. A tropical fruit grown in southern China, which when sliced crosswise looks like a star, giving it the name "star fruit.''
5. Fudan University is a prestigious institution of higher education located in Shanghai.

6. A well-known line from Lu Xun's short story classic "Kong Yiji," written in 1919.

7. Kong Yiji, the protagonist in Lu Xun's story by the same name, was a traditional scholar of the classics who failed to pass the official examinations. Reduced to beggary and mocked at by the townspeople, he struggled to keep face in spite of it all.

8. Changing two characters in a common Japanese men's name (pronounced Ishi Taro in Japanese) creates a homonym which translates to "Ravaging Wolf."

9. Changing two characters in a common Japanese women's name (pronounced Nakai Ginshi in Japanese) creates a homonym which translates to "Money Lover."

10. A contemporary Chinese woman writer, popular particularly in the south and Hong Kong.

Rejecting Fate

Han Chunxu

I've passed into another time.

Never has my heart torn so painfully, every last residue of feeling destroyed from within. I tremble with mad impulse; no longer can I bury all that's inside. Shasha, I stand wide open before you.

Shasha, can you imagine? On a simple canvas cot. Every agony God gave woman in the creation of new life was mine. But from it came nothing: I am not a mother.

Little one, how can I tell you! This small life, unborn and yet already sentenced to death. Shasha, he (she), with feet firmly planted in the soil of our universe, called to me, called to the blue sky above. Knowing. Knowing that he (she) was a real living being of flesh and blood, of a soul. What am I doing? The blood of murder stains my hands. I don't know anymore. I twist in agony, my eyes grasping, seeking ... I tremble, gasping for breath, reaching out instinctively to grab on to something, but all that come back are fingers, fingers and this hopeless struggle ... I wish I could die ... really wish ... I could leave this world with the small life in my womb.

I am not human. I am not a woman. He (She) breathed with me for six months. I am the one who strangled him (her), I am the one who strangled the soul of my own passion!

Shasha, and I must tell you, it was the fruit of our most perfect moment of passion.

* * *

Shasha, a miracle came to me in a dream: that small life was yet inseparably one with me. Without a cry, he (she) serenely faced heaven and passed from this earth.

I am a mother.

I am his (her) mother.

I struggle to hold on to what is no longer one with me, stopping up the torrent of blood from my heart. And I must know: "Is it a boy or girl?" Their eyes (the eyes of these women doctors) cut me like knives: "You still have the face to ask?"

No more brutal answer can be found.

I am but a filthy slur, that which I have borne, a disgrace. Suddenly there is only black; I know nothing.

* * *

All has died, already dead. Shasha, when I opened my eyes with a groan, an unbearable emptiness came pressing down — I wanted to cry; I wanted to cry out loud, but nothing came out.

All that I had hoped for, was it just an illusion?

Who knows to cry for the crimes humanity commits against life?

Life, do I understand life? Shasha, I have to ask myself this.

I want to rise up, run far away ... but ... every nerve in my body clenches me, holds me.

How I wish I could be a real woman, as lovely as a poem, a woman who understands love, who knows how to love, who loves with warmth, with passion, with delight; to be a *lover*, a *wife*, a *mother*. And to experience all the sensibilities of a woman for myself. I'm not afraid of the pain that comes with love, nor the solitude. I want to let my life drown every moment in feeling. I want to let my life unfurl and blow, like the air, like sunlight.

Shasha, is this my mistake? Am I not a woman!

Can there be anything more disheartening, more stifling, than those hateful looks of scorn?

The air I breathe here is the bitter cold of night's darkest hour. I am a pale streak of cloud rejected by the moon's bright beams.

The mothers here shine with pride and a kind of holiness. Creators of those tiny sprouts of life, they bask in their husbands' tender affection. They rejoice at the first stream of milk to jet from their breasts. The room breaks into laughter watching that small, thin mother's flustered attempts to hold her baby. A young couple peers intently into the face of their new child, arguing about who she looks like. Here is a wonderful celebration of life, an eternally pure, sweet oasis from the world.

I know what they're whispering behind my back — "outside lover," "unmarried and pregnant" — names only we Chinese could come up with. Names that will get their full usage out of me.

My heart laughs in anguish. What else can I do?

I don't regret anything.

Shasha, my one sorrow is that I could not break free from their filth and courageously become a mother.

I thought I was whole, but here, here I've been completely shattered. I'm wound up inside as tight as an alarm clock.

I can only weep silently in my heart.

The standards humanity lays down for itself both wrap us in layers of pain and sow between us barriers to understanding.

Isn't that so?

If they (the women) can cherish the fruit of their own passion, why is it they can't treat me — treat my small one already in heaven — with the same genuine love of life?

Is there really a hierarchy of difference inherent in that mingling of body and soul?

I lie here in my anguish and think about us (us women). Some say we were put on earth for the sole purpose of propagation. They say it's our bounden duty, our vocation. Shasha, don't think I'm so terrible. I can't help thinking: of all the children born in China, how many were conceived in a perfect moment of giving and receiving? How many?

I can be proud.

The stars outside dilute and fade; my vision is blocked by the coming darkness.

I know the greatest human fear is the fear of death. And I know we won't live forever. But how many of us lucidly value this brief life? How many of us take our lives out into the boundless natural world and really live! I can't help but look at myself and see the piles of great dead boulders I've stacked up in the riverbed of my life.

Something suddenly confuses me, makes me feel life is crammed with things I can't understand. All that I valued about myself seems a ratty imitation.

How pitiful. I've never been so worn down, so exhausted…. I'm already buried.

*   *   *

Shasha, at a time when I should have cared for nothing but the blue sky and white clouds, I fell in love with two people — my teacher and my father. The men I've loved since all bear the faint imprint of those two, those two who took the blue sky and white clouds from my heart….

I'll never forget. Never forget his pressed blue Sun Yat-sen suit and spotless black cloth shoes. Never forget his steady, sure gait, the way he planted one foot firmly before lifting the other. I liked his writing on the board, so careful and neat, just like the red characters on my calligraphy sheet.[1] I could feel his warm, deep voice reach down to my heart every time he read the text.

It was one day at lunch when we sat solemnly eating our simple meal. He brushed past and stooped to pick up the piece of corn husk biscuit my classmate had just spit on the floor. Chewing it down, he declared indignantly: "Students, we must not forget the days when all we had were tree leaves and burlap sacks to eat.'' I was suddenly looking into the face of a stranger.... The stench of that chewed biscuit, already fermented, seemed to rise from his stomach and fill my air. It wasn't long before the whole school was talking about my beloved teacher — as if he'd faced a martyr's death. How I wished I could yank out my heart and wash it clean in the rain! Then use it to cover that terrible stench.

To this day, I can't figure out why that fire crackled so violently. Those weren't freshly cut tree branches, and only oil could have blazed out that noxious wet heat; its sharp snaps burned fear in my heart. I buried my face in my mother's bosom, afraid to look at the Red Guards[2] in their green army get-up, afraid to look at the red fire. Afraid, most of all, to look at my father's face glowing in the light of the flames. I was terrified he'd rush at them with raised fists — then go straight for the fire. Over the piercing sound of the loudspeaker: "Revolution is no picnic,"[3] came my father's cool praise: "Good job, Red Guard fighters. They're burning well.''[4] I couldn't believe my ears. I wanted to go over and crack open my father's skull to find out what he was really thinking. Ever since I was a toddler I knew about that wall of books in our home. I knew my father always washed his hands before opening a book. I knew my brother had once gotten a good spanking for taking a book without asking. Everything was changing ... everything.... I cried as if my heart would break, as if I'd lost something very important....

You can't tell me people don't have it in them to shed a genuine tear, to dream a real dream, to feel a true emotion — I just don't believe it.

We Chinese may all put on the same look; we may all have inherited our ancestors' watered-down emotions, but I dare say that nobody can live a life that is so innocent, so pure and simple. How full of hidden secrets the heart when comes time for the final plunge! If someone were to collect revelations of the souls passing into heaven, wouldn't they be overwhelmed by the loneliness and illusion, passionate love, hope, cries in the dark ... to come showering from this real world of living beings?

Shasha, don't think I'm crazy. Don't think I'm a bad woman who can't control her emotions. You are so spotlessly pure; my thoughts stand naked before you.

And the nights, when I stared up at the stars, how often did I think I'd go crazy! Once I felt so all alone: there were only the two of us, myself and that shadowy moon. I remember talking, sharing my thoughts, when it began to wrap itself in a dim cloud. I cried and begged it to wrap me up with it, to let my soul disappear into the haze. But it paid me no mind. I longed to knock it down with my fist and throw half into the ocean, half into the river. Never let that moon be whole again.

I'm suffocating. This must be what it is to go crazy.

Since the day I realized my existence, all I've wanted is to become a whole person. If not completely whole, then at least true.

*   *   *

The babies' cries, the laughter in this room, cut at my heart. I'm like a piece of garbage pulled from the trash and tossed in the corner. What spring, what faraway shore, can wash the chill from my bones and restore the warm brilliance?

Shasha, when I loved him, loved him with such a passion, I'd tremble all over. Awkwardness would overtake me, words fail me. And when I'd finally found his eyes, something inside me would topple, like a slave; if before me he stood a mighty king, I was the dirt at his feet. Everything I had, body and soul, I was ready to give him. For him to hold me in his arms, take me in his deep gaze, I didn't care if he'd love me in the future. The present was all I needed. That was enough.

I am a woman who loves men. I love their magnanimity, their imprudence; I love all the things about them we women can never be. And I hate them. Hate all the things that let them keep on going. Love to them is just one part of life. When they love you, they want you to fit into their world, but they'll never waste their life on you.

Shasha, it was too late by the time I understood that. I now regret letting myself go so completely. Love, I now know, also requires distance. I wanted him to give me all the love that flowed through his veins; I wanted him to live for me; I wanted to breathe only air that passed through his lungs. Ah, Shasha, I had it all mixed-up. He was my everything, my life.

That's the foolish love of women. Drunk with illusion, we burn our past worlds to ashes and end up a binding nuisance. That's our tragedy. That's the mistaken love I traded my life for.

*   *   *

This hazy white day feeds my loneliness and sorrow.

Back from the delivery room, she snuggles close against her husband's chest. He softly smoothes her tangled hair and she smiles, peacefully. I weep.

I think of us, and that place where the moon rose bright and clean, that place where the night air floated balmily, where the ocean kicked up splendid froth beneath the azure sky. Shasha, I can't forget, though the memory brings only pain.

That night at Marco Polo Bridge, the moon slanted west and disappeared behind a bank of clouds. We tore off our clothes and, falling to the ground, let the stone bridge marker stand proudly as our roof. To live! To live is to feel; we broke through the cloud bank and found the brightest star beside the moon. The mosquitoes came in for attack. Go ahead, eat your fill. We clung to each other. In that great deep silence, the world was ours — what greater happiness can there be!

We'd found the loveliest shore in all of Asia. It ran to the edge of the world, with us standing in bare feet on its silky sands. We faced the sea, the waves brushing toward us in neat rows. Then would come a surge, a grand green wall, pouncing playfully, surfacing foamy white.

Nobody but us. The sea and sky opened for us alone, purified us in their wash, transfigured us.

We played with the surf. We scooped up the fine sand to build a golden wall, but a wave came and mercilessly rolled over, leaving not a trace. Ha, ha, we laughed, pointing with fingers of sand, then bent to build anew.

I'd never played so happily, so earnestly, with the sea. To be human! Knowing for certain the ultimate destruction of our wall, knowing it's all a game, but insisting on proving ourselves to nature with sand. To be so perfectly human!

At the coming of dusk, the sky deepened and laced in the edges with puffs of rose. The sea paled, drawing a line at the horizon where all had been one.

That was nature. But what about us? *In the long river of sensation, were the beautiful moments only that—fleeting moments?*

Shasha, I don't regret. I never thought later why I'd done it. Why think about it? I'd thrown myself in completely — isn't that the only way to live?

What is it we shouldn't forget about the love, so Chinese, that Zhang Jie writes of in "Love Must Not Be Forgotten?"[5] A love like that, so shrunken, so pitiful, so hideous....

Love is great, powerful, and it's not enough for me to just say those words — I must feel it for myself, even if it means a bump, a scrape, a fall into the river....

Shasha, why is love's visit to our lives so short? Has it fit so well into civilized regulations? Only once, only as a prelude to marriage, and if you can't comply, you'll be yoked and branded.

No. Like the sun, the rosy clouds at dusk, like the

stars, love should companion our every living moment.

I dare to say the best thing in life is love. Human virtue itself springs from the soil of love, and without it, how dull-witted, how mediocre we would be. Love helps us transcend ourselves.

Shasha, I've never felt this exhilarated, this stirred up — the world seems suddenly to have grown very large. But I don't even have the strength to sit up and drink water. I've lost too much blood.

You know, induced labor at six months is just like giving birth. The only difference is their fruit was ripe and ready to drop; mine was cut as it grew on the stem. I suffered in labor as much as they, but I don't even know the sex of my child. He (She) didn't scream out a newborn's cry, but just the same, soaked in the blood of his (her) mother's womb. I'm no different from those other mothers, my heart as full with a mother's love.

*　　　*　　　*

That's him ... that's him ... just as I had pictured in my dreams, lying peacefully at my side ... every line in his face so innocent, so happy....

Ah, my little morning star. I want to take you out into wild open meadows and let you run and run. I want you to know you belong only to yourself, that you never have to do anything you don't want to. I want to teach you what it is to live, to have your own will, to transcend. I want you to become the noble master of yourself.

But I've lost that. Destroyed it. Cut it painfully away.

Shasha, I'm exhausted. All this crazy thinking is wearing me down. I don't ask for only happiness or love. What is happiness anyway? What does it give? It's pain that follows you through life.

But I thank the pain and unhappiness. I learn through its ridicule. It brings me wealth, emotional wealth.

*   *   *

How could a dream frighten me so, fill me with such empty illusion! I saw my spine slip to the ground; clutching it against my chest, I raced for the hospital. Then I saw my head clamped between two high mountains, floating somewhere above red clouds.

Dreams. I've never trusted them, never let them run my life. A dream's a dream and nothing more.

*   *   *

Now, Shasha, now I wish I were healthy. Healthy enough to climb from this bed and run outside. Outside to that boundless sea of red grass. Outside to the blue mountains of sundown. Outside to that moment when the sun and moon hang together in the clouds. To cast this hurt and hopelessness into the burning crimson sea. To let the sun give succor to my life, let nature permeate my blood. To release my spirit to the open and let fire and ice, life and death, love and hate, brew into these hot tears; and then in solitude, in solitude recover that deep, enduring experience.

We go through this life, Shasha, forgetting to meld with nature. We know only to shrink ourselves under the eaves, happy with our cup of tea, busy with our talk of neighbors. We know only to prove who we are, to tighten our belts so we can buy a stereo (with or without the cassettes). We know only two lifeless words: should and shouldn't. Never comprehending the wealth of language and consciousness that nature in its every turn extends to us. Whenever I see the phrase "It's better to stay confused"[6] hanging on someone's wall, I feel only death and ignorance in the room.

You must know, the true calling of every person who comes into this universe is to realize her own existence, not to just scrape by *living*.

I can't recall ever leaning for so long against the wall.

It's not that I'm such a proud person. There are times when my spirit shakes and wants to curl up inside. Shasha, it's often when I'm happiest that the awareness of death strikes me. When my life does finally rend, I'll let my spirit go peacefully with the flesh. *I won't be like those who wait until the last moment to realize their existence.*

Agitation takes over where sorrow has left off. I'd give anything to leave this spiritless place and run to hold you in my arms. One more thing: I want to take my own road, the road that leads toward life and the sun. I want to grow in my own soil, mold myself from my own clay. Even though I'm weak, even though people will say: You're too young.

Afterword

(The following was taken from a conversation with the author about her inspiration for this story.)

I was twenty-five. When my time came, my husband took me to the gynecological hospital, where I was given a bed in a narrow, brightly-lit room with two other women waiting to deliver. I learned the pain and joy of birthing; the deepest link between women, it is an experience of life foreign to every man.

Sometime during the eight hours I lay in that room, I saw the orderlies wheel in a hospital cart. They put the woman by the wall where I could see, over the contorted profile between, the dark mass of her tangled hair. Labor pains cut short my attention; her moans came to me, like a comfort, through the screen of my own torment. Then she was quiet, and I saw her lift herself unsteadily to half-sitting. "Is it a boy or girl?" she whispered hopefully. The two women doctors in attendance stared at her in disbelief. The older said with a sneer: "You still have the face to ask? Next time you come in here, you better own up and tell the truth. Don't say it's your first time."

She crumpled back onto the canvas mat, unconscious. The blood I saw pour from her heart rendered my own pain meaningless.

Later, when the contractions quickened, I was taken into

the delivery room. I gave birth to a beautiful little boy. Space is a problem in China, especially in the big cities. Our recovery room, my home for the next four days, was a bustling public arena with fifteen beds and non-stop traffic of nurses and family. The girl with the tangled hair was kept by the window on a cot. Ignored by the rest, she told me her story.

At eighteen, she'd gotten pregnant with the man she loved, a married man several years her senior. She'd wanted to go through with it. She wanted his child, even though he'd backed out and refused support. For a while it seemed she could hold up, but the pressure got too great. After six months, she decided to abort.

My own pain had sprouted into a body of perfect living joy; hers had burned at the stake, was still burning, choking her with the ashes of memory, licking her with the flames of ridicule and disdain. Hadn't she the right to be a mother as I? Hadn't she known every moment of the life growing inside her and loved it as all the mothers in that room who turned their backs and refused to speak to her, a "bad woman"? Doesn't love teach us to be greater than ourselves?

What I saw in the hospital that week set me on a course of introspection about love and the realization of our natural selves. Our heritage of antiquated ideas about correct moral behavior chains us into an acceptable "normality" that defies the true path to life. Blind to ourselves, we cannot see others. That is our plight, a plight I see as unique to the Chinese experience.

Notes

1. Children learn to do calligraphy in school by tracing with a brush over practice sheets of red characters.
2. In the Great Proletarian Cultural Revolution (1966-1976), Mao Zedong invoked the support of China's fanatical revolutionary youth to ferret out "those in the Party who take the capitalist road." The result was the creation of the Red Guards, youth in their teens to early twenties who, at the climax of their career, occupied Party headquarters and government buildings, ousted public officials and roamed the country ransacking, burning and smashing everything they could find intellectual, foreign, official or old. Books, priceless heirlooms and old photographs were some of the greatest losses for many families. (See Note 5 of the

Introduction for more on the Cultural Revolution.)

3. Mao Zedong's idea that revolution through class struggle requires conflict and sometimes violence. Directly translated: "Revolution isn't treating your friends to dinner."

4. Indicating the pile of books being burned by the Red Guards before his eyes.

5. Zhang Jie's "Love Must Not Be Forgotten" opened a new phase of contemporary Chinese literature when it appeared in 1979 for its revelation of a woman intellectual's inner emotional world and the confrontation of a previously tabooed subject—extra-marital love. As the narrator suggests, love in this story is not expressed through passionate abandon but rather through illusion, memory and sacrifice.

6. This saying, attributed to a Qing Dynasty painter and calligrapher, can also be translated as: "Confusion is hard to come by." It's better, in other words, to go along in life maintaining a safe level of confusion. Don't think too much, don't become too clear, or you'll create problems for yourself.

The Authors

Bai Fengxi was born in 1934 in Hebei Province. She joined a theatrical troupe in 1949 when she was fifteen and continued to act for the next thirty years. She began to write in the late 1970s. Her most important published work is *The Women Trilogy* (1988), a compilation of three plays focusing on the problems women face in present-day society. A national prize-winner, it was published in English by Chinese Literature Press in 1991. Bai is a nationally recognized playwright with the Chinese Youth Art Theater.

Han Chunxu was born in 1955 in Beijing. Her plans to study medicine were interrupted by the Cultural Revolution, when she was assigned a job as a salesclerk in 1970. Work in the shop, however, became inspiration for her writing; she published several short stories and articles before transferring to the *Workers Daily* newspaper as a literary editor in 1979. This turning point in her career was marked by a degree from the Chinese Institute of Journalism. Her first collection of short stories, *Rejecting Fate* (1988), has been followed by numerous essays and other works of non-fiction. Han is a member of the Chinese Writer's Association and the Chinese Prose Poetry Society.

Li Xiaojiang was born in 1952 in Henan Province. She worked in the countryside for three years during the Cultural Revolution before being assigned a job as fitter and driver in a machine factory in Wuhan, Hebei Province. In 1979 she began postgraduate work at Henan University in European and American literature, delving for the first time into the study of women's issues through literary comparison. She began to publish theoretical articles on the topic in 1983, and in 1985 introduced a new course on women's literature to the curriculum of Zhengzhou University, where she'd been assigned to teach after graduation. In 1987 Li established the first non-governmental Women's Studies Center in China; she has edited twenty some volumes in the academically-oriented *Women's Studies Series*. Her published works include two books in the series, *The Probe of Eve* (1988) and *On Women's Aesthetic Consciousness* (1989), as well as numerous theoretical books and papers. She organized the first non-governmental international women's studies symposium in 1990 and is presently preparing to establish a national women's museum in Henan Province.

Liu Xihong was born in 1961 in Guangdong. She graduated from high school in 1978 and began work at the Wenjindu Customs Office in Shenzhen in 1980. Her first piece of fiction was published in 1984; her first collection of short stories, *You Can't Make Me Change*, came out in 1987. Liu's work, centered in the Guangzhou-Shenzhen area, generally depicts young, independent women in daily, real-life situations. Liu is presently living abroad.

Ma Zhongxing was born in 1931 in Taiyuan City, Shanxi Province. She received degrees in acting from the Central Academy of Theatrical Arts in 1951 and the Beijing Film Institute in 1953. Her acting career was cut short by the Cultural Revolution, when she was sent to an iron and steel factory in Taiyuan to work in the propaganda department. In 1981 she returned to the Beijing Film Institute as an associate professor of literature. Ma has published academic papers, short stories and essays. She is now retired and writes at home.

Tie Ning was born in 1957 in Beijing. She graduated from high school in 1975 and spent four years working in the countryside before returning to Baoding City as a fiction editor for *Hua Shan* magazine. Tie has published one novel, ten novellas and more than seventy short stories, as well as collections of essays and articles. Her short stories "Ah, Fragrant Snow" (1982) and "June's Big Topic" (1984), and novella *The Red Shirt Without Buttons* (1982) have all won national awards. Her stories have been translated into eight languages and published in the quarterly journal *Chinese Liter-*

ature. *Haystacks*, her first short story collection in English, was published by Chinese Literature Press in 1991. Tie is a professional writer with the Hebei Branch of the Chinese Confederation of Literary and Art Circles.

Wang Anyi was born in 1954 in Nanjing, the daughter of woman writer Ru Zhijuan. Raised in Shanghai, she went to Anhui Province in 1969 to be "re-educated by the peasants." She published her first essay in 1975 and in 1978 began work as an editor for the magazine *Childhood*, put out by the China Welfare Society in Shanghai. In 1982 *Lapse of Time* won the Best Novella of the Year Award; her trilogy of "love" novellas in the late eighties brought acclaim and controversy. Wang's work has been widely translated and published in the quarterly journal *Chinese Literature*. *Lapse of Time*, a collection of short stories and the title novella, was published in English by Chinese Literature Press in 1988. *Baotown* (1985), the tale of life in a small village, was published in English by W.W. Norton and Company in 1989. Wang is a professional writer with the Shanghai Branch of the Chinese Writer's Association.

Xiang Ya (Zhao Shaoling) was born in 1951 in Hebei Province. The Cultural Revolution cut short her schooling; in 1969 she was sent to Inner Mongolia for three years. Upon return to Beijing in 1974, she worked in an electrical equipment plant before transferring to the Beijing National Library. She attended night school and received her degree in Chinese Literature in 1985, having published her first article in 1984. Her work, primarily non-fiction and interview-based, focuses on various aspects of modern experience, from ideas about sex to the lives of flight attendants. *Women Speak* has been adapted into a movie by the Shanghai Film Studio titled *Golden Fingernails*. Zhao is presently living abroad.

Further Reading
Recent Collections of Contemporary Mainland Chinese Women Writers in English

Bai Fengxi. *The Women Trilogy*. Beijing: Chinese Literature Press, 1991.

Born of the Same Roots: Stories of Modern Chinese Women. Edited by Vivian Ling Hsu. Bloomington: Indiana University Press, 1981.

Cheng Naishan. *The Blue House*. Beijing: Chinese Literature Press, 1989.

Contemporary Chinese Women Writers II. Beijing: Chinese Literature Press, 1991.

One Half of the Sky: Stories from Contemporary Women Writers of China. Translated by R. A. Roberts and Angela Knox. New York: Dodd, Mead and Company, Inc., 1988.

Seven Contemporary Chinese Women Writers. Beijing: Chinese Literature Press, 1982.

Ru Zhijuan. *Lilies and Other Stories*. Beijing: Chinese Literature Press, 1985.

Shen Rong. *At Middle Age*. Beijing: Chinese Literature Press, 1987.

The Rose-colored Dinner: New Works by Contemporary Chinese Women Writers. Hong Kong: Joint Publishing Co., Ltd., 1988.

Tie Ning. *Haystacks*. Beijing: Chinese Literature Press, 1991.

Wang Anyi. *Lapse of Time*. Beijing: Chinese Literature Press, 1988. (Published also in San Francisco, California: China Books and Periodicals, Inc., 1988.)

Wang Anyi. *Baotown*. Translated by Martha Avery. New York: W. W. Norton and Company, Inc., 1989.

Zhang Jie. *Heavy Wings*. Translated by Howard Goldblatt. New York: Grove Weidenfeld, 1989.

Zhang Jie. *Love Must Not Be Forgotten*. Beijing: Chinese Literature Press, 1986. (Co-published also in San Francisco, California with China Books and Periodicals, 1986.)

Zhang Xinxin and Sang Ye. *Chinese Lives: An Oral History of Contemporary China*. Edited by W. J. F. Jenner and Delia Davin. New York: Pantheon Books, 1987. (Published also under the name *Chinese Profiles* in Beijing: Chinese Literature Press, 1986.)

Zhang Xinxin. *The Dreams of Our Generation and Selections from Beijing's People*. Cornell University East Asia Papers 41, Ithaca: Cornell University China-Japan Program, 1986.

图书在版编目（CIP） 数据

我要属狼：中国当代女性文学选：英文/金婉婷
编译.
– 北京：新世界出版社，1996.8 重印
ISBN 7 – 80005 – 124 – 2

I. 我 ...
II. 金 ...
III. ① 短篇小说 – 作品集 – 中国 – 当代 – 英文
　　② 中篇小说 – 作品集 – 中国 – 当代 – 英文
IV. I247.7

我 要 属 狼
—中国当代女性文学选

(美) 金婉婷　编译
(Diana B. Kingsbury)

*

新世界出版社出版
（北京百万庄路 24 号）
北京大学印刷厂印刷
中国国际图书贸易总公司发行
（中国北京车公庄西路 35 号）
北京邮政信箱第 399 号　邮政编码 100044
1994 年（英文）第一版　1996 年北京第二次印刷
ISBN 7 – 80005 – 124 – 2
02500
10 – E – 2669P